'Out the back' of Ceduna in remote South Australia, Aunty Sue mob and a crew of greenies are undertaking the difficult, dirty and deeply satisfying work of 'rockhole recovery'. They care for country in vigorous rejection of the state's native title regime. Eve Vincent eloquently tracks the enterprising struggles of Aunty Sue against a long history of devastating ruptures endured by Aboriginal people. 'Against Native Title' *is a fine-grained, perceptive and forceful account of the challenges and world-changing possibilities of cross-cultural alliances and new ways of belonging.*

Melinda Hinkson
Associate Professor of Anthropology, Deakin University

Country always had to be looked after, and still needs to be. If that is a task of central concern, can one afford to be diverted by the native title process? This book carefully describes Aunty Sue Mob's ways of caring for country and maintaining cultural continuity. Her resistance to native title is not just a refusal, but a means of gathering further allies to a cause that will only gain strength in today's more environmentalist context. This is an inspiring account as well as good ethnographic writing. Eve Vincent pays attention to what is going on in a situation, which means adding reality to it in the form of agencies driving the situation until it becomes an event, consequential in ways that zigzag right up to 'government policy', just as the mob slips out of town to get something practical done.

Professor Stephen Muecke
Jury Chair, School of Humanities, University of Adelaide

Professor Emeritus of Ethnography, Environmental Humanities, School of Humanities and Languages, University of New South Wales

Adjunct Professor, Nulungu Research Centre, University of Notre Dame, Broome Campus

Eve Vincent has produced a vital and timely book. Her insights into the relationships between people and country highlight the replenishment provided to Aboriginal communities through their deeply intimate contact with land and each other. 'Against Native Title' *also examines the obstacles encountered by communities in defence of country, cultural balance and histories of deep time when faced with forces and institutions of state barely able to scratch the surface of Indigenous life. Vincent's scholarship, driven by both an intellectual and ethical exchange, offers a model of connectivity that would benefit all in the country.*

Professor Tony Birch
Bruce McGuinness Research Fellow, Moondani Balluk Academic Centre, Victoria University

For Jane Vincent, David Vincent and Judy Vincent

'Against Native Title'

Conflict and creativity in outback Australia

Eve Vincent

First published in 2017 by Aboriginal Studies Press
Reprinted in 2026

Aboriginal Studies Press
is the publishing arm of the
Australian Institute of Aboriginal
and Torres Strait Islander Studies.
GPO Box 553, Canberra, ACT 2601

Phone:	(61 2) 6246 1183
Fax:	(61 2) 6261 4288
Email:	asp@aiatsis.gov.au
Web:	www.aiatsis.gov.au/aboriginal-studies-press/

Aboriginal and Torres Strait Islander people are respectfully advised that this publication contains names and images of deceased persons, and culturally sensitive information.

National Library of Australia Cataloguing-In-Publication data is available at www.trove.nla.gov.au

ISBN: 9781925302080 (pb)
ISBN: 9781922059383 (epub)
ISBN: 9781925302103 (Kindle)
ISBN: 9781925302127 (ebook PDF)

Cover image: *Sue Coleman Haseldine, 2010*. Photograph: Jessie Boylan.
Detail: *Rockhole after heavy December rain*. Photograph: Eve Vincent.

Contents

List of images

Acknowledgments

My foremost thanks go to Aunty Sue, and to her extended family, for folding me into their lives so warmly and teaching me much with great patience. I wish also to thank the woman I call 'Aunty Vera', who looked after me with tenderness.

This book was originally a PhD thesis, undertaken in the University of Sydney's anthropology department. Gillian Cowlishaw, my PhD supervisor and firm friend, challenged and nurtured my thinking at every turn. I will remain forever grateful to her. Yasmine Musharbash was an inspiring co-supervisor, and I thank her for her involvement in my doctoral project and ongoing support.

Many friends have offered encouragement as I slowly rewrote the thesis into a book, in fits and starts. Thank you Tanya Serisier, Jane Lydon, Jessica Whyte, Clare Land, Rebecca Giggs, Sascha Fuller, Rose Butler, Liz Humphrys, Camilla Pandolfini, Katie Hepworth, Banu Senay, Anna Clark and Alison Clark. None of the research or writing would have been possible without my long and strong friendship with Breony Carbines, whose insights are everywhere in this work. I am also immensely thankful for my collaboration with Tim Neale and for all our conversations. Belinda Burbidge cast an exacting eye over numerous draft chapters, which I greatly appreciate. Thanks to my old mate Clare Brown for the Adelaide sojourns and for our road trip out to the Far West Coast in 2014, and to the delightful Julie Beare for sharing her plant knowledge with me. Thanks also to the talented Jessie Boylan for permission to reprint some of her photographs here.

I thank sincerely all of my colleagues in the Department of Anthropology at Macquarie University for providing a collegial and intellectually stimulating workplace. While I am reluctant to single out any one of my excellent associates, I must discharge some more particular debts. I thank Greg Downey for being such a wonderfully supportive Head of Department, Lisa Wynn for mentoring me, Kalpana Ram for her scholarly example, and Chris Houston, Jaap Timmer and Chris Vasantkumar for their lovely friendship. I gratefully acknowledge the support of a Macquarie University Faculty of Arts publication Subsidy.

Thanks are due to all the team at Aboriginal Studies Press, particularly Rachel Ippoliti and Isabella Edquist for their hard work. Aboriginal Studies Press supported my aspiration to write a book that we hope will be accessible to a broader readership: Janet Hutchinson provided intelligent and sensitive editorial advice in this regard. I thank two anonymous reviewers for their insights into the original manuscript, as well as the press's Publishing Advisory Committee for astute feedback.

Parts of this work have appeared in previous publications. *Griffith Review* carried a short essay based on this book, 'Outlaw One', in the February 2017 'State of Hope' issue (no. 55). A much earlier version of the argument about native title's impact on Aboriginal identities appears in '"Sticking up for the land": Aboriginality, mining and the lived effects of native title', *Australian Journal of Human Rights* (vol. 19, no. 1, 2013), and a short version of the argument about Koonibba Mission appears in 'The Making of "Mission Mob": Koonibba Lutheran Mission as a Site of Memory', *Journal of the Anthropological Society of South Australia* (vol. 37, December 2013). Two essays consider the role of greenies in more depth, 'Hosts and Guests: Interpreting Rockhole Recovery Trips', *Australian Humanities Review* (no. 53, November 2012) and 'Kangaroo tails for dinner? Environmental culturalists encounter Aboriginal greenies', in Eve Vincent & Timothy Neale (eds), *Unstable Relations: Environmentalism and Indigenous people in Contemporary Australia* (University of Western Australia Publishing, 2016).

I thank my parents David and Jane Vincent for their unwavering support. My aunt, Judy Vincent, and my mum have provided truckloads of help over many years, sharing the hard labour and joy involved in looking after my little ones. I couldn't do what I do without them. Thanks are due to Jen and Jim Reside, whose support I also treasure.

I reserve my most loving gratitude for Shane Reside and our two beautiful boys, Ned and Billy Rose. Shane, somehow, miraculously, made it possible for me to write, in this crazy busy shared adventure called life: I owe him the deepest thanks.

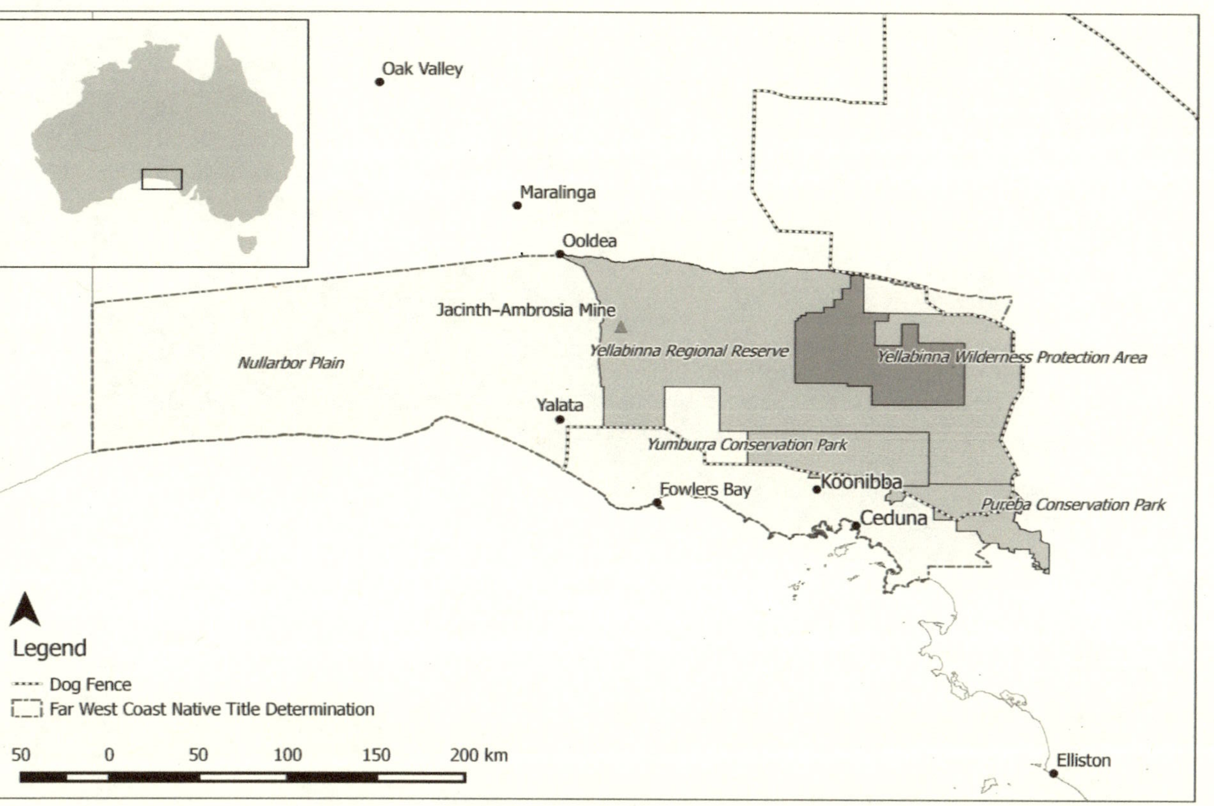

Map of Ceduna and surrounds

Introduction

'All mixed up'

This book is about a specific group of Australian Aboriginal people's experience of a divisive native title claim in the small town of Ceduna, South Australia. Here, as in other communities across Australia, the process Indigenous people engage in when they register and pursue a native title claim has had a profound impact on the identity of many Aboriginal people.

The central character is Sue Coleman Haseldine, a Kokatha woman aged in her mid sixties. Sue has staked out a position 'against native title' and here I attempt to understand why.

Ceduna is a dusty outback town perched atop a ragged coastline. Located 800 kilometres west of Adelaide, on the north-west extremity of the Eyre Peninsula, it is the last major 'service town' beyond which looms the flat, tree-less Nullabor Plain and the South Australia–Western Australia border. Ceduna, outlying farmlands and various pocket-sized localities together have a total population of around 3,500, a quarter of whom identify as Indigenous.[1]

Central to local life are questions of race relations and entrenched inequalities. Despite rapid changes over recent decades, an intact racial hierarchy, which institutionalises white dominance and normalises Aboriginal subordination, remains a fact of life. The relationship between Aboriginal people and whitefellas here is characterised by a central contradiction: between lived intimacy, on the one hand, and social distance and separateness on the other. Here, whitefellas and Aboriginal people share bedrooms, surnames, histories, workplaces, football fields, the schoolyard and the bakery queue. Sue says, 'We know there's no getting rid of white people now. Which is good. We are all mixed up anyway.' And yet, in contemporary Ceduna, there lingers the 'carefully divided world of the past', when Aboriginal and non-Aboriginal people inhabited 'different social realms'.[2] Considerable energy is directed towards the maintenance of race-based identities: this is a place where whether you're black or whether you're white, 'matters'.[3]

I first visited Ceduna for a week in November 2006. I had been involved in various environmental and social justice campaigns as a Melbourne-based activist, and was especially heavily involved in a campaign called 'Irati Wanti (The poison, leave it)' against a proposed nuclear waste dump in northern South Australia. The Kupa Piti Kungka Tjuta, a council of senior Aboriginal women living in Coober Pedy, initiated Irati Wanti in 1998, and fostered close working relationships with urban environmental organisations and campaigners over the course of their successful seven-year campaign. I was part of a small group named the 'Melbourne Kungkas' from 2000 to 2004.[4] It was a close friend from those Melbourne Kungkas days, Rhiannon, who first suggested I seek out Aunty Sue, whom Rhiannon had gotten to know.

At our first meeting, Sue slung an arm across my shoulders and gave me a firm squeeze. 'Welcome to our country,' she said gruffly. As a white Australian, 'born of the conquerors', in poet Judith Wright's words, I have long been afflicted with a variety of postcolonial anxiety about having inherited the legacy of violent dispossession.[5] It felt wonderful to be welcomed. That November I slept on a rusted spring bed-frame and thin foam mattress out on the verandah at Sue and her husband Gary's farm. Aunty Sue spent the week acting as a guide for Rhiannon and me: we picnicked out bush, lost money on the Melbourne Cup, waded into warm water at low tide to claw razor fish out of the mudflats, and spent the weekend camping with around twenty members of Aunty Sue's extended family behind a beach where uneven waves thwacked at a rocky shoreline.

These days I treasure a light-hearted friendship with Sue and in person call her 'Aunty Sue' in order to address her 'respect way', as it is said in Ceduna, not to indicate that I have adopted a familial relationship with her. Except in Sue's case, I use pseudonyms throughout this book. In earlier publications arising from this research, I also used a pseudonym for Aunty Sue, calling her 'Aunty Joan'. Her public status and recognisability have steadily increased over the decade since I first met her in 2006, to the point that any attempt to disguise her real name in this book would be farcical.

Aunty Sue has drawn others to her. I refer to the broader group who look to her for everyday moral and political guidance as 'Aunty Sue Mob'. This loosely shaped, always fluctuating social grouping comprises somewhere between ten and twenty adult members of Sue's extended family.[6]

My decision to call the people I work with 'Aunty Sue Mob' was carefully taken. It makes no sense to describe them as 'the Kokatha'. First, this strikes me as a brittle and outdated ethnographic construct. As American anthropologist Gerald Sider explains, this notion implies 'discrete, bounded, culturally and socially distinct societies', mystifying the ways in which this very model is produced throughout involvement in, rather than pre-exists, colonial processes.[7] Further, many Kokatha-identifying people in Ceduna have been centrally engaged with the native title claim, including a few of Aunty Sue's close relatives, who have distanced themselves from her critique.

Aunty Sue Mob largely corresponds to members of an incorporated body, which represents this particular family group's interests, and facilitates their applications to funding bodies for grants to support their cultural and conservation projects. However, the bureaucratic conditions of maintaining incorporated status are resented; instead of using some version of the solemn, unwieldy and very long name of this body—a title generated to satisfy institutional requirements—I opt for a term that arises out of my observations of everyday dynamics, and makes use of the local vernacular.

Membership of Aunty Sue Mob is not fixed or predetermined, it hinges on involvement; this is a term that foregrounds the decisions of those people who throw their lot in with Aunty Sue, whether wholly or momentarily. As will become clearer, I hope to avoid the trap of reproducing and relying too heavily on the very categories that the native title claims process has had the effect of reifying. I have a greater need for a shorthand way of describing the people in Aunty Sue's family group who take their cue from her than do those to whom the label refers, and use 'Aunty Sue Mob' much more frequently than they do.

While 'Indigenous' is increasingly favoured over 'Aboriginal' in Australian scholarly settings, the word 'Aboriginal' is far more commonly used in Ceduna, which is why I prefer it. Aboriginal people in South Australia generally self-identify as Nungas, and I also make use of this term, which enjoys wide currency among both Aboriginal and non-Aboriginal residents, or whitefellas, of Ceduna. A<u>n</u>angu, rather than Nunga, is used by northern South Australian and Central Australian Aboriginal people; the term means 'person' in a number of Western Desert languages, and is used here to refer to those Aboriginal people who are oriented to the remote communities of Yalata and Oak Valley that lie north-west of Ceduna.

Living with native title

Aunty Sue Mob might seem a politically inconsequential handful of people who live in an environmentally marginal 'out-of-the-way place' peripheral to the global economic order.[8] However, their perspective demands to be taken seriously, as they disrupt a narrative of political progress vis-a-vis Indigenous rights in land.

At the end of 2013, nearly eighteen years since native title claims were first lodged in the Ceduna region, the Federal Court of Australia found that Aboriginal people on the Far West Coast of South Australia held native title rights and interests over approximately 80,000 square kilometres. This was a consent determination, in which a mediated—or negotiated, rather than litigated—outcome was reached. The determination secures native title holders' rights to 'access and camp in the area, enjoy the land, teach and conduct ceremonies and protect sites of significance'.[9] But by this point Aunty Sue Mob had long since 'turned their back' on the claim, refusing incorporation into this slow-moving process. Why, exactly, has this particular group been sufficiently agitated to take up and articulate a position outside of and 'against' native title? And why do they hold out against the vision of their future offered by the resource extraction ventures of the mining industry? I grapple in this book with the emotionally charged, sometimes contradictory answers Aunty Sue Mob hurl at these questions.

Native title legislation followed the 1992 High Court of Australia case of *Mabo v Queensland (No 2)*. The Mabo judgment rejected as erroneous the idea that the legal doctrine of *terra nullius*, a land without owners, applied to the Australian continent. The colonial presumption that Indigenous inhabitants did not hold any proprietary rights to land owing to a perceived lack of social organisation and political institutions was regarded as 'repugnant and inconsistent with historical reality'.[10] Numerous historians have since clarified that the British Crown did not explicitly invoke the doctrine of *terra nullius* when founding the colony of New South Wales in the late eighteenth century. The doctrine that 'proclaimed land inhabited by hunters and gatherers to be ownerless' became widespread in legal thinking only in the nineteenth century.[11]

In Mabo, the High Court affirmed that prior to colonisation Indigenous peoples across Australia held title, in common, to their land under their own laws and customs.[12] Their native title was not extinguished by the mere assertion of sovereignty, or dominion, by the British Crown.[13] The subsequent legislative response to the High Court decision, the *Native Title Act 1993* (Cth) (NTA) did not grant new rights; the act provided a mechanism to determine whether or not the common law native title rights derived from Indigenous laws and customs continued to exist, in cases where Indigenous people had maintained a connection with their land since colonisation. The act also provided a mechanism for the native title rights determined to exist to be recognised.

Native title can be seen to form part of the land justice Indigenous activists had long fought for and, from the mid-1970s, increasingly secured.[14] Yet this legislation has had unforeseen consequences.

For Aunty Sue Mob, native title is not necessarily a vehicle for the acknowledgment and affirmation of Indigenous relations with their country. The claims process involves amassing information that will verify claimants' continuity of connection to the country of their ancestors, using archival and oral sources. As part of this process, many Nunga residents in and around Ceduna have rediscovered and reinvigorated their 'tribal' identity as members of a group called Wirangu, attaining traditional owner status and moral authority in the process. Others, including Aunty Sue Mob, express their ongoing loyalty to the Kokatha 'tribe', despite their perception that Kokatha people have been recast as traditionally dwelling in the desert and as no longer technically belonging to the place in which they have lived out their whole lives.

In fact the 2013 determination took great care to emphasise the shared trade, ceremonies and communication between three language groups, Mirning, Kokatha and Wirangu, in pre-colonial times, and to describe their intensive intermingling in the post-contact period. However, what was also clearly stated was the fact that these groups inhabited three distinctive geographic areas in times past. It was this picture of the past, which came to light in the mid-1990s, that rocked Aunty Sue Mob's understanding of their own place in the world.

Wirangu people understand themselves as a coastal people, whose country stretches inland as far north as Ooldea.[15] Over the last two decades, local discourse has increasingly recognised Wirangu people as the traditional owners of the coastal regions where people now reside. Yet many Ceduna Nungas, regardless of their more specific identity, express a close attachment to the place they call home and understand it as their rightful country—in this fishing town, the coast is also valued as the locus of leisure and a source of sustenance.

It is no exaggeration to say that Aunty Sue Mob have experienced native title as a powerful incitement and unwelcome imposition—as something that has emanated from the state, that has resulted in their own *affective* dispossession, and out of which they have gained only enemies. Further, and importantly, they argue that native title exists to facilitate and expedite the expansion of the mining industry into this area, and the disturbance of precious country that entails.

Aboriginal people have been inveigled to reimagine and redefine themselves on the state's terms, in order to satisfy the criteria of legislation anchored in notions of recognition and redress. Thus the claims process, which unfolded between the mid-1990s and late 2013, became a force for the production of a new and not always welcome reality, thoroughly reorganising local Aboriginal identities over the course of this period.

At the outset it is necessary to say something about my use of the shorthand term 'the state' throughout this book. I have perhaps succumbed to the temptation to treat 'the state' as if it were a thing-like thing, to which it is possible to attribute solidity and uni-directionality. In fact, 'the state' is far from a monolithic and an intentional actor, and the workings of state power produce instead complex 'state effects'.[16] However, Aunty Sue Mob have experienced 'the state' in these more monolithic terms and frequently refer to it in this way. The state, or in Sue's usage 'government', has made invitations and imposed upon them, 'dictated' to them, undermined and tricked them, seeming to promise an acknowledgement and extension of their rights in land, yet serving to facilitate instead the expansion of extractive industry interests, which in turn threaten their lived relations with country. I have found somewhat unavoidable a merging of this way of thinking about the state with my treatment of it.

My main concern in this book is the everyday, lived and frequently painful effects of native title. I deal with native title's capacity to reconstitute and rearrange Aboriginal relationships and social worlds—that is, native title's 'constitutive role in the production of indigenous social reality'.[17] More attention needs to be paid to Aboriginal analyses and experiences of native title; arguments about the native title process and its lived effects are only rarely heard in the public domain.

More broadly, the destablisation sometimes unleashed by the native title claims process sheds light on the acute contradictions that characterise the contemporary Aboriginal predicament: putative recognition of Indigenous rights, interests and cultural difference also potentially undermines aspects of Aboriginal people's complex, multiple lived identities, produced through colonial histories. In response to a confusing situation, which initially ensnared them, Aunty Sue's family have engaged in a struggle to reproduce and remain loyal to their self-understanding, rebuffing what they interpret as an attack on the terms of their identity as Kokatha people. Throughout this book I refer to this as a 'struggle for self-definition'.

A prolonged period of conflict left wrecked relationships and bitterness in its wake, but also saw Aunty Sue's family forge new alliances with non-Indigenous environmentalists. This book then is as much about creativity and storytelling as it is about frustration, fighting and refusal. Sue's pursuit of a renewed relationship with sites of cultural significance and her conservation efforts in a mineral-rich region emerge as inventive undertakings which serve, in part, to forge a space 'beyond native title'.[18]

On one level then, this book deals with Aunty Sue Mob's experience of the native title claims process, and the everyday effects of native title. At another level, I discuss more broadly the impact of historical discontinuities on the Aboriginal realm. These first two foci tell of conflict and fragmentation: these are experiences that produced Sue as a critic and spurned her refusal of mining and of the very legitimacy of native title. Later in the book I turn to all that Aunty Sue Mob embrace, celebrating what French scholar Michel de Certeau might have called their 'makeshift creativity'.[19] At this point I detail and attempt to understand Aunty Sue Mob's capacity to shape a meaningful response to this destabilisation. Far from this group being productively understood as politically perverse and obstructionist, their deeply held views find expression in everyday actions that are inspired and life-affirming. Specifically, I consider the significance an initiative called 'Rockhole Recovery', which Aunty Sue organises and which sees Aunty Sue Mob members and invited urban-based environmentalists travelling together 'out the back' to visit, tend and restore important cultural sites.

In going out to clean rockholes, Aunty Sue Mob stress that they are doing something that they have 'always done': they consistently foreground cultural continuity. I find helpful anthropologist Diane Austin-Broos' proposal that continuity is 'worked at through imagination'; cultural traditions do not propel themselves forward through time.[20] Cultural theorist James Clifford places even more emphasis on this point, proposing that cultural 'endurance is a process of becoming', and contemporary Indigenous peoples 'reach back selectively to deeply rooted, adaptive traditions'.[21] Clifford is here proposing a way out of measuring indigeneity via fixed notions of 'authenticity', emphasising process and the translation of old practices into new. Aunty Sue Mob's imaginative and practical efforts, as well as their spatial practices, are all directed towards deliberately maintaining their own longstanding cultural traditions. Yet in doing this thing they have always done, it will become clear that Aunty Sue Mob are *also* doing something original, as it occurs in a new context and has new, exciting and highly political effects.

* * *

I lived in Ceduna for twelve months in 2008 and 2009. I was an activist turned anthropology student, and in that period conducted much of the fieldwork that forms the basis of this book. I enter the picture then as a kind of 'hybrid scholar-activist', attempting to manage a dual identity as a 'greenie' and a researcher.[22] I continue to feel accountable both to the people I write about and to the task of 'cultural critique', that is the imperative to produce academic knowledge that questions current relations of power.

The American anthropologist Charles Hale, who works in Latin America, is optimistic about the admittedly difficult task of remaining both loyal 'to the space of critical scholarly production and to the principles and practices of people who struggle outside the academic setting'.[23] Hale celebrates research methods I have used (and which many researchers not calling themselves activists also use): an emphasis on collaboration, dialogue and dissemination of the outcomes of my research efforts. However, I stop short of following him the whole way, as I especially seek to maintain a degree of distance between Aunty Sue Mob's criticism of other Indigenous political strategies in Ceduna and my own understanding of these. Put simply, I do not take Aunty Sue Mob's enemies as my own.

More prosaically, these multiple aspects of myself, the greenie and ethnographer, which I sometimes roughly conceived of as a former and a future self, were contained within the one body: that of a sleep-deprived new mum, as I arrived with my ten-week-old baby. Anthropologists and greenies were both known entities to Aunty Sue Mob, but anthropologists had come to be associated with the process of collating a native title claim, which by early 2008 had unravelled from Aunty Sue Mob's perspective. I looked, talked, acted and dressed like a scruffy greenie from the city who liked to knock around with blackfellas. It was as a greenie and potential political ally that I was welcomed; ambivalence and occasional suspicion surrounded my role as novice ethnographer.

Yet it was as a mum that I established a commonality with many people in Ceduna, consciously seizing the possibilities for relating to others that my new motherhood created. Shared experiences are a powerful basis for relating to and taking mutual enjoyment in one and another, and these formed the starting point of many empathic conversations with Nunga mums as well as young rural white women, whose classed cultural mores, I came to see, radically contrasted with my own. I dragged minya (little) Ned with me everywhere: he gnawed gummily on a gristly wombat bone, crawled into rock pools, and watched 'bush telly'—the fire. He was, as Uncle Gary liked to say, a 'little bush baby'.

Despite the sense of commonality fostered and enjoyed, comments on this by criminologist Lisa Maher resonate for me. Maher, who was pregnant in the latter stages of her ethnographic research with women drug users in Bushwick, Brooklyn, argues:

> While experiences of pregnancy and mothering may provide some basis for establishing common ground, they are not cultural universals, and individual women's experiences of pregnancy [and motherhood] are both ontologically fractured and far removed from each other according to the social, economic, and cultural sites in which particular pregnancies are situated.[24]

My experience of being a new mother in a place where the social, economic and cultural conditions and expectations surrounding motherhood were vastly different from my own served to continually draw my attention to the classed and culturally-specific nature of motherhood, itself a profoundly embodied experience. The most obvious difference—constantly commented upon, sometimes with discretion but often not—was my age as a first-time mum, an ancient thirty.

I made eight return trips to Ceduna between 2009 and 2015. If I was received more as a greenie than ethnographer throughout 2008 and 2009, I am certainly seen as more academic than greenie now that I spend my time teaching in a university in Sydney, rather than being involved in the world of protests and Aboriginal-led environmental campaigns.

I make heavy use throughout of colloquialisms and vernacular categories as well as quotations from recorded interviews. I conducted a series of wide-ranging interviews with Aunty Joan Mob members and other Ceduna locals, most of them in early 2009 after I returned to the West Coast after Christmas. I had by then spent the best part of a year establishing relationships with people, which allowed me to collect what the American anthropologist Philippe Bourgois describes as 'meaningfully contextualized life-history interview[s]'.[25]

I also spell Kokatha words according to Sue's guidance: she has a strong preference for phonetic renderings, which make the prospect of pronouncing them less intimidating to readers. This stance is consistent with her suspicion of specialised forms of knowledge, including that held by linguists, as well as her celebration of ordinary and improvised methods of laying claim to the world.

Ethnographic biographies and the everyday

Throughout this book I use both the substance of Aunty Sue's own life experiences—as well as the penetrating insights, aphorisms, little gems and grimly funny tales she produces about those experiences—to illuminate the dilemmas and struggles of a distinctly Aboriginal predicament. As a discipline, anthropology's original focus on different collective forms ('tribes' or 'societies') occluded much focus on individuals' lives.[26] In the late 1950s, however, celebrated anthropologist WEH Stanner sketched a portrait of Daly River man Durmugam, describing him as an initiated Nangiomeri man with a strong 'sentiment for Aboriginal ways', who 'wanted to live a blackfellow's life' and 'venerated his culture'.[27] All of this also struck me about Aunty Sue, but what it means to strive to live a Nunga life in her own times, and in this social and political context, is of course vastly different from the scenario Stanner described. Also like Durmugam, Sue has a 'hot belly' for her rights.[28]

'Stanner's Durmugam', anthropologist Jeremy Beckett reminds us, offered readers a picture of a man whose physique, vitality and commitment to the Aboriginal religious life captured Stanner's imagination on the frontier, as it contrasted with the cultural 'decay' and moral degradation that Stanner associated with colonial contact.[29] I am conscious of my own role in creating this portrait, and am also aware that Sue has carefully presented herself to me.

The late Marjorie Shostak, an American anthropologist, describes the frustrations she experienced in finding !Kung women to converse with and interview, until she started recording narratives. Nisa took on the job of teaching Shostak with seriousness and clarity, relishing the interview situation and the conversations recorded by the 'machine that grabs your voice'.[30] Shostak's book about this time is a testament to a singular connection; *Nisa: The Life and Times of an !Kung Woman* was first published in 1981. Another pioneer of ethnographic biographies as a distinct genre, renowned anthropologist Vincent Crapanzano, highlighted his own role as an 'active participant' in the life history of the illiterate Moroccan tile-maker Tuhami. Crapanzano became Tuhami's interlocutor, and his questions produced a 'change in consciousness' in Tahumi.[31]

Other anthropologists describe being sought out rather than seeking their biographical subjects: Mexican 'Indian' woman Esperanza Hernández entrusted Ruth Behar with her story, which travelled across the militarised USA–Mexican border, as well as the border between the spoken and printed, genres of writing, and relations of power.[32] Esperanza's efforts at persuasion remind me of anthropologist Nancy Scheper-Hughes' description of the impoverished mothers of a Brazilian *favela*, jostling for her attention, seizing the 'opportunity to tell a part of their life story'.[33]

Nothing so profound as a change of consciousness was produced in Sue through her exchanges with me. Yet, as in the examples above, Sue was already seeking the means to amplify her voice, and to facilitate the circulation of 'her story'. She found one in the filmmaker Ali Russell, whose 2010 documentary *Keeper* focuses on Sue's anti-mining position, and now screens on Australia's public Indigenous TV channel, NITV. She found another in me. My task, of course, also involves critical engagement with the broader issues she has directed my attention to, rather than providing here a facsimile of her messages.

Numerous Australian anthropological sources carry vivid biographical sketches as part of larger discussions. Gillian Cowlishaw was interested in the person of Frank Doolan, a passionate and articulate Koori man who moves between Sydney, Dubbo's riverbank and the outback town of Bourke, and who personifies 'a particular critique of Australian society ... as well as a conviction that another Aboriginal story needs to be told'.[34] Doolan is also a published poet and maintains an enthralling Facebook page in which he describes himself as a 'Public Figure': he has, then, many ways of accessing an audience. His voice is not necessarily mediated by academic interest in his persona, and neither is Sue's, even if it is here. Deborah Bird Rose once captioned a portrait of Hobbles Danayarri, the former Kimberley stockman, 'master storyteller and political analyst'; Danayarri produced compelling narratives that commented on the moral content of the colonial encounter.[35] Beckett beautifully captured the analytical bent of Aboriginal drover and raconteur George Dutton, and also collaborated with Aboriginal bushman Myles Lalor to publish his rich recollections.[36]

Like these men, Aunty Sue has grasped something fundamental about the condition of being Aboriginal in a contemporary settler colonial society, that is, something general beyond her particular individual experience. Wary of the kind of inquiries undertaken through formal institutions she often says proudly that the 'bush is my university'. Similarly, Gary never tires of telling me about taking a foolhardy anthropologist out the back one time, and her getting lost: 'She was a doctor of something, but she had no fucking brains.' Nonetheless, I propose Aunty Sue is best understood as a perspicacious, grassroots intellectual, treating her words and analysis as a generative force that propels this book.

My approach is also indebted to experimental ethnographer Kathleen Stewart's work on stories and the everyday in *A Space on the Side of the Road* and *Ordinary Affects*. My book might be, in some ways, about native title, but it is primarily about ordinary people's everyday experiences; this is about what happens around kitchen tables rather than in the courtroom.

In writing of contemporary American society Stewart notes 'the terms neo-liberalism, advanced capitalism, and globalization … [and their putative characteristics] do not in themselves begin to describe the situation we find ourselves in'. Stewart does not deny the reality of the forces and systems these words 'try to name', but resists the urge to see them as 'dead effects imposed on an innocent world'. Instead, Stewart is intent on evoking 'the ordinary', which she understands as 'a shifting assemblage of practices and practical knowledges'.[37] Ordinary, miniscule and daily 'forms of living' are comprised of moments both banal and significant, beliefs and practices that are at once incoherent, contradictory and axiomatic, and the intimate, painful and lived effects of severely constrained possibilities.[38]

It is ordinary forms of living, arguing and creating that I bring to light in this book, rather than the workings of the native title legislation. Like Stewart, I found that the possibilities for everyday local action and narration are in excess of the limits life's circumstances set, even in colonised spaces. Stewart might describe these spaces as 'occupied', as well as 'exploited and minoritized'.[39] Like Stewart, I place the authors of ordinary activity in the foreground—it is Aunty Sue Mob's insights, experiences, hopes, fears and frustrations that lie at the heart of this book.

As is already apparent, this book also bears the influence of anthropology's decades' old 'self-reflexive turn' of the 1980s, which saw the role of writer and researcher itself highlighted, and is very much the outcome of a 'constructive negotiation involving at least two… conscious, politically significant subjects'.[40] Aunty Sue has read over and commented upon this whole work prior to its publication, liking some of my ideas and being less impressed with others. I have made minor amendments at her request, and she was closely involved in the selection of the photos that have been included.

And I reveal something of myself in this work, on occasion making myself 'vulnerable'.[41] To conceal the shifting basis of my relations with Aunty Sue Mob would be to obscure 'under what conditions' the information contained here was 'obtained', the disclosure of which is stipulated in that most canonical work of classical anthropology, Bronislaw Malinowski's *Argonauts of the Western Pacific*.[42]

There are other reasons I am unwilling to erase the angst, anxiety and ambivalence that are my constant companions in the highly politicised space I occupy as a white anthropologist working in Aboriginal Australia. I regard these as 'political emotions'.[43] My sense of discomfort has not its primary source in my psyche or personality but in the social. These feelings arise out of Indigenous challenges to non-Indigenous quests to acquire knowledge of and seek access to Indigenous worlds, as well as many Aboriginal people questioning the right of non-Aboriginal people to speak authoritatively about the kinds of questions I tackle.[44] Personal identity, it is worth noting, has long been installed as the *a priori* source of political authority in the post-1970s identity-based new social movements.[45] Further, I include my moments of uncertainty because these kinds of feelings found expression in my everyday relations with Aunty Sue Mob members, sometimes inhibiting them.

Chapter 1

Heading 'out the back'

Grip of a fighter

'The wind is my hairdresser,' says Aunty Sue, stepping out into her dusty yard and letting the hot north wind rush through tangled thick black hair. A wire clothesline stretches across the dirt yard, tractors and car carcasses rust away in a nearby paddock, dogs run out madly to greet approaching cars, and in the middle of this scene Sue stands with a cigarette in a curled hand. Sue lives on a wheat farm with her white-fella husband, Gary, near the small, isolated town of Ceduna. From her yard a strip of flat, grey-blue sea can be glimpsed to the south. North of the chip-dry paddocks, 'out the back', lies a vast stretch of bush; stunted mallee scrublands roll away on sandy waves.

The task of the hairdresser is to subdue and shape hair, human hands and tools bringing this naturally occurring stuff under their control. Sue styles herself in conscious opposition to this, subverting the human will/natural forces hierarchy. She is drawn to images of wildness and rebellion, joyfully submitting to the wind, which here represents the unpredictable and powerful forces of the natural world with its capacity to overpower human designs and desires.

The philosopher Richard Klein understands smoking as 'a wordless but eloquent form of expression'.[1] Sue pinches her cigarettes between her thumb and first finger in a smoking style that is distinctly edgy. This is the grip of the fighter: the knuckles are bared.[2]

Sue embodies a kind of refusal to have her passions tamed, and a disregard for others' expectations. She is 'against native title', despite the fact that native title legislation is designed to recognise Indigenous connections to land, and subsequent rights and interests in it. She is 'against mining' too, even if it promises the economic salvation of remote and regional Aboriginal worlds such as hers. Her experience of these complexly entangled issues will emerge in time. For now I add that for all her toughness, Sue both refuses *and* embraces. While she is locally well known for the things she is against, in this moment she also meets the wind, playfully embracing a certain wildness she believes is in us all.

That 'outlaw one', Aunty Sue

Aunty Sue spent her childhood on the Koonibba Lutheran Mission, located approximately 45 kilometres west of Ceduna. As a young woman she met Gary, whose family has farmed in this wheat-growing district since the early years of the twentieth century; in the late 1960s they danced together to the jukebox in a Greek café in the adjacent port town of Thevenard. Sue raised her own six children (one deceased), as well as 'growing up' a host of other kids, and is now a grandmother and great-grandmother. My focus is firmly on her most recent phase of life, and her public identity as activist, 'rebel', or, as she puts it, 'outlaw one'.

Sue has a brown, sun-beaten face creased with deep smile lines; spindly stars radiate from the edges of her eyes. She also has the gift of the gab. Her warmth and humour, as well as her ability to craft a narrative and to generate insights out of ordinary occurrences, have made a lasting impression on me, as well as on many people around her.

Aunty Sue wears tracksuit pants and floppy tee-shirts. In 2007, she was awarded the inaugural South Australian Premier's Award for 'excellence in Indigenous leadership in natural resource management' and in 2013 she was recipient of the South Australian Landcare award in the Indigenous Land Management category. Sue donned 'glad rags' at the ceremony for the first award, but kept on her beloved 'trackies' beneath her skirt. She would cheerfully accept a prize for fighting against the aggressively pro-mineral extraction policies of the very state government whose representative shook her hand, but she would not give up being herself in the moment she did so. Two favourite tee-shirts give further insight into her cheek, both given to her as presents from environmentalists. One features armed Native American Indians and says, 'Homeland Security. Fighting Terrorism Since 1492.' The other declares, 'Black by popular demand.'

Born on the mission

Storytelling is a vital human imperative. In telling a story, distance between the storyteller and the events concerned is established. In the process, anthropologist Michael Jackson writes, a 'degree of agency is recovered', and 'a balance re-established between our need to determine the world to the same extent that it is felt to determine us'.[3] One of the narratives that Sue has most masterfully shaped is the story of her own life. Born on Koonibba Mission in 1951, Sue frequently says that she has 'always been a rebel'. Her siblings remember her as a 'tomboy' growing up. Aunty Sue told me:

> I used to go with all the men, which was pretty much unheard of. There'd be one little girl who'd travel everywhere with the men coz all the other girls had to learn basket weaving and stuff, but I learned on the land, our culture. So I was really lucky in that respect.

Sue travelled out bush in a two-wheel sulky, drawn by a horse. 'Our people have been walking that country for years so having a horse and sulky was a little bonus,' she says.

She was the particular favourite of one of her mother's younger brothers: he spoilt her 'something rotten' and gave in to her demands to go everywhere with the men. With her uncles and grandfathers, Sue went bush for days at a time. 'They took me right out the back there.'

Sue now thinks that she was taken bush for a reason:

> Old grandfathers used to look after me, take me places—I think they took me there just [because] I had memory, coz I

> can remember things. That's why I'm fighting now. I think they already knew that 'this one here is an outlaw'. Coz I was always called outlaw. 'Outlaw one will get a back up later on in life.'

Sue traces her current willingness to fight 'government' on the issue of mining to her childhood experiences. Her grandfathers entrusted cultural knowledge to her about particular rockhole sites, permanent water sources scattered in the scrub 'out the back there', believing she would be inclined to get her 'back up' and be willing to 'stick up for the land'. Moreover, as she explained to oral historian Sue Anderson and archeologist Keryn Walshe in 1996, her dogged 'hatred for government' stems from the fact that she harbours 'a fair bit of hatred for the system that took the brother away'.[4] This is a reference to her experience of 'Welfare' and the splitting up of her family after the end of the mission in 1963.

Sue and Gary's farmhouse, built in the 1950s, has thick crumbling stone walls, which keep it cool in the scorching summers. The couple is usually to be found sitting around their kitchen table, its laminex surface cluttered with condiments, foodstuffs and stacks of paper—Aunty Sue's 'piling cabinet'. The kitchen walls overflow with family photos, and the cupboards with collections of jars. There is always some kind of activity underway: fish soak in the sink before being gutted; bargain-price nectarines are stoned and stewed before being frozen; a crossword is being filled out.

Gary is a retired wheat farmer who left school at the age of fourteen and started his working life 'lumping' or loading wheat bags onto boats down on the wharves at Thevenard, the small port town adjoining Ceduna. He met Sue when he was about 20:

> I thought, 'Geez, she's a beautiful girl.' And we sort of went together for a couple of years and then I married her, then we had six kids, and we're still together.

'Never had one fight,' he joked. 'We've had lots of them.'

Gary remembered that when he and Sue married:

> There wasn't very many people who married dark girls; at work people used to look down on the dark people and I could never work out why but it was just the way it was ... [M]y parents were a little angry to start with, but then they fell in love with my wife just the same as I did, and they loved her.

Certainly there might have been local talk about his marriage to Aunty Sue, concedes Gary, and about their 'brown-skinned babies'. But of those who talked, he told me, 'I don't give two shits about them!'

His spirited defiance suggests that judgments were commonplace and psychic energy was required to overcome them. Another Ceduna whitefella of the same generation, who also married an Aboriginal woman in the late 1960s, boasted that he had settled the same matter among local whites with his fists.

Walking through the paddocks one day, Aunty Sue and I looked up to see a bunch of crows chasing an eagle through the sky. The eagle ducked and weaved, and the crows came at it from every side, pecking and harassing it. 'Go Crows!' Aunty Sue called out, in her husky smokers' voice.

Sue barracks for the Adelaide Crows football club, a stirrer in a Port Adelaide stronghold. But she also identifies herself with the sharp-eyed, observant crow, and refers to herself sometimes as 'an old crow cackling'.

She has a strong singing voice that is both rough and sweet. I thought she was skilled in the Situationist art of 'detournement'. The Situationists were radical French artists and thinkers of the 1960s. In Mackenzie Wark's *The Beach Beneath the Street* he explains that detournement 'treats all of culture as common property to begin with, and openly declares its rights'.[5] Aunty Sue delights in such acts of 'unauthorized appropriation', which produce subversive meanings. She alters selected fragments of country and western lyrics so that they become irreverent ballads about local Ceduna characters—one featuring white farmers ready with a shotgun. She taught me an amended lullaby that I sung to my own babies: *I see the moon and the moon sees me / Smiling through the leaves of the old gum tree / I hope that moon that shines on me / Shines on the one that I love.*

Native title on the West Coast

Out bush one day Sue mulled over the fact that 'government' named the railway line that runs from Adelaide to Darwin, 'the Ghan'. And yet, she said, the government 'was locking up all those Afghans in Baxter [Immigration Detention Centre]'. 'Hang on,' Sue continued, 'why am I surprised by that?' She paused for effect. 'That's what they do to us.'

According to numerous theorists, the liberal multicultural nation state sometimes reaches out to acknowledge, celebrate and even incorporate Aboriginality into its self-understanding, desiring to respect cultural difference.[6] But late liberal states also move to manage, contain and cordon off the perceived threat of difference, often in violent ways. In the case of the Ghan, Australia gestures retrospectively to honour and incorporate the experiences of a dominated people previously subject to racial prejudice and violence. Yet, as the sheer brutality of Australia's asylum seeker system demonstrates, the federal government also retains the power to manage the national space, excluding others in the present.[7]

Native title is an exemplary case of a late liberal settler colonial state grappling with the 'recognition' of Indigenous difference, as native title rights arise from Indigenous peoples' distinctive cultural traditions. Anthropologist Elizabeth Povinelli has brought to light the conditions imposed on the state's embrace: difference is seemingly valued but the multicultural state recoils from too much difference, or 'radical alterity', revealing its intolerance. Since the 2002 publication of Povinelli's groundbreaking *Cunning of Recognition*, the nation-state's limited romance with Indigenous cultural difference has waned. Indeed, as political theorist Elizabeth Strakosch writes, 'The progressive multicultural state that recognizes and dispenses entitlements … already seems like a figure of nostalgia'.[8]

In the policy era ushered in by the 2007 Northern Territory Emergency Response ('the Intervention'), extensions and evolutions of both sovereign and disciplinary forms of state power have meant possibilities for being culturally 'otherwise' are ever shrinking, argues Povinelli.[9] Put more simply, the current moment insists on the integration of Indigenous individuals into the mainstream capitalist economy, justifying coercive interventions into the lives of those Indigenous people who are deemed to lack the capacity to work.

These complex developments are beyond the scope of this work. Here I note simply that no epoch neatly supplants another. In one sense, native title might seem like a creature properly belonging to a more optimistic time—a period in which it was hoped that Mabo might come to mark a rupture in Australia's colonial history, and form part of a movement towards collective redress. In fact, as anthropologist David Martin has perceptively shown, the *Native Title Act* simultaneously evokes indigeneity in two different guises. The claims process asks Indigenous people to present their identities in a 'singular and traditionalist' mode, in order to secure native title rights. At this stage of the process Indigeneity is desired in a familiar sense, as 'authentic' and shared cultural difference. Yet the agreement-making provisions of the same act are predicated on Indigenous people partaking in interest-based negotiations with third parties. Native title claimants and holders typically seek to secure employment commitments from resource companies, business development opportunities and so on. In this moment, Indigenous people's active engagement with the capitalist economy rather than collective attachments to country is centred: indigeneity is refigured as best served by incorporation into the contemporary state and employment market.[10]

In response to recognition's 'cunning' or its 'trick', Mohawk scholar Audra Simpson shows that Indigenous peoples might instead 'refuse' that which they have been offered.[11] For Simpson, 'there is a political alternative to "recognition," the much sought-after and presumed "good" of multicultural politics'. The alternative is refusal, which Simpson says, involves 'a willfull distancing from state-driven forms of recognition and sociability in favor of others'.[12] Rather than making themselves recognisable by enacting the kinds of 'contortions' involved in becoming an ethnologically legible Indigenous cultural subject, that is to say the right kind of Indigenous person on whom recognition might be bestowed, many Mohawks of Kahnawà:ke direct their political energies into assertions of nationhood and questions of membership. The energies of Aunty

Sue Mob are more diffused, and the scope of their modest actions more local in scale, but Simpson's argument clearly applies.

These are my questions: What are some of the unintended consequences and unpredictable social forces unleashed by involvement in native title claims? What kinds of Aboriginal life experiences and identity formations are rewarded within the native title process? And what kinds of Aboriginal experiences of the colonial encounter—of movement, disjunction, dislocation and discontinuity—jeopardise the basis of an efficacious claim to traditional owner status? Where the answers to these questions lead to disillusionment, what does the resulting politics of refusal look like?

To return to more concrete details: the late-2013 Federal Court decision on the West Coast resolved the largest native title claim in South Australia. The claim joined together the claims of the following cultural groups: Mirning Peoples, Wirangu Peoples, Kokatha Peoples, the descendants of Edward Roberts, Yalata Peoples and Maralinga Tjarutja (Oak Valley) Peoples. Aunty Sue Mob are 'proud Kokatha people' but they did not participate in the latter stages of the claim. Why not?

The backstory to this complex claim, and their eventual rejection of its terms, runs something like this: since the mid-1990s, the rightful ownership of this country became the subject of a bitter local contest. The turn to the colonial archive, which research for native title claims invariably involves, has seen the re-emergence over the past two decades of a near-forgotten 'tribal' category. A group of people in Ceduna have now come to identify as Wirangu. I am at pains to acknowledge that many Wirangu-identifying people are excited by the revelatory and empowering opportunities for self-discovery that native title has underwritten. Those people who understand themselves as Wirangu now assert that they are the traditional owners of the coast; Kokatha people are increasingly 'properly' understood in the anthropological literature as Western Desert 'migrants', whose traditional estates—those lands over which they can claim rights of traditional ownership—lie in the arid north, far beyond their well-known world.[13] Those termed 'migrants' live less than 50 kilometres from the birthplace of their grandparents.

In this book I wrestle with a political problem. Aunty Sue Mob have found their own reality being defined from the outside; a redefinition that has been so pervasive as to undermine Aunty Sue Mob's capacity to enjoy some modicum of authority on the subject of *their own understanding of themselves*. The native title system, they intuit, has reproduced the colonial dynamic in which outsiders and experts parse the 'truth' of their Aboriginal identity.

Since the 1990s, through their experience of the native title process, Kokatha people in Ceduna see themselves as having been recast as inhabitants of country that they do not rightfully belong to. There is no precise moment or dramatic event I can direct the reader to, to explain *exactly* how this happens: this was a subtle process in which the acquisition of new knowledge saw an adjustment of the significance accorded to what it meant to be, primarily, Wirangu and what it meant to be, primarily, Kokatha. Kokatha-identifying people cannot claim the much-respected mantle of 'traditional owner' over the Ceduna area, without this designation being called into question. For Aunty Sue Mob members this whole process, which I describe in more detail in later chapters, has involved much anguish as the substance of a relationship to country in which they were born and brought up—country that they have intimate knowledge of, and a strong attachment to, and in which they have lived out their whole lives—has been undermined.

Anthropologists Benjamin Smith and Frances Morphy's important edited volume, *The Social Effects of Native Title*, argues for such a shift in focus towards what they call the 'social effects' of native title.[14] Smith and Morphy begin by noting that the role of the native title system is in 'delimiting and forcefully re-shaping the character of Indigenous ties to traditional lands'.[15] These authors highlight Indigenous people's ambivalence about engaging with a system that, on the one hand, entails submission 'to the state's authority over the contemporary existence of Indigenous property rights', and prospects for securing formal recognition of Aboriginal relations with their land and water on the other.[16] The latter point is not to be discounted. Not only does native title provide a vehicle for securing long sought-after legal rights and interests, which can be accompanied by or leveraged for economic opportunities, but also it is important to remember that native title claimants seek to 'affirm and promote their relationship with country'.[17] 'Country' for many Aboriginal people is a living entity, imbued with the presence of ancestral beings whose activities are described in the creative epoch commonly known as 'the Dreaming'. However, Aunty Sue Mob's stance on the trade-off Smith and Morphy identify cannot be understood without also grasping the impossibility of successfully opposing—in absolute terms—mining within native title-related negotiations.

'Too good for miners'

Just north of Ceduna lies a series of designated areas largely devoted to conservation, which are open to the public for camping and driving; they are popular spots for Ceduna locals and four wheel drive (4WD) enthusiasts. Indeed, over 85 per cent of the Far West Coast native title determination comprises national park, reserve or wilderness area, the determination area encompassing the entirety of the Yellabinna Regional Reserve, the Yellabinna Wilderness Protection Area, and the Yumbarra and Pureba Conservation Parks.[18] My 2008–2009 fieldwork was undertaken in the midst of Australia's richest mining boom, which, it is now widely acknowledged, has peaked. Falling commodity prices have now underwritten a transition away from investment in exploration to production. At the time of my fieldwork, however, Yellabinna Regional Reserve and Yumbarra were under intensive mineral exploration, their geological sub-stratum being especially rich in heavy mineral sands deposits.

Two geological provinces meet in this region. The Gawler Craton underlies the greater part of South Australia; the Eucla Basin extends from the western Eyre Peninsula into Western Australia. The Gawler Craton is prospective for uranium, gold and copper deposits, among other minerals, and the Eucla Basin is prospective for heavy mineral sands, among other minerals. BHP-Billiton's gargantuan Olympic Dam uranium and copper mine, located near Roxby Downs, is part of the Gawler Craton Basin.[19]

The passing of the *Native Title Act* in late 1993 ushered in a period in which group names, often called 'tribes' in Ceduna, emerged as ascendant and were then codified. This period, roughly the mid- to late-1990s, coincided with the beginnings of increased interest in mineral exploration in the region.

As I have summarised elsewhere with Tim Neale, native title provides claimants and holders with no rights to veto or consent over resource extraction or development. However, most third party land uses, such as mining, trigger opportunities to negotiate compensation or 'benefit' packages with developers.[20] Legal scholar David Ritter calls this a 'native title market', whereby Indigenous groups have their consent to trade.[21] Third parties are delivered security and a 'social licence' to operate; state and territory governments benefit from royalties and infrastructure investments; and Indigenous stakeholders secure some mix of financial payments, employment targets, training, preferential procurement policies, and so on. In Australia as well as internationally, the mining industry has made much of its embrace of a new era of 'agreement-making'; however, as Ritter points out, such agreements are now mandated by law in Australia.

In Ceduna in the 1990s a situation emerged in which numerous mining companies were seeking exploration rights in the region. These companies were, it is now alleged, impatient to identify and enter into negotiations with the relevant native title claimant group, just as these groups were in the very process of forming and their members consolidating an understanding of their identities in primarily 'tribal' terms. These processes unfolded in tandem, resulting in much confusion and division.

The Yumbarra Conservation Park, which lies most immediately north-west of Ceduna, was controversially 'reproclaimed' in 1999, from a single-use conservation park into a multi-use park, in order to allow exploration and mining to take place within the park. How did this park's conservation status come to be downgraded? Environmental campaigners Greg Ogle et al explain that 'aerial geological surveys in the 1990s revealed a large anomaly under the surface of the Park of a type which have been found to be highly mineralised elsewhere in the Gawlor Craton'.[22] The mining industry lobbied to have Yumbarra 'opened up' while conservation groups campaigned to 'maintain its strictly protected status'.

The South Australian Liberal government's 1999 re-proclamation was opposed by Labor in opposition. However, when Labor came to power in South Australia in 2002 it proved reluctant to reinstate Yumbarra's status as a single-use conservation park, despite nothing ever having come of the anomaly. Instead, then Labor premier Mike Rann appeared to offer a sweetener, proclaiming a 500,000-hectare portion of the Yellabinna Regional Reserve a wilderness area, and banning mining and exploration in the northern corner of this reserve.[23] Regional reserves were, in themselves, new categories of reserves designated in 1987, which explicitly provided for mineral exploration and mining to take place in areas simultaneously recognised to have conservation value.[24]

In Ceduna I was told, 'Nobody was going to dig anything until the mining companies decided that they could make a buck and the state government decided they could make a buck.' Then, these parties said, 'Let's have a look at those blacks over there and see what they think? We might get some greedy ones ... who want to make a buck as well and screw the rest.'

Many Indigenous groups across Australia stand to potentially benefit from the right to negotiate statutes contained under the *Native Title Act*. A majority of the mines in Australia are adjacent to Indigenous communities whose ties to kin and country make their populations the ideal workforce, it is argued, for projects located far from the nation's major urban centres.[25] However, as American anthropologist Kirk Dombrowski points out, this Indigenous habit of 'staying behind' contrasts with global rural-to-urban movements, and has been underwritten in Australia, Canada and elsewhere by successful land claims which have, in turn, fed the 'voracious appetite of capital for the raw material basis of modern manufacturing'. Today, the poverty in remote Indigenous communities is too often naturalised as a cultural phenomena, according to Dombrowski, obscuring the fact that while life at these economic and environmental peripheries has become 'marginally more possible', this state of affairs has facilitated massively profitable mining projects.[26] Further, it is clear that Indigenous groups with greater political and economic resources routinely achieve more equitable agreements in this profoundly inequitable contractual landscape.[27]

In Ceduna in the 1990s claimants found themselves in a highly pressurised situation with many forces in play. I have been told that this period presented an opportunity for those Nungas who previously knew little about their genealogy or seemed to have a minimal interest in the Aboriginal past. Most Aboriginal people in Ceduna today can trace Wirangu, Kokatha and other antecedents. However, people came to express their 'tribal' identity in singular terms—although this is not always the case—and bitchy criticism is directed at those who 'can't make up their mind about who they are'.

It was put to me with great venom that 'those who didn't know what their tribal group was' ended up, around this time, 'picking one'. And, it was alleged, these decisions were primarily strategic: 'You pick the one, probably, pick the one that's got the dollars, or the one that's got the big mouths.' Cynicism attends many of the personal decisions made around this time of the Wirangu's (re)emergence or, in anthropologist James Weiner's terms, their 'elicitation'.[28] Anthropologist Ben Scambary describes a similar situation in the Pilbara, where individuals might seem to divide their allegiances between language groups on an ad hoc basis. However, closer examination reveals these shifting identifications involve decisions made with regard to many factors, including 'positioning oneself to be in receipt of resources associated with the native title claims process or mining agreements'.[29]

The resolution of the Far West Coast claim in 2013 clarified exactly the extent and nature of the native title still held in this region. But years before, in December 2007, the Far West Native Title Group had already signed an Indigenous Land Use Agreement (ILUA) with Western Australia-based Iluka Resources, which covers a mine called Jacinth-Ambrosia.[30] Sue tags this an 'Illegal Land Use Agreement', and remains a vehement opponent for the mining proposed in this region. At the event of the signing of the agreement, Aunty Sue Mob members staged a silent protest at the local oval, dramatising the fact that their opposition to the coming mine was not being listened to. 'We don't have a political voice,' Sue told me. 'We don't have any rights at all because we won't join up with native title.'

In 2010, Iluka began mining and processing the mineral sand zircon at the Jacinth-Ambrosia site on the far western edge of the Yellabinna Regional Reserve, approximately 200 kilometres north-west of Ceduna. Iluka, one of the largest tenement holders of exploration licences in the region, has certainly not assumed the role described elsewhere, in which maintenance of roads, and provision of essential services, for example, might become the responsibility of mining companies rather than a reduced neoliberal state.[31] Iluka has, however, a visible presence in local life, acting as a major sponsor of both whole-of-community and specifically Indigenous events and initiatives.

Zircon is used in ceramics, such as floor and wall tiles. Here, the lives of outback residents become caught up with global processes: the rapid urbanisation of China makes profitable the mining of minerals trucked through Ceduna: 'uneven and awkward links' such as these are the interconnections that make contemporary global capitalism.[32] Jacinth-Ambrosia has a predicated life of ten years; under the agreement with the native title group, Iluka has a target of 20 per cent Indigenous employees, which the company states has been met since 2012.[33] This mine is in the Eucla Basin. Other significant deposits, including of uranium, have been found 'out the back' but at the time of writing no other project has moved beyond the 'feasibility study' stage. Mining hovers around the edges of this story: a possibility, prospect or threat that now recedes as the boom peters out. Indeed, in early 2016 Iluka announced it would suspend activities at Jacinth-Ambrosia as a result of this downturn; the suspension began in April 2016 and will remain in place for 18 to 24 months.[34]

In sum, Aunty Sue Mob perceive that those Ceduna Nungas who are most enthusiastic about mining, and are best positioned to benefit from it, are those who earlier fully embraced the native title claims process. She accuses some Aboriginal people of being willing to give their 'signature', or 'sell the land', 'for a few pieces of silver'. Those who are thus inculpated are sometimes called 'mining mob', sometimes 'native title mob'. Again, there is no right of veto over mineral projects afforded under the *Native Title Act*, and negotiations can become both ugly and wearisome. 'Native title mob' and 'mining mob' remain synonymous in Aunty Sue Mob's usage.

Chapter 2

'Rockholes all over the place'

Rockhole Recovery

How do Aunty Sue Mob respond to all I have outlined so far? Sue, especially, channels her dynamism into organising a twice-yearly event. Every six months she leads a camping trip out into the bushland that lies beyond her dusty yard, heading 'out the back'. These trips are named 'Rockhole Recovery', or in the vernacular simply 'rockhole trips'. They comprise six, sometimes seven, days of 4WD travel and involve visiting a series of rockholes—permanent water sources scattered across semi-arid country, and significant cultural sites connected to the Seven Sisters Dreaming complex.[1] The trips are ongoing, and take place each September, as the Seven Sisters or Pleiades constellation makes its appearance in the spring skies, and in March, before the Sisters slip beyond view.

Aunty Sue Mob jointly undertake these rockhole trips with interested non-Aboriginal visitors. They are not a commercial venture; trip participants 'chuck in' to help cover the cost of fuel and food. Aunty Sue Mob have affectionately tagged their guests 'greenies': these greenies are best described as grassroots environmental activists and are based, mostly, in Melbourne, Adelaide and Sydney.

The rockhole trips are collaborative ventures. Aunty Sue first made contact with greenies in 2003. At a bush camp called Kulini Kulini, over 300 anti-nuclear environmental activists met at the invitation of the Kupa Piti Kungka Tjuta—a council of senior Aboriginal women based in Coober Pedy.[2] The gathering was part of the successful campaign against the siting of a nuclear waste dump in northern South Australia. Here, Sue 'got up and asked for help'.

Sue formed a close bond with an anti-nuclear activist who responded to her request. Interpersonal relationships with Aboriginal identities are desired and exalted by environmental campaigners of this ilk. No doubt this activist recognised that Aunty Sue's request for help also represented the potential beginnings of a friendship—here lay an invitation to enjoy closeness with a charismatic Aboriginal authority, someone with a deep feeling for her culture and country.

In March 2006, Aunty Sue, in collaboration with this dynamic greenie, organised the first rockhole trip. Aunty Sue quickly encountered other 'greenies' from within this same social-political-cultural milieu—including, eventually, me.

Rockhole Recovery participants visit either three or four named rockhole sites over the course of each trip; the route varies slightly each time according to which rockholes Aunty Sue deems it a priority to visit. Participants empty rockholes of gunk, debris, rotting animal remains and dirty water, leaving them empty for the next rain to replenish these ancient water sources.

My own interpretation of rockhole trips is as follows: Rockhole trips are an inspired undertaking at the margins that express Aunty Sue's extant vision of the world. My sense is that these trips can be productively understood as a response to the political crisis produced by this mob's protracted encounter with the native title claims process. Aunty Sue Mob explain to greenies that the trips involve, in part, the reproduction and reinvigoration of a traditional cultural practice, the careful tending of these special, sociologically significant places. I'm certainly not saying that I think Rockhole Recovery trips are about something other than what Aunty Sue Mob say they're about. Rather, I think these trips are *also*, and crucially, a vehicle for the reproduction of Aunty Sue Mob members' self-understanding—as Kokatha people living on Kokatha Country. Rockhole trips involve Aunty Sue Mob travelling through country, being on country, sleeping on country, getting tired, sweaty and filthy working on country. All of this provides a means for them to claim, express, enact and live out their relationship with this country, with their bodies, on their own terms. Thus their struggle for self-definition is advanced.

On another level again, Rockhole Recovery can be understood to represent Aunty Sue Mob's determined expression of opposition to mining in this country, writ large. Rockhole trip routes traverse those conservation parks that are overlaid with a patchwork of exploration licences. On my first rockhole trip, undertaken in March 2008, I collected a flyer that stated:

> Every March and September [Aunty Sue Mob] and [the greenies] colloborate on a 4WD journey monitoring and cleaning significant soaks and water holes within the Yellabinna Regional Reserve and Yumbarra and Pureba Conservation Parks, which are under siege from SA's mining boom.

The flyer includes a quote from prominent Aunty Sue Mob figures:

> WE HAVE BEEN CAMPAIGNING FOR PROTECTION OF THIS REGION FOR MANY YEARS. SHORT TERM PROFITS FROM MINING WILL NEVER OUTWEIGH THE NATURAL AND CULTURAL VALUES OF THIS LAND, AND WHAT IT MEANS TO OUR PEOPLE. OUR MESSAGE TO THE STATE GOVERNMENT AND ANY MINING COMPANIES IS 'MUNDOO YUMADOO ILIGA' WHICH MEANS 'LEAVE THE LAND AS IT IS'.

The flyer is now a creased and torn piece of A4-sized paper, folded in quarters and smudged with sweat. It forms part of my collection of scrappy ephemera, the value of which lies far beyond its mnemonic function. In studying the white bureaucrats charged with addressing the dire health of Northern Territory Indigenous people, the ethnographer Tess Lea treated policies, data, charts and diagrams as cultural 'artefacts', which gave material form to public servants' desire for analysis and outcomes.[3] Flyers—spelling mistakes and all—are among the artefacts I collected while conducting this research. In the space shared and shaped by Aboriginal people and their greenie supporters, passionate and stark sentiments are cobbled together, reproduced ad hoc, and disseminated quickly and cheaply. The flyer is small, jammed with text of varying shapes and sizes, and too-dark black-and-white photocopied photos. Its texture and 'unprofessional' character is not something I wish to hide; instead it points to the value Aunty Sue accords extemporaneity, as well as her carefully maintained remove from state and federal government funding sources and processes.

Rockhole Recovery participants travel in a slow, snaking 4WD convoy along soft, sandy roads, the conditions of which have greatly improved because of the access mining companies' exploration parties now enjoy to this remote area, an irony Aunty Sue Mob appreciate. 'We used to call this killer track!' Aunty Sue Mob members frequently comment when travelling one particular route, before jokingly offering thanks to 'the miners' for widening roads and clearing overhanging trees for them.

Aunty Sue Mob reinscribe these routes for their own purposes, in order to maintain a relationship with country that they wish to see protected from development. The traces of exploration parties' travels are literally overlaid with the tracks made by Sue's convoy. Aunty Sue Mob hold an absolute position as to the future of their country—they do not want to see any mining proceed in this particular swathe of bush, under any conditions. 'Too good for miners,' Aunty Sue once fired back, her eyes flashing, after I commented on a particularly beautiful spot we visited on a warm spring day.

Aunty Sue has summarised her opposition, stating:

> There are rockholes all over the place: special, sacred sites all over the place. You can't negotiate. The land is the land, and I've been saying all along, 'The land is not negotiable.'

Thus Aunty Sue Mob say they are determined to 'stick up for the land'. They hold out against the vision of their future that influential Indigenous public intellectual Marcia Langton and others outline—mining is often held up as the saviour of remote and regional Aboriginal worlds.[4] Aunty Sue Mob extend an invitation to urban-dwelling environmentalists to participate in Rockhole Recovery as guests in their country, in order to establish and maintain a political support base that they anticipate drawing upon in the future. Further, rockhole trips and other trips out bush signal Aunty Sue Mob's refusal to accept the terms imposed by the *Native Title Act*, a refusal to see their relationship with this country undermined because it does not satisfy the requirements of a 'traditional' relationship, in a strict sense.

Rockhole trips can be seen to be about maintaining, expressing, enacting and enjoying a relationship to country. Moreover, rockhole trips involve being on one's country and living out a relationship with that country via sweaty, smelly physical activity, which is what the task of cleaning out the rockholes involves. In this way Aunty Sue Mob convey and experience their relationship with country by means of a sensuous physicality that stresses a contrast between the process of outlining people–country relationships to satisfy the state's requirements, in words, and the process of expressing and living this relationship, with bodies.

Native title produces new realities in places like Ceduna, as the relationships between people who have long associated and inevitably see each other frequently are altered. Rockhole trips are an example of a group of people's efforts to respond to native title by creating something beyond and outside of native title, producing in effect an alternate reality. Rockhole Recovery is key to the creating of such a reality, to dwell in and to savour, even if only fleetingly.

I do not delve into the Dreaming stories that link these sites. My attention is turned instead to the conditions that have generated a situation in which the possessing, disclosing and circulating of Dreaming stories and other kinds of cultural knowledge represents an extremely fraught undertaking. The reasons for this are bound up in the conflicts generated by the local native title claim process.

Aunty Sue Mob are caught in a double bind: rockhole trips are one means by which they legitimate their own cultural authority, emphasising their familiarity with and attachment to these sites to a local audience, as well as to visiting greenies, who are in turn regarded as emissaries of the imagined nation. In other words, Aunty Sue Mob are acutely aware of wider expectations about what 'real' Aboriginality looks and sounds like. At the same time, they fear the consequences if the stories, meanings and even names associated with particular sites, which they wish to demonstrate that they know, circulate too freely. The fear is that other Aboriginal people will claim to 'know' things they don't *really* know, or at least did not know until they learnt them from the Aboriginal people who 'really' hold this understanding. Once things are set down, Aunty Sue Mob perceive, it's there for 'anyone to read': people might read it and claim 'they've know it all their lives'. 'Knowledge' is thus treated as something that needs to be held over time, and something that directly links contemporary people with their antecedents, whose social identities were fundamentally sourced in the stories for and metaphysical dimensions of country.

It is the experience of these kinds of tensions—over the rightful proprietors of cultural knowledge, over the significance that country holds today—as well as the broader conditions that give these conflicts shape that I hope to analyse. For this reason I also refrain from specifying or naming the particular rockholes visited over the course of Rockhole Recovery. The sites themselves all have a number of names. One, for example, bears a European woman's name on all the maps I have seen of this region. Sue is grateful to the 'lovesick explorer' whose naming of this feature has meant that the alternate Aboriginal name for this site is only in limited circulation. I routinely use the Aboriginal name for this site in conversation, but not another 'deeper' name, which is only sometimes expressed, and not within my rights to utter. I err on the side of circumscription throughout this book.

Histories of rupture

In the early 1970s, the social scientist Charles Rowley wrote a major three-volume analysis of the present state of Aboriginal Australia.[5] In *Outcasts in White Australia*, a map separated the continent into two zones: colonial and settled Australia.[6] The line marking these boundaries is perforated in sections, including just north of Ceduna. Here, presumably, there was movement in and out of different settings: north of the broken line representing what are today called remote Aboriginal communities; and south and east of the line representing the shared social domains of cities and towns.

Ceduna lies on the very edge of what Rowley designated as settled Australia.[7] Rowley may have designated the sparsely populated north as 'colonial' in 1967, contrasting this with 'settled' Australia, but today it is clear that bounded and Aboriginal and non-Aboriginal worlds do not exist even in the communities of the so-called 'remote' north, permeated and produced as these communities are by the presence of actual non-Aboriginal people as well as entanglements with the logic, knowledge systems of, economic ties to and cultures of the Australian nation-state.

Conducting research in a small rural town where whitefellas outnumber Nungas, I remained acutely aware that Aboriginal people in remote northern settings have remained the enduring object of anthropological fascination and elicit a broader public interest.[8] The notion that 'settled is lesser' is well understood by Aunty Sue Mob members who live with this as an everyday reality.[9] Frequent comment, in tones varying from wounded to wry, is made by individuals who fear that their cultural authority might be doubted by tourists and politicians on the basis of them failing to conform to the 'pernicious fantasy of the "Indigenous look"'.[10]

One of my main concerns is the relationship between Aboriginal identities, colonial history, movement and change, whether chosen, induced or coerced. Experiences of discontinuity are the legacy of the colonising process, yet this fact sits uneasily along the recent emphasis on cultural continuity within Australia. Writing in the early 1950s, Stanner emphasised 'sameness, absence of change, fixed routine, regularity' as the 'main dimension' of Aboriginal 'thought and life'. Stanner greatly admired this quality of 'abidingness' and supposed that the Aboriginal 'value on continuity' was so high that Aboriginal people had become 'a-historical in mood, outlook and life'.[11]

Anthropologists have also placed a high value on continuity, in the process paying inadequate attention to colonialism, as anthropologist Francesca Merlan argues. Merlan warns that 'to pass over the question of change is to abdicate the effort to understand contemporary complexity' as well as to implicitly endorse the value of cultural authenticity as uncorrupted cultural difference.[12] Merlan explains that pre-colonial Aboriginal 'tradition' is the 'currency of indigeneity' within the late liberal state.[13] This currency circulates, and is traded in, in unpredictable ways. Aboriginal people, especially in the south-east of Australia, can be deprived of rights in land due to a perceived deficit of traditional culture, as in the well-known Yorta Yorta native title case, which was finally decided in 2002.[14] In this scenario, Justice Olney concluded that the 'tide of history' had washed away Yorta Yorta native title rights. On the other hand, Indigenous people living in 'remote communities' are frequently pathologised as retaining a surfeit of traditional culture incompatible with 'modern' social norms.[15]

Interestingly, an emphasis on continuity is evident even among those recent ethnographers who have worked in south-eastern Australia, where the disruption to pre-contact cultural forms has been greatest. The contributors to Ian Keen's groundbreaking book on 'settled' Australia, *Being Black*, which was first published in 1988, took issue with the emphasis of earlier south-eastern scholars on 'acculturation' and the 'disintegration' of the normative content of localised and distinct Aboriginal social and cultural forms.[16] Writing against the notion of a cultureless remnant, or the popular idea that Aboriginal people in south-eastern states were socially marginal people, who had retained little of their cultural traditions, the contributors to Keen's anthology made a vital contribution to our understanding of colonial contact. The works published in *Being Black* stressed that not only in the north but in 'settled' Australia too, cultural continuity was everywhere in evidence, documenting the perpetuation of distinctive cultural traditions, sets of meanings and social relations, all in massively hostile conditions. In a similar vein, contributions to Peggy Brock's 1989 *Women, Rites & Sites: Aboriginal Women's Cultural Knowledge* demonstrated the retention and renovation of land-based cultural knowledge in South Australia, specifically that held by Aboriginal women.

Yet this focus on continuities, even in south-eastern settings, runs the risk of diverting attention away from the historical and political conditions in which Aboriginal life stories are enmeshed. As is now well established, the definition of Aboriginality has in of itself constantly changed over time: legal scholar John McCorquodale's analysis of 700 pieces of legislation yielded '67 identifiable classifications, descriptions or definitions' used from the time of white settlement to the late 1990s.[17]

In the inter-war period, assimilationist thinking gained ground in Australia. In this model, it was the Aboriginal capacity to change—to effect discontinuity—which was coerced, approved and rewarded by state government policies. In the context of native title, it is the quality of remaining most unchanged—the capacity to effect and demonstrate continuity—that is demanded, approved and rewarded by federal government legislation. As Indigenous legal scholar Irene Watson writes:

> Who we are is often navigated from a violent space within which Aboriginality is measured for its degree of authenticity, and where those who do the measuring are ignorant or deniers of the history of colonialism.[18]

How are we to think through this history of profound discontinuities in the midst of a scenario that now valorises cultural continuity?

Aboriginality as an unstable identity category

Again, I take contemporary Aboriginal identities as always interrelated with state effects, and co-constituted through relations with other actors such as environmentalists and local whitefellas. If this is the case, then historical ruptures, indeterminacy and shifts in identities are as much to be taken account of as cultural continuities.

Like all identities, Aboriginality is an unstable category, constantly being defined and refined by external actors and forces, and about which competing and contradictory ideas swirl in the same place and in the same moment. However, the experiences and effects of such instabilities are unevenly distributed, and in this case the costs and burdens are high. For the Martinique-born anticolonial thinker and psychiatrist Frantz Fanon, the experience of colonised blackness was to be 'sealed in crushing objecthood'.[19] 'The white man has woven me out of a thousand details, anecdotes and stories,' wrote Fanon.[20] 'I am overdetermined from without.'[21]

Aunty Sue Mob's story makes clear that Aboriginality is an especially overburdened and over-determined category of experience. Since the publication of Edward Said's *Orientalism*, much has been written about 'constructions of Aboriginality'.[22] What I am interested in is the effects of *living* simultaneously alongside, with and/or against these many 'constructions'. Sue's own lifetime has spanned traceable historical shifts in the possibilities available to her for living and expressing her Aboriginality. Thus, like many Aboriginal people in contemporary Australia, Aunty Sue Mob members are compelled to enact an ongoing dialogue with manifold and contradictory discourses about the significance of the particular qualities of their own lived and embodied existence, as the value accorded to their cultural traditions, for example, is ever shifting. According to Indigenous public figure Michael Dodson, to speak of Aboriginality is to enter a 'labyrinth full of obscure passages, ambiguous signs and trapdoors'; Aunty Sue Mob seek to wend their way through this labyrinth.[23]

I may have already given some sense of the condition of living with multiplicity, if we pay closer attention to the not-quite-interchangeable and shifting terms I use to refer to Aunty Sue Mob members. Aunty Sue Mob members sometimes style themselves as and are described as Kokatha people, sometimes Nungas, sometimes Aboriginal people, and sometimes seeking to remind others of their Irish ancestry.[24] Of course, living with multiplicity in contemporary Australia is not an experience unique to Indigenous people. But for Aboriginal people this multiplicity carries a risk, and its reality is not so much to be denied as backgrounded. Indigeneity remains an essentialised as well as deeply 'territorialised' identity formation.[25] By that I mean Aboriginality is commonly seen as sourced in an innate, internal reservoir of spiritual feeling for ancestral land and is regarded as suspect where these qualities are perceived to be attenuated.

How then do Aunty Sue Mob navigate their own particular and hazardous course between being-as-Aboriginal object and being-as-Aboriginal subject, to employ existential philosophy's terms and find a way to live in the present?[26]

The historical revisions I glossed above involved violent and sometimes sudden transformations. The maintenance of a viable and coherent sense of their own identities in the midst of these interpellations requires constant imaginative work on the part of Aunty Sue Mob.

Aunty Sue Mob members must find a different course to that of Fanon, as they find Aboriginality frozen and objectified through mechanisms that many hoped would serve to repair, even reverse, the injustices of the racist, colonial past. Aunty Sue Mob are recognised, desired, called upon and sometimes venerated—particularly by environmentalists—as well as being pointed at, marked, spurned and reviled, if never as literally as Fanon was. And so, Aunty Sue came to perceive, native title moves to redress the injustices of the colonial period but through this *very same process* reproduces colonial relations between the nation-state and Aboriginal people. The native title claims process has been experienced by Aunty Sue Mob as overriding their reality and as allowing and disallowing certain Aboriginal identities, determined on the state's terms, reproducing a colonial dynamic.

What underwrites the re-emergence across Australia of 'tribal' identity categories is the conception of cultural identity that the influential Jamaican-born cultural theorist Stuart Hall so lucidly outlined: the notion that one's 'true' cultural identity lies waiting to be discovered, excavated and brought to light. Importantly, Hall did not dismiss the powerful effects of this process of 'rediscovery' for those involved, and in Aboriginal Australia this development certainly predates native title legislation.[27] But one of the effects of the investment in the process of rediscovery of pre-contact identity categories has been the disavowal of the possibility of living with and the celebration of an alternate kind of identity: that formed through colonial history. This was the model engaged in urban Aboriginal Australia in the early 1970s, the time in which, for instance, the Aboriginal flag was designed and acted to unify peoples whose commonality was their structural, historically produced position vis-a-vis the colonial relation.[28]

Hall famously wrote of identity in this other, and in his view more productive, sense, as a matter of 'becoming' as well of being:

> It is not something which already exists transcending place, time, history and culture. Cultural identities come from somewhere, have histories. But, like everything which is historical, they undergo constant transformation.[29]

In the present it has become increasingly impossible to fully embrace an Aboriginal identity that speaks of and to constant transformation. An identity that is formed through the vicissitudes of history is a liability, diluting one's claim to authentic Aboriginality. Yet, as Hall reminded us, it is only if we take account of identity in this second sense that we can 'properly understand the traumatic character of "the colonial experience"'.[30] The colonial experience of the past is indispensible to understanding contemporary Aboriginal identities, and not an impediment to accessing their truth. The events I describe in this book also reveal the disturbing character of Aboriginal experiences of the settler colonial present.

A return to everyday experience might help ground this more specialised discussion for the general reader. Aunty Sue was born into a world in which she was categorised as 'half-caste' and has vivid memories of hiding from 'Welfare' so that she could remain living with her Aboriginal grandparents, mother, uncles and siblings. She was discouraged from speaking Kokatha, the language in which her grandparents were conversant. Lutheran missionaries hoped she would receive a Western education. Yet she came of age in a period of rapid transformation. The policy of assimilation was being dismantled, and in the 1960s the progressive South Australian Labor Premier Don Dunstan began the legislative reforms that would usher in the self-determination era.

Now a great-grandmother, Aunty Sue has participated in state-funded Kokatha language documentation programs, and is engaged to teach Nunga and white school children how to make wurlies, bent-bough dwelling structures. Sue, of course, has other skills. She is a rural girl, long married to a farmer. At the 2008 Ceduna Oyster Festival I saw her win her heat of the wheat-bag sewing competition with a strong and skilful stitch. She did not take out the title.

Aunty Sue evaded both the Lutherans' attempt to educate her, because it involved leaving behind her home and family, and attempts to incorporate her into the Aboriginal community-controlled organisations that flowered throughout the self-determination policy era, which began in the mid–1970s with Gough Whitlam's election. She preferred instead to live on the economic margins throughout this period, sending her kids to harvest seafood and to fish for 'a feed'. While she now enjoys limited validation of her long-standing and avid interest in pre-contact Indigenous cultural practices, as her role at the school demonstrates, she has simultaneously refused to engage with the native title claims process, rejecting the opportunity to deal with mining companies as a claimant and, as I later elaborate, scorning the turn to the archival record to authenticate contemporary identities.

Aboriginality then has undergone broad shifts since the turn of the twentieth century to the present: as something to be eliminated, then 'uplifted' through assimilation policies, and as a means of augmenting what might be called governmentality in the self-determination era.[31] And now, via the native title claims process, it is desired as uncontaminated, 'authentic' cultural difference.

Chapter 3

The making of 'mission mob'

Home

Koonibba, says Aunty Sue's sister Vera, was—is—home. I interviewed Aunty Vera in her quiet lounge room in early 2009. She told me, 'I was born at Koonibba, I was baptised at Koonibba, I was confirmed at Koonibba. And I suppose I'll be buried there.' In an earlier interview in 1997 with Sue Anderson and Keryn Walshe, Aunty Vera insisted on the centrality of Koonibba to her identity. 'It is my birthplace. My afterbirth was buried there, so it's very significant. It's our home.'

In the last years of the nineteenth century, Sue and Vera's great-grandfather, Micky Free, began gathering Aboriginal people to a site selected for a mission to begin the task of scrub clearing. In 1963 the gates of the Koonibba Lutheran Mission were torn down and the South Australian government assumed responsibility for the running of the settlement which was later to become Koonibba Aboriginal Community, now governed by an elected council. As Sue describes:

> They took down the big front gates at the mission, because it had 'Koonibba Lutheran Mission' and they took—just ripped them off. They didn't want them anymore. Which I thought was sacrilege, because they were really pretty.

Throughout most of the twentieth century, West Coast Nungas organised and expressed their collective identity around the shared experience of life on Koonibba Mission. The native title era has generated new tensions and possibilities around the way local Aboriginal people identify themselves. 'Tribal' identities, which were certainly retained on the mission, have re-emerged as the principle referent for Aboriginal self-understandings in recent decades. Indisputably, 'tribal' identities and the associated nomenclature—Kokatha, Mirning, Wirangu and Pitjantjatjara—have risen in prominence as identity categories in Ceduna, as they have across Australia.[1] An understanding of the Koonibba experience remains vital, so as to grasp the basis of an identity formation that has been largely but not fully eclipsed.

At Koonibba, under conditions not of their own making, West Coast Nungas consolidated their number and remade themselves into a new collective, 'mission mob'. Indigenous media scholar Frances Peters-Little has criticised non-Indigenous historians for failing to recognise the import of missions and reserves to contemporary Aboriginal people's identities. Writing about her own Kamilaroi elders, she asserts 'missions and reserves have become as vital to their identity as sacred sites and ceremonies of significance'.[2] I collected a wealth of material about Koonibba from storytelling sessions and through interviews; the centrality of the mission to West Coast Nungas' identities certainly demanded my attention. At Koonibba, generations of West Coast Nungas played as children, went to school, fought, loved, buried their afterbirth and their dead. Around the campfire and around the kitchen table at the farm, stories about growing up at Koonibba were frequently told. On rockhole trips, many greenies evidently enjoyed listening to these recollections of an evening.

In filling out these accounts I draw extensively on Peggy Brock's excellent account of Koonibba in *Outback Ghettos*, endorsing her reluctance to emphasise the all-encompassing capacity of the missionaries to re-make people. Instead, as Brock wrote, 'I suggest that we should see Aborigines making themselves rather than being made.'[3] I also rely heavily on Kokatha-Mirning woman Iris Burgoyne's *Mirning: We Are The Whales*. Burgoyne was born at Koonibba in 1936; her memoir was published in 2000. Also invaluable is the memoir of the former Koonibba pastor, Clem Eckermann, which was published posthumously in 2010 as *Koonibba: The Mission and the Nunga People*. Eckermann served at Koonibba as a teacher and assistant pastor from 1941 to 1942, then as a pastor and superintendent from 1946 to 1953, and again as pastor and superintendent from 1960 until the mission's end in 1963.[4] Using interviews conducted by me as well as those done by Anderson and Walshe, I focus on the lived, everyday experiences of mission mob, after outlining the historical circumstances of its establishment.

Aboriginal-European contact on the West Coast

The entity now known as 'South Australia' came into being in 1836, nearly half a century after a British penal colony was established in New South Wales in 1788. A private commercial company founded the South Australian colony and distributed land to free citizens.[5] In Britain much debate preceded the convict-free South Australian experiment. Promoted and designed by ambitious capitalists and social reformers such as Edward Gibbon Wakefield, the colony was created at a time when humanitarians dominated the British Colonial Office. Previously active in anti-slavery campaigns, they expressed concerns about Indigenous people's rights in land and insisted that Indigenous people be regarded as British subjects.

The 1834 *Waste Lands Act*, which authorised the establishment of the colony, set out the plan for 'systematic colonisation' by claiming land described as 'waste and unoccupied'.[6] Yet an 1836 Letters Patent, which defined the exact boundaries of the 'Province of South Australia', stated that nothing in that patent:

> shall affect or be construed to affect the rights of any Aboriginal Natives of the said Province to the actual occupation or enjoyment in their own Persons or in the Persons of their Descendants of any Lands therein now actually occupied or enjoyed by such Natives.[7]

Historian Henry Reynolds, whose pioneering research focused on frontier violence in Australia, explains the relationship between these two documents, and the schism between the South Australian Commission (the company promoting the venture) and the Colonial Office.[8] The Commission effectively drafted the *Waste Lands Act* and had it rushed through parliament in haste, a process roundly criticised in humanitarian circles.[9] However, before the Commission could dispatch the first boatload of colonists to the colony, the Colonial Office was required to issue a Letters Patent. The clause cited above was intended to enshrine Indigenous property rights.[10] The Letters Patent, according to Reynolds, 'created a sense of crisis among the would-be colonists already frustrated by long-delayed departure'.[11] Reynolds argues that the Commission, from the outset, 'aimed to outwit the zealous reformers in the Colonial Office'.[12] The *Waste Lands Act* was never amended, as the Colonial Office desired, and the Commissioners were in a position to interpret what constituted 'occupancy'. The Commissioners worded their promises carefully. Reynolds concludes, 'The leading figures ... knew all along that they would claim, on arrival in South Australia, that Aboriginal property rights, even the right to occupation and enjoyment, did not exist.'[13]

Further, the fact that Aboriginal people were considered British subjects 'did not alter the realities of settler violence and Aboriginal resistance to invasion'.[14] Aboriginal people in South Australia, as elsewhere, were impacted on by the alienation of land for specific types of capitalist developments.[15]

In the early 1840s European pastoralists established a toehold on the lower Eyre Peninsula at Port Lincoln, an area in which whalers already had presence.[16] By 1842 this isolated pastoral settlement was 'in a state of siege' due to Aboriginal attacks on settlers and stock[17] and the settlers almost abandoned it.[18] Historian Robert Foster's detailed work on rations distribution in South Australia shows how, in some instances, 'rations became a tool for controlling frontier conflict'.[19] Port Lincoln was a case in point, rations eventually providing the means for 'securing' the settlement.[20]

By 1860 a permanent European presence was established on the West Coast, atop Eyre Peninsula, with the founding of the pastoral station Yalata west of Fowlers Bay.[21] A rations depot was established at Fowlers Bay in 1862.[22] The Ceduna Museum is crammed with a crazy jumble of donated bird egg collections, football club medals, sea opals, a German hymn book, petrified wood, chipped-off pieces of the Berlin Wall, a seahorse, 'unusual small tools', Aboriginal stone implements, typewriters, rusted lamb bells and smudged kerosene lamps. It also holds a photo of the Yalata homestead, as well as the cracked, leadlight glass window from above its door. A handwritten note is sticky-taped to the window: 'This run ran over 120,000 sheep at its peak.' Local historian Jim Faull describes the Yalata property in the late 1880s as 'a vast sheep empire'.[23]

The early pastoral economy was labour intensive: Aboriginal people were engaged as builders, to sink wells, and as fencers, shepherds and outstation keepers. Eckermann stressed that 'no strife' arose over access to watering grounds; in fact, interestingly, wells tapped into the underground basin 'made considerable new sources of supply available to the Nungas'.[24] Eckermann mentioned the spearing of the explorer Darke at Waddikke Rocks as a rare example of a violent encounter on the West Coast.[25] However, accounts of several violent clashes recorded at the time are easily available to the most casual reader. In 1858 an Aboriginal person speared a member of an early well-sinking party who was working for the squatter WR Swan. Soon after one of Swan's shepherds was killed. Faull describes an 'elaborate and macabre execution' carried out at the site of the shepherd's murder.[26] He also notes examples of near sadistic cruelty on the part of early pastoralists who exploited Aboriginal labour.[27]

Nunga oral histories tell of further frontier violence in this region, and especially of a massacre at Elliston. Historians Robert Foster, Amanda Nettelbeck, and Rick Hoskings, the authors of *Fatal Collisions*, deal with various versions of this event as it is rendered from 1880 to the present in newspaper accounts, a novel, Aboriginal oral history and local debate. Intent on also establishing the verifiable facts about the case, they conclude that the 'legend' of the Elliston Massacre aggregates details of a series of different events from 1848 and 1849.

Most versions of the massacre begin with the 1848 murder of hutkeeper John Hamp, whose body was found some distance from his hut, having set out from his hut to cut timber unarmed.[28] In May 1849 five Aboriginal people died after eating arsenic-poisoned flour stolen from a hut. This event may have precipitated the payback murders of Captain Beevor and Anne Easton.[29] Three weeks later, a group of armed whites pursued their Aboriginal attackers down the Waterloo Bay cliffs. According to the available documentary evidence, this resulted in two or three Aboriginal men's deaths, while five others were arrested in possession of stolen goods. Four of those apprehended were charged with various offences, and subsequently escorted to Adelaide. Two of these men were tried and convicted of Beevor's murder; they were sentenced to death, escorted back to the district and hung from a red gum outside Beevor's hut.[30] Three other men were tried for Easton's murder but were acquitted for lack of evidence.

Burgoyne's memoir appeared in 2000, the year before *Fatal Collisions*. Her account of the Elliston massacre reworks, in vivid detail, some of what is outlined above. Burgoyne says that, 'a camp of about two hundred Aboriginal people lived on the outskirts of Elliston'.[31] Two men went out hunting from this camp and the next day a farmer wrongly accused the two of stealing some missing sheep. A judge from Adelaide sentenced the two to hang. The two men's trial, according to Burgoyne, was held at night in a big shed in Elliston.[32] 'The Aboriginal people stood outside in the dark, peeped through the window and watched the two men as they pleaded with the judge.'[33] Burgoyne has here Aboriginal people bearing witness to the workings of a cruel new order, while they remained 'in the dark', simultaneously excluded and outside of its grasp.

According to this version, on the night following the trial the two wrongly convicted men were hung in the centre of town: 'Those innocent fellows hung there all the next day, while the Aboriginal people mourned them.'[34] The next night, Aboriginal people removed the bodies. After burying their countrymen, Aboriginal people:

> snuck around to the boarding house where the judge slept and coaxed him outside with a whoobu-whoobie, a device that made different sounds like an engine, a dog growling or a horse neighing. When the judge emerged they grabbed him, knocked him unconscious and hung him in the very same place.[35]

Swift retaliation followed, according to Burgoyne, as the townsfolk took 'the law into their own hands':

> The police rounded up farmers with about ten horses and rode out to the camp. They herded all the Aboriginal men, women and children like animals and forced them off the cliffs at Elliston. People tried to escape, but they were cut down by whips, sticks and guns.[36]

The massacre's three survivors recounted these scenes up and down the coast. These events are said to have taken place in 1839, with 'another massacre' occurring in the same area ten years later. 'No Aboriginal person has lived in Elliston ever since,' says Burgoyne.[37]

Aunty Vera remembers the Elliston massacre story being narrated with force and immediacy at Koonibba. 'The old history,' she told Anderson and Walshe, 'was handed down very, very strongly.'

It is well known that what WEH Stanner persuasively termed the 'great Australian silence' prevailed in the national histories of the twentieth century, systematically denying the presence of Aboriginal people in Australian history.[38] Yet in local contexts, lurid, gothic and explicit accounts of frontier violence flourished—most notably in the period after the realities of frontier life faded from immediate memory and became part of colonial mythology.

Foster et al document a crucial shift: at the local level, the frontier was portrayed in the late nineteenth century and into the twentieth century as a site of Aboriginal depravity and outrage, and European courage and resourcefulness. Settler violence had a crucial function within these representations: this was the stuff pioneer stock was made of as they subdued a savage landscape and expunged a savage presence. Numerous versions of the Elliston massacre are grotesque: the hutkeeper Hamp is decapitated; in some his sawn-off head is found in a camp oven. Representations of these kinds of 'treacherous' acts signified the Aboriginal 'power to wreak disorder and destruction', the fear of which 'legitimated much of the redemptive violence produced on the colonial frontier'.[39]

In the late 1960s and early 1970s, as Aboriginal people were rapidly gaining political and social status, this situation—again, at the local level—was quite changed. The civil rights body the Federal Council of Aboriginal and Torres Strait Islanders (FCAATSI) planned to build a memorial to those killed at the Elliston massacre at a place where, it claimed, 250 Aboriginal people were driven to their deaths in 1846.[40] This plan was met with concerted local opposition and went unrealised until 2017. In the 1970s, local opponents were intent on sanitising and denying the violence of the past.[41] Settler violence no longer had a redemptive function nor served to enhance the reputation of settlers as pioneers; instead it rendered both their individual legacies and the colonisation process morally questionable.

While I know many people related to Iris Burgoyne, the only version I have heard of the Elliston massacre in Ceduna stresses that while some people were driven to their deaths, *most* Aboriginal people survived, hiding in caves at the base of the cliffs. This version does not allow for a wholesale loss of Aboriginal people or cultural knowledge in a single moment. Instead it has Aboriginal people again bear witness to the brutality of the frontier, but ultimately survive to both reproduce Aboriginality over time, and to reproduce and circulate testimonies about settler violence. Aboriginal people survive not out of luck but due to their skills and cunning, by hiding and successfully eluding the finality of the fate that settlers would have them meet.

What then of Pastor Eckermann's desire to render the history of dispossession uneventful and consensual? Other white locals also trivialise Aboriginal responses to colonialism in this region as passive and ineffectual. In the Ceduna Museum, as well as objects, I found local memoirs, stacked higgledy-piggledy on the shelves. EE Lutz's account of his years on the West Coast between 1893 and 1961, provides one such example. Lutz says, of the Aboriginal people that gradually 'came in from the bush, loaded with spears, boomerangs, waddies etc':

> They looked rather savage and made one feel a little jittery … Although always well armed, it was surprising how soon their courage vanished! When for the first time, two natives saw a man on a bike riding towards them, they headed for the scrub, thinking 'muldarby' (devil) was chasing them![42]

Lutz presumes to access Aboriginal people's consciousness, infantilising them and portraying them as representing no real threat to the

European taking of the country. He uses the phrase 'time marches on' as a refrain throughout his memoirs, casting dispossession as an inevitable *effect* of history, rather than a fact of history—a historical process, involving the actions of human actors.

Aboriginal people also feature frequently in the reminiscences of old settlers collected in a local oral history publication.[43] There are two notable things about the part Aboriginal people are allotted in these 'pioneer tales'. First, Aboriginal people are always in subservient roles, either calling on settlers to ask for tea, sugar and clothing, or aiding white settlers becoming established on the land by doing menial jobs. Second, while these contemporary tales are careful to recall and set down the names of any families or identities who had a presence on the West Coast in the nineteenth century, they never name Aboriginal individuals, just refer to them as 'natives'. It is also striking that many of the white surnames celebrated in this collection are also strongly associated with Aboriginal families in Ceduna: Aboriginal people adopted the names of prominent white families with whom they had an association, sometimes indicating that Aboriginal and non-Aboriginal people today have a shared white settler in their genealogy.

By the 1880s kangaroo hunters had set up camps on and around the Nullabor Plain with the aim to eradicate kangaroos, considered vermin.[44] Both pastoralists and kangaroo hunters employed Aboriginal people 'utilising their hunting and tracking skills and knowledge of the country'.[45] However, there is evidence that Aboriginal women were frequently abused in the hunters' camps.[46] By 1894, when the kangaroo hunters left the area because of a lack of water and game, it was reported that Aboriginal people were starving as the result of increased pressure on their food sources.[47]

The pastoral leases granted from 1860 expired in 1888. There was 'strong demand' in the colony of South Australia for new agricultural land.[48] Subdivision of larger pastoral properties started, with numerous smaller agricultural units with either Right to Purchase leases or Perpetual Leases becoming available. Agriculture, mostly wheat cropping, used the land much more intensively than pastoralism 'and represented a formidable attack on Aboriginal ritual and economic activities'.[49] By the turn of the century the food supply situation was critical and the period was marked by more frequent violent encounters between Aboriginal people killing sheep for food, on the one hand, and shepherds, the new farmers and their families on the other.[50] It's at this crucial juncture that missionaries arrive on the West Coast.

Clearing the scrub: early days on Koonibba

In August 1897 Pastor Kempe, formerly of the Central Australian Hermannsburg Mission, visited the West Coast for the purpose of identifying a suitable site for a Lutheran mission. Local settler William McKenzie took Kempe to the Hundred of Catt, an area of thick mallee scrubland, in the pouring rain, leading him to the camp of Micky Free and Sara-Rose Button.[51] These are Aunty Sue's great-grandparents, and also the grandparents of Iris Burgoyne who writes that her grandmother made tea for Kempe and McKenzie in the billy, sweetening it with sugar used from a tree, called womma.[52] Then, Free led Kempe and McKenzie through dense mallee woodlands:

> The timber became thicker and thicker, until it was almost impenetrable. They had to leave their vehicle in the middle of the scrub, and continue … on foot. The whole block was criss-crossed from every direction and inspected by [their] keen and knowledgeable eyes. In places there was low, in places, high scrub; in places small open plains. Everywhere, they startled and set into flight the great variety of animal and bird life. Abundantly convinced that the land was suitable for agriculture, and accompanied by their admirable and competent guide, they arrived, completely exhausted, back at the vehicle.[53]

The Lutheran Church secured a lease in the Hundred of Catt with a right of purchase in two years. Eckermann thought that the name 'Koonibba' was possibly based on a poor transliteration of the term 'Kuru Hibla' or 'iris of the eye', which may have been the name given to the Koonibba rock-hole, a permanent water source on which the mission depended.[54] Aunty Vera, however, said to me slowly, 'Koonibba. See—goona …'

Goona, or shit, was a word I knew well. According to Aunty Vera, Koonibba meant 'pile of shit'. Aunty Sue told me the same thing, adding, 'The Nungas had the last laugh over the missionaries on that one.'

Micky Free features as a compelling figure in all accounts of the Koonibba Mission. Free, also known as Willis Michael Lawrie, was the son of Michael Lawrie, a London-born Irishman who worked as a boundary rider, and Tjabiltja Catlin Mingo, a Mirning woman. One of Free's many descendants told me that Michael Lawrie, 'the Irish fella', jumped ship down at Eucla, atop of the Great Australian Bight. Micky Free and Tjabiltja were married in a traditional firestick ceremony.[55] Free's long and varied working life involved, among other things, periods as a leaseholder of a block of land in the Hundred of Catt; as a kangaroo hunter; and as a guide for an exploration party in the Warburton Ranges.[56] He taught himself to read English while patrolling the dog fence. Aunty Sue and Aunty Vera's mother, interviewed by Anderson and Walshe, says she remembers him, in later life, living alone in a tin hut on Koonibba. In 1947, at the age of seventy-nine, Free spent his last morning cutting wood in the scrub, before collapsing as he climbed out of his buggy on his return home.[57]

While he did not settle there permanently until 1906, Free was instrumental in gathering people at Koonibba to begin the task of scrub clearing, necessary for the establishment of a farm. Between 1898 and 1901 Koonibba was without a pastor. It was effectively a farm, overseen by a white, Lutheran-appointed manager who welcomed Aboriginal people as workers, or simply to camp undisturbed on the church's lease. Koonibba Mission took over the function of distributing government rations to the old, sick and to children from a local settler and also distributed rations in return for work.[58] In the early years of the mission it was the ready food supply that attracted Nungas to Koonibba. Even after the first missionary's arrival, says Brock, 'Many resented the work required from the able-bodied, preferring to go to Denial Bay or Penong where they could camp without labour demands and still obtain food.'[59] Instilling a work ethic was an early and major objective of the missionaries and they wrestled constantly with the need to provide food, so as hold Nungas to Koonibba, and an ideological reluctance to issue rations except as a reward for work.[60]

Scrub cutters worked with axes and bare hands. Horses were used to drag the felled trees and the cleared areas were burned.[61] Free had previously acted as a foreman on Aboriginal teams already employed as scrub cutters around the district; indeed in years to come Aboriginal workers continued to command better wages cutting scrub as well as shearing off the mission than on it.[62] The task of 'snagging' was particularly arduous and disliked on Koonibba; this involved 'cutting back to ground level the stumps and shoots on the cleared ground'.[63]

A memorial to the early scrub cutters is on display in the Koonibba Community Council office today. It is based on an early photo of the clearing underway: a silver plaque depicts the same scene in relief. The text praises the hard labour involved in pulling out the tough mallee trees, with their nobbled roots, in order for the workers to build 'a place to call home'. When I interviewed Aunty Sue Mob member Jamie he proudly explained that he was descended from one of the early scrub cutters. But when I went to Koonibba with a visiting Melbourne friend she raised an eyebrow on reading the dedication, commenting drily, 'Presumably they already had homes.' My friend did not recognise, and indeed could not be expected to know, that Nungas are proud to see something of their own past in the contemporary landscape. Her viewpoint reflects more widely shared progressive assumptions, in that Aboriginal people are rarely credited desires and aspirations for modernity or new experiences. Ceduna Nungas, however, perceive both that their ancestors' world and homes were destroyed *and* that their ancestors helped make a new world (which was certainly not of their own design). In popular local narratives, white 'pioneers' are alone venerated as establishing the early towns and economies of the region, in a distant period characterised by hard labour and deprivation. The scrub cutting plaque recognises Aboriginal creative efforts against this local backdrop of denial.

Koonibba offered, in Brock's terms, a 'refuge' to Aboriginal people increasingly displaced by new land use and on the brink of starvation, providing, especially, a 'safe haven' for their children.[64] Thus in Koonibba, local Aboriginal people intuited and seized the potential for establishing a stable base from which to camp as a large group (something becoming increasingly difficult in the district), to re-energise ceremonial life and to collect a regular food supply. Furthermore, at Koonibba, the seeds for an emergent collective identity were sown.

Brock says of the early Koonibba population, which fluctuated greatly:

> The Lutherans were told that there were 500–600 Aboriginal people on the West Coast in 1898. The Wirangu, Kokatha and Mining [sic] moved throughout the district. The west coast area was able to support very large gatherings … It was not unusual for 200–300 people to meet together for ceremonies. In the first years of the mission, groups of between 150–200 would gather, preparatory to moving on to ceremonial grounds.[65]

After the bulk of people moved on for ceremonies, only a handful remained at Koonibba, 'the old and sick and a few people of mixed descent who did not want to participate'.[66] This situation was to gradually change after the arrival of Koonibba's first pastor.

Chapter 4

Spectres of 'Welfare'

Spiritual struggles

In December 1901 the German-born and American-educated Pastor Wiebusch arrived at Koonibba. Wiebusch set about learning the names of everyone present, conducting roll calls every evening at six o'clock. Wiebusch, says historian Peggy Brock, ran the mission on 'extremely strict principles' rewarding hard work, obedience and spiritual 'progress' over the course of his tenure.[1] The mission day began at 7:45 am when a flag was raised to indicate mealtime and then school, and closed with evening sessions in the camp where Wiebusch played hymns on his violin. 'Nungas,' says Eckermann, 'were amazed at the sounds that he could extract from this "block of wood".'[2]

As at other missions, Wiebusch was evidently intent on establishing disciplined routines of the kind French thinker Michel Foucault described in *Discipline and Punish.* Aboriginal people's 'bodies' were to be 'subjected, used, transformed and improved' into working bodies.[3] This objective was not easily realised; hymn singing precipitated the singing of traditional songs and ceremonies, which on occasions continued for several days, leaving people too exhausted to do any farm work.[4]

Eckermann devoted almost half of his account of the Koonibba mission to the Wiebusch years (1901–1916), shaping a linear narrative of progress. Nungas come out of 'darkness' and into God's light: church attendance grows, baptismal class numbers gradually swell, ceremony attendance dwindles. Eckermann also narrates a story of material progress: buildings are erected and then, as they crumble, are gradually replaced by larger, more solid and sophisticated structures. There are 'challenges': a perpetual water shortage; a severe drought from 1914 to 1916; local anti-German sentiment during the same period, which finds expression among mission Nungas;[5] and the financial problems which were to dog the mission throughout its history. All of these are conceived as 'set-backs', slowing but never diverting the 'stream of Time'[6] that carries goal- and future-oriented people such as Europeans along, and into which Aboriginal people had been swept.[7]

Wiebush and his wife, says Eckermann, cared lovingly for Koonibba Nungas, however much their moral sensibilities were offended by their cultural practices.[8] Eckermann relays that Wiebusch heard of a case of infanticide in the Fowlers Bay area and witnessed the 'touch-penis greeting rite' practised by subincised men in the region.[9] Other 'repellent' Aboriginal cultural practices described by Eckermann include whole animal eating, and an elaboration of Daisy Bates' discredited accounts of cannibalism.[10]

Accounts of the past have much to teach us about the present moment within which they are written. Why would Eckermann commit himself to a graphic evocation of this particular version of the Aboriginal past? I think that Eckermann sought here to expose a form of liberal bad faith. Addressing a contemporary audience, Eckermann was seeking to redeem the reputation of mission work in a climate he perceived as hostile to the history of missionaries' hubris, and which would judge harshly Wiebusch and others' attempts to destroy Indigenous worlds. So Eckermann positions himself on the defensive noting, 'I know that to concede that such infanticides actually happened is to invite condemnation as one guilty of racial prejudice.'[11] He challenges his readers to accept these 'real-life' Nungas, conjuring up images of radical otherness intended to test the limits of liberal tolerance, and weaken the moral case against the missionaries. It is in the 'censoring of repugnant customs,' says Povinelli, that the 'nation forgets its own intolerance', an insight that Eckermann seems to have grasped, as he tries to revive suppressed feelings of repulsion and intolerance, in order to encourage in his readers an affective identification with the missionary Wiebusch.[12]

Eckermann, too, may have regarded those West Coast Nungas encountered by Wiebusch as living in a state of material and spiritual poverty, but he was at great pains in his memoir to dignify the Koonibba identities with whom he worked. While Eckermann imagined traditional beliefs to centre on malevolent spirits, leading him to conclude that 'the Gospel answered a deep-felt need to be set free from fear', Brock shows Wiebusch's converts engaged in involved and lengthy struggles, both within themselves, with other family and community members who disapproved of their decision, and with Wiebusch, whose style was autocratic.[13] Conversion was not undertaken lightly, on either side. Koonibba Nungas continued to live within a rich cultural milieu and '[t]he majority of people were not seeking out an alternative set of beliefs'.[14] Brock concludes, 'Their religious life was vigorous and had not as yet become seriously undermined by European colonialism', despite the immense pressures and difficulties confronting them.[15]

Indeed, from Wiebusch, Eckermann relates constant movement between Koonibba mission and north to Tarcoola and the Gawler Ranges for initiation ceremonies.[16] While the population had 'stablised' by the time of Wiebush's departure in 1916,[17] and Eckermann says the last 'walkabout' took place in 1924,[18] movement for ceremonies evidently continued for some time after this.

Where Eckermann concludes God offered freedom, Burgoyne says of life on the mission, 'we were robbed of our freedom'.[19] Micky Free, she says, was 'eventually brainwashed', frightening his daughters into going to church.[20] Aunty Vera told Anderson and Walshe that she remembers Free cracking a stockwhip in the air and then being marched into church after she'd been playing in the quarry:

> And he would sit right up the back by the door and as soon as he saw a head move—and he'd sit right on the aisle—he would creep down the aisle … So you never moved in church. You sat there with your muddy feet and muddy face and hands and mud dripping off your clothes if you'd been playing in the dirt and you never moved. And you sang when you had to sing.

The process of converting Koonibba Nungas did not reach a neat endpoint. In 1934 Pastor Mueller reported that the last of the 'camp natives' had been baptised. However, according to Eckermann, 'new catechumens continued to come into Koonibba territory from the hinterland to the north and west, asking for instruction for baptism'. These were Kokatha people who mostly lived at Ooldea but also 'came to and went from Koonibba at will'.[21] The Koonibba population then continued to fluctuate, to some extent, throughout its entire history.

Koonibba Children's Home and assimilation

At the Koonibba Children's Home, a residential institution, generations of boys were trained up to work as farm labourers and girls as domestics. Its legacy has proved the most controversial aspect of the Koonibba experience.

The last decades of the late nineteenth century, a period of economic downturn, were characterised by government disinterest in Aboriginal affairs. A widespread belief that Aboriginal people were fated for extinction underwrote this period and, in a desire to cut spending, the state limited its role to amelioration of only the most desperate circumstances via basic rations distribution. Into the vacuum left by 'government's withdrawal' came philanthropic and church groups.[22] However, just as Koonibba was becoming established, the South Australian government began 'again taking an active role in Aboriginal affairs', partly motivated by the public's realisation that the population of Aboriginal people of mixed descent was rapidly increasing rather than decreasing.[23]

The *South Australian Aborigines Act 1911* ('the Act') was modelled on Queensland's 1897 protectionist act, *Aboriginals Protection and Restriction of the Sale of Opium Act 1897 (Qld).* The Act represented a 'belated attempt to protect Nunga people' from the destructive effects of contact, including alcohol and sexual abuse.[24] The resulting legislation was repressive. Amended twice, in 1934 and 1939, the Act remained the basis for administering Aboriginal lives in South Australia until 1962.[25] Christobel Mattingley and Ken Hampton summarise, 'Our people bitterly resented it and its effects, which are still felt today.'[26]

At Koonibba the repressive facet of 'protection' found its clearest expression in the Koonibba Children's Home. The Home opened in 1914, entered a period of decline in about 1955 and closed its doors in 1963.[27] In building it the church incurred a huge debt, which was to 'haunt the mission board for many years' and have profound ramifications: later, Aboriginal labour was effectively exchanged for donations to the mission as children, especially girls, were sent out to work for Lutheran families in South Australia and Victoria.[28] The Home housed children whose parents continued to move either around the district, for itinerant work, or through their country, because they continued to live mobile, tradition-oriented lives. Either way, most Home children's parents did not reside permanently on Koonibba.[29]

Under the Act the Chief Protector of Aborigines became the legal guardian of all Aboriginal children in South Australia under the age of twenty-one.[30] Koonibba mission staff were extremely concerned about provisions in the Act relating to 'half-caste' children. The Protector had the power to take charge of all 'half-caste' children found 'wandering or camping' with Aboriginal people and put them under the control of the State Children's Department.[31] In 1912 the Protector warned the Koonibba missionaries directly that 'neglected' children of mixed descent were to be removed from their parents and that 'if these children were to remain at Koonibba the accommodation would need to be upgraded'.[32] Eckermann relates that the mission decided, 'with the full approval of the concerned parents … that a children's home should be built at Koonibba'. The Home was to ensure children stayed in contact with their families: children were only ever placed there voluntarily and parents could 'visit daily … so that family bonding would be maintained'.[33] The Home was conceived then out of genuine concern, in order to circumvent aspects of the 1911 Act. Yet it evolved into an institution with aims entirely congruent with nation-wide policies of Aboriginal child removal, severely curtailing children's contact with their kin and setting them on a course to assimilation into white society.

In *Survival In Our Own Land: 'Aboriginal' Experiences in 'South Australia' since 1836* Audrey Kinnear (nee Cobby) recounts, 'There were fifty of us in the Home. We were one big happy family and my memories of life in the Home is mostly of happy times.' While discipline was instilled, Kinnear's memories of the home environment are mostly warm: 'Amongst the Home kids there was a strong sense of togetherness. We were a big family sharing our happy and sad times and problems.' The discipline, hard work and routines endured, reflected Kinnear, 'stood me in good stead throughout life' and she offers sincere thanks to the Lutheran families who 'opened up their homes and hearts to support me through my passage through life'. Kinnear's mother was a Yankunytjatjara woman, removed to Yalata because of the Maralinga nuclear testing program. It was with sadness that she 'vaguely remembers' the mothers of Home children coming to Koonibba and camping in the bush near the church. Kinnear continues:

> Us kids used to sneak to the camp and they gave us rabbits and *guldas* [sleepy lizards] cooked in coals—they were delicious and we shared with the other kids. Our mothers stayed a few days then disappear.[34]

Once a child was voluntarily installed in the Home they were not allowed to leave. Historian Cameron Raynes refers to the residents as 'inmates', highlighting that young single women were effectively trapped, working there under a rule known misleadingly as 'the 21 rule'. As Raynes explains, this rule 'stipulated that young Aboriginal women should not be allowed out of the home until the age of 21 [as they were under the guardianship of the Chief Protector], unless to marry'.[35] However, Raynes' archival research brought to light cases of women being held in the Home for much longer than this; they continued to be a source of free labour, assisting with cooking, cleaning, sewing, washing, ironing and mending.

Mission women also worked in the home, including Iris Burgoyne's mother, and Aunty Sue and Aunty Vera's mother, now deceased. The latter told Anderson and Walshe she was never paid for any of the work she did in the Home. Aunty Sue related to the same interviewers that her mother developed close bonds with three boys there, brought down from Yalata and Ooldea 'because they weren't full blood Aboriginals'. 'One of them boys to this day calls her "mum",' said Aunty Sue.

The church board's debt was eventually cleared during the Debt Liquidation Campaign of the 1930s, with help from Lutheran congregations in South Australia and Victoria. In return for Christian generosity, the Home provided domestics and farmhands to these areas for years to come: girls and boys were trained up in the home and then 'sent out'.[36] On this subject, Aunty Vera commented, 'But I'm not sure that you'd consider them part of the Stolen Generation, because they did come back.' Her doubt points to the difficult task of grasping the legacy of the Children's Home.

Extensive Australian scholarship demonstrates that from about the 1930s state-based assimilation policies had as their object the dissolution of Aboriginal identities via the 'absorption' of people with Aboriginal descent into white Australian society.[37] The violence that accompanied this process—physical, sexual and institutional as well as spiritual—has been the subject of emotional and ideological Australian public debates since the late 1990s. The 1997 report of the National Inquiry into the Separation of Aboriginal and Torres Strait Islander Children From Their Families concluded that, between 1910 and 1970, 'not one Indigenous family has escaped the effects of forcible removal', public revelations which culminated in then prime minister Kevin Rudd's 2008 apology to the Stolen Generations.[38]

For his part, Eckermann seemed stunned by the fact that he was called to appear before the aforementioned inquiry in Adelaide, stressing that the rationale of the Home was never to *permanently* sever children's ties to their family.[39] The residents of the Children's Home were, after all, placed there 'voluntarily', in contrast to the stories of removal by means of coercion, deception, compulsion and sheer force that the inquiry brought to light. But the families who entrusted their children to the care of the Koonibba Children's Home did so with a full awareness that if they did not do so their children might well be taken away, and all contact with them lost. The Home cannot be represented as separate from the policy of forcible removal, and innocent as to its effects, as it relied on the spectre of removal for its own *raison d'être*.

Furthermore, it is clear that once placed in the home, Aboriginal children found themselves committed to an institution with a disciplinary function. Missionaries acquired enormous discretionary powers over every aspect of the children's lives; the children's labour, especially the girls', was exploited. For example, children were usually allowed to spend the Christmas holidays with their parents but Raynes shows that the release of 'inmates' over this period did not always occur. In 1946 Eckermann tried to keep children at the Home over this time. Raynes shows that Eckermann was genuinely concerned about the education of these children, fearing they would fail to return after the holidays. Moved by Aboriginal distress, he eventually reneged.[40]

'Pretty openly acknowledged'

The questions surrounding the Home, 'Welfare' and assimilation pressures are pressing ones for Aunty Sue and her sisters, and further biographical detail is needed to explain why. Vera is Sue's eldest sister, and the first child of a Kokatha woman from the mission and a local white farmer. Anderson and Walshe questioned Aunty Vera's mother directly about her relationship with this whitefella, but she was reluctant to talk about her love affair with a man she met while working milking cows on a neighbouring farm. When she first fell pregnant, Aunty Vera's mother ran away, fearing her own parents' reaction. She returned before Aunty Vera, the first of six children to this man, was born.

Aunty Vera and Aunty Sue's white father was involved, to a limited extent, in their family life. He regularly brought his children clothes and food, and he delivered Christmas presents. Aunty Vera vaguely remembers going out to the farm to stay with him and travelling with him 'from time to time' into Ceduna. Aunty Sue told Anderson and Walshe:

> Before my father died, he used to come out to the mission all the time with the back of his ute full of fruit and vegies and stuff—just loaded up with food—and he would pull up there and I would be like a big queen on the back of the ute, throwing the kids apples and oranges and stuff.

Aunty Vera says, however, their father did not like the fact that all the food he took to the mission was shared out among kin, worrying that his children were missing out. He sometimes stood by his truck while his children ate in front of him, an image that speaks both to his affection and his distance from Aboriginal cultural mores.

In Ceduna, Aunty Vera told me, 'People actually knew who we were, they knew who our father was.' She continued, 'We weren't openly discriminated against but I believe we were talked about around the kitchen tables.'

Their father had another, older white family, on a nearby farm. This family acknowledged the relationship with Aunty Vera's family. Vera refers to her father's white children as 'brothers' and 'sisters', and Aunty Sue remembers their father's first wife showing them kindness after the mission closed and the family experienced severe hardship.

> Yeah, yeah, that was pretty openly acknowledged, even by his wife, dear old soul. And when we … left the mission … his wife was wonderful, she just treated us—I don't know where she got the patience to teach me anything, but she treated us like we were her own kids, and that was a big thing for that woman to do coz she was ridiculed in the white society … but she just stood up strong and accepted us.

While 'white society' talked about them, Aunty Vera and Aunty Sue's mother was 'a bit of an outcast' on the mission, shunned, especially by Aboriginal men, for having 'all these kids and no husband'. And mission children, too, sometimes teased Aunty Vera and her siblings for being 'half-caste'. Today, Aunty Sue likes to ham up that they were neither black nor white in colour, but 'the creeeeam in between'. But her sisters remember being made painfully aware of a stigmatised difference. I met up with Aunty Vera for lunch one day in Ceduna and told her I'd been in the library, watching footage of the 1952 Koonibba Jubilee. I had looked for her in the children's running races but didn't see her. 'I'm the minya [small] white one,' she said with some bitterness, challenging me to acknowledge that she should have been easily identified in the footage as fairer than the rest. The footage is blurry, sped up and washed out, and I honestly couldn't distinguish her.

Aunty Sue insists that Lutheran missionary staff consistently warned the whole community about impending visits from 'Welfare', enabling children who were not living in the Home to head out bush. Aunty Vera also remembers escaping Welfare by heading out bush, but says this was done in defiance of *both* government officials and the missionaries:

> Welfare was a big terrifying feature of mission life for us, for us kids. We used to run away from them, but Mama and Papa [her maternal grandparents] and them adults knew where we were … and when it was dusk we'd wander home to the [mallee] shoots between the community and the footy oval and sit there and Mum would bring some food down for us to eat, some tea, cause during the day we caught our own galahs and found our own eggs in the birds' nests.

Then, 'we'd wait until all the lights went out at the missionaries' houses, and then we'd go home and go to bed'. Again our conversation turned to the question of the 'Stolen Generations' narrative, as it had come to circulate publicly. In this exchange Aunty Vera pinpointed more precisely that certain experiences remain invalidated by that narrative, such as the omnipresent *threat* of removal, which was a defining and frightening feature of her own childhood.

> If we happened to be caught at school when they [the Welfare] came—you can imagine we never wore shoes there, but we had shoes that we had to force our feet into, and that was … very painful wearing those shoes, because the missionaries might say 'you gotta wear shoes' and take us away if we don't. That was a big threat. A lot has been spoken about the Stolen Generation, but very little if anything has been spoken about the emotional suffering of the people who weren't actually stolen but who were under threat of being taken away.

Vera concludes these reflections by noting, 'That was very traumatic.'

Connections with Koonibba

The significance of Koonibba as a source of contemporary Aboriginal identities is by no means straightforward. The mission experience was 'traumatic' in parts, as Aunty Vera says. And yet, as I go on to detail, it also inadvertently provided the conditions to maintain *something* of the very way of life those missionaries explicitly set out to supplant. Aboriginal people came to settle permanently at Koonibba, signalling the end of a way of being for mobile hunter-gatherers. Lutheran missionaries sought to transform their Aboriginal converts: they were to become sedentary, domesticated, working, individuated subjects, possessed of Christian moral values. Yet today, 'mission mob' cherish their connection with Koonibba as it is seen to afford them access to firsthand experiences of land-based cultural practices such as food collecting. A childhood spent on the mission is in some cases associated with the transmission of cultural knowledge pertaining to certain sites that lie in the scrub just beyond the mission.

On the one hand Nungas express regret at the fact that Aboriginal people who had previously shared in an identity as 'Koonibba people' or 'mission mob' have now differentiated themselves as either Kokatha or Wirangu, in part because of native title. On the other, memories of life on Koonibba are used as a basis of differentiating local Nungas as 'authentic' or as lacking in credibility, in precisely the terms belonging to native title. Time away from the mission makes one vulnerable to the charge of inauthenticity, or of being an opportunistic 'Johnny-come-lately'.

Koonibba is remembered then as somewhere where knowledge of 'the old ways', and of language, was kept alive. As other scholars have pointed out, the relationship of the mission to Aboriginal cultural practices maintained since prior to colonial contact is by no means obvious.[41] The missionaries discouraged but did not ban the speaking of Indigenous languages, yet this only saw a heightened importance attached to efforts to teach language 'behind the missionaries' backs'. The missionaries endeavoured to displace a land-based cosmology and to ensure ritual practices were discontinued, yet today Nungas in Ceduna equate growing up on the mission with an opportunity to learn something of their cultural traditions. Specifically, ceremonial gatherings continued at the mission, in secret, into the 1950s. And Koonibba Nungas continued to maintain a relationship with country contiguous to the mission as they went hunting in order to supplement their meagre ration supply.

Memories of mission childhoods are, in fact, memories of time spent out the back. 'We had the run of the mission,' says Aunty Sue. 'We were free.'

Chapter 5

Memories of the 'old ways'

Camps and cottages

According to historian Peggy Brock, in its early years Koonibba was divided into 'two poles': the mission settlement and the camp on its fringes. 'As the mission became established, the camp remained physically and ideologically separate.'[1] What the missionaries imagined as a transition from one way of being to another was initially symbolised by the move from wurlies and humpies in the camps to stone cottages, which were preferentially allocated both to the converted and to the most indispensible workers. Eckermann deploys the same symbolic-cum-spatial distinction when he comments that the Children's Home gave children the opportunity to know more than 'the lifestyle of the wurley'.[2]

Burgoyne describes daily life in the camps on the fringes of the Koonibba Mission in the 1940s. She explains that 'many of the old people' from Talewan, Ooldea and the Bight area resided in these camps on the outskirts of the mission. Those she calls 'camp people', 'lived in the bush', and ate lizards, emu eggs, wombats, kangaroos and fruit. As a young girl she often visited the camps for something to do. 'We could not afford a television or radio,' she relates, so instead the children 'flopped down on the blankets and talked' with the old people. It was here that she learned about 'Mirning culture, rules and Law'.[3]

Camp life, then, was not just an important aspect of the early years on the mission but a long-term feature of Koonibba life. Aboriginal people continued to visit Koonibba for periods of time—from Ooldea and further north—up until the 1950s, and camp on the edges of the mission settlement. In 1996, Aunty Sue told Anderson and Walshe:

> Other people used to come ... we would have to go to corroborees and that was the whole community had to go, kids and all ... And they'd be there for a week or so ... next morning you'd get up and the camp was gone, just like that.

While camp and settlement were certainly distinct and 'ideologically separate' spaces *from the point of view of the missionaries*, camp Nungas were a part of the lives of those living and growing up in stone cottages. Burgoyne tells of a childhood spent moving between these spaces, regularly visiting and spending time with her kin. Camp people also occasionally visited their kin now housed in cottages, if they needed to check on or look after someone. However, Burgoyne remembers, 'they [camp residents] much preferred to drink their cup of tea outside, rather than go inside the house'.[4] Furthermore, those Aboriginal people living in houses did not necessarily use their domestic space in the way it was designed to be used.

Aunty Vera and Aunty Sue's mother grew up in a two-room home on the mission: one room held a woodstove and kitchen, the other room slept their grandparents and the twelve children. Damper was sometimes cooked in the ashes in a fire outside the house, and as there was very little crockery, people simply ate with their fingers. Many people opted to sleep outside, under the stars, on hot summer nights. Such re-fashioning of domestic space occurred, and continues to occur, across Australia.[5]

Those people who lived in houses on Koonibba routinely went to Denial Bay for the summer. Today the Koonibba minibus often brings people from Koonibba Community down to the beach at Denial Bay on hot summer days. With music blaring from the car stereo, community members cook up food in the picnic area, swim and wade in the shallows, and sometimes dance in the car park adjoining the jetty.

Throughout Vera and Sue's childhood, the Koonibba mob built wurlies and slept on seaweed mattresses at Denial Bay. Aunty Sue

Mob have strong memories of these camps. While Vera remembers Clydesdales pulling a dray down to the camp spot, Sue remembers arriving 'on the back of the mission truck'. She says, 'The missionaries would drop us off there and we'd stay there for a couple of weeks of the holidays.' At Denial Bay, the community simply camped in the scrub, as Aunty Sue described to Anderson and Walshe:

> We just went and got the seafood you know, what we could get—fish, crabs, razorfish—whenever the tide was out, there was always heaps to eat there. I remember Granny having this great big black pot—she was always making noodles in it to feed everybody—it was huge. But then there was a lot of people too.

Sue is suggesting that it was possible to experience a form of camp life, even if one normally lived with one's family in a house. Aunty Sue told Anderson and Walshe that she grew up in a three-room 'big house, big solid stone thing', on the mission, which also had a 'sleep-out'. Their grandparents had the sleep-out, a large family occupied each of the other two rooms, and a single uncle slept by the fireplace in the kitchen. Yet Aunty Sue Mob's memories of the Denial Bay camps are treasured in the way Burgoyne treasures her time visiting camps on the mission. This was a place where a version of the 'old ways' was taught and lived. Memories of summers at Denial Bay centre around the gathering and sharing of food: collective, kin-based bonds and food-collecting skills are emphasised.

Further still to this sketch of camp(s) and settlement, I would add a third space: the fringe camps many Koonibba people resided in on the outskirts of towns in the district, including Ceduna, Wudinna and Port Lincoln. These camps formed part of Koonibba Nungas' 'beats', in Beckett's terms.[6] Indeed, as much as the Lutherans initially encouraged and rewarded a commitment to Koonibba, conditions on Koonibba necessitated movement off the mission for economic reasons.

Up until 1921 Koonibba was a fully functioning cattle and wheat farm, with full employment of Aboriginal men its policy, and self-sufficiency its goal. Aboriginal people undertook farm work under the supervision of a white overseer or, when they were not available, 'the more reliable Aboriginal workers (mostly of mixed descent) acted as supervisors'.[7] While working men left during World War One to take advantage of a European labour shortage throughout the district, after the war's end they were back on the mission.[8] By this time the period of full employment—whereby labour was demanded in return for a combination of wages, rations and clothing—had succeeded in its objective. It had ensured a potential pool of converts had reason to remain on the mission, and enabled close supervision of the newly converted. This period resulted in a generation of Koonibba women who were trained housekeepers, and men who were 'capable teamsters, shearers, wheat lumpers, stevedores, stone masons, carpenters and blacksmiths'.

In 1921 the church board, heavily in debt after the building of the Children's Home, decided to abandon full employment, as it could not afford so many wages on a 12,000-acre property with poor soil, and to switch from cattle to sheep.[9] While the last decision created more work in the short term as fences were sheep-proofed, and the policy change took some years to implement, increasingly Koonibba men had to seek work off the mission, mostly in the region's towns but also on farms. By the mid-1930s the church had given up on farming altogether, leasing the mission's land to local white share-farmers, who employed just one or two Aboriginal men at any given time.

Vera and Sue's maternal grandfather, or Papa, had been trained on Koonibba, and was an accomplished stonemason who worked both on the mission and around the district. Aunty Vera remembers, as a little girl, jumping up and down on the piles of sand Papa was using for his mortar at the site of a house that still stands in the centre of Ceduna today—and getting into trouble for her efforts. Aunty Vera recounted to me that she once told the then mayor of Ceduna this but he denied it, asserting that *his* father had built that house. Aunty Vera told me, 'I swear to almighty God that Papa built that house and not [the former mayor's] father! But see because we're black people nobody is going to take notice of us.'

As well as being a stonemason, Papa was a 'gun shearer', much sought after around the district for his speed and skill. He travelled the district with his brother, also a shearer, on a pushbike.

Increased mobility

The 1921 change in policy at Koonibba coincided with opportunities for greater mobility on the West Coast, via cars and a new railway line, and the advent of telephone communications with the outside world.[10] Aunty Vera and Aunty Sue's mother told Anderson that mission Nungas often purchased second-hand cars from nearby farmers. Brock says:

> Cars became a common sight on the West Coast. The mission bought its first car in 1925 ... By this time some Aboriginal people had already acquired their own cars with wages they had earned, not only farms but on the railways and at the new deep sea port at Cape Thevenard. Cars gave them increased mobility and independence at a time when they might have to travel long distances in search of work.[11]

Koonibba men, sometimes alone and sometimes with their families, went to live for periods in improvised fringe camps on designated reserves on the outskirts of towns such as Ceduna, Wudinna and Port Lincoln. In Ceduna, men obtained work on erratic terms, loading wheat and gypsum at the Thevenard deep-sea port, and then, in the late 1950s and early 1960s, building Thevenard's wheat silos.[12] During the 1940s, families moved to Wuddina either to work with the railways or on the building of the Tod River Pipeline;[13] and families moved to Port Lincoln in the 1940s, initially to work at the freezing plant and on the wharves.[14]

Iris Burgoyne describes life in Ceduna at this time:

> The government set aside land for Aborigines to settle but provided no housing or sanitation. All we had was a water tap. We made humpies and wurlies and relieved ourselves in the bush. We collected large bags of seaweed and made mattresses. We did the best we could. We washed ourselves with hot water in old tins and buckets.[15]

Descriptions of the rudimentary nature of fringe camps on the outskirts of rural towns at this time are also found in the early anthropological writings about south-eastern Aboriginal Australia.[16] Brock describes the general atmosphere in Ceduna as 'hostile' to the Aboriginal presence. Against this hostility, assistance and acts of kindness made a lasting impression. Burgoyne recounts:

> Non-Aboriginal women that our mothers worked for gave us blankets, towels, pillows and tins of food. Their husbands would deliver old pieces of canvas to our camp, which made our shelter along with sticks and boughs.[17]

Burgoyne describes hunting for food or walking the 5 kilometres into town for supplies. 'Kind people offered us lifts back to our camps,' she writes, providing a list of names of these 'fine gentlemen'. Men from the camp worked loading boats at Thevenard: 'My heart flickers with gratitude for the dear old Greek shop owners in Thevenard. They allowed Mirning people credit for food until our mothers paid the bills.'[18]

Aboriginal children were effectively barred from white schools in the district. Similar stories are recorded elsewhere.[19] In the 1940s, the Ceduna primary school refused to accept Aboriginal children, arguing that a school was provided for them at Koonibba. The 45 kilometres was, of course, an impossible distance to travel daily at the time.[20] The policy, as elsewhere, was inconsistent over time, and the justifications for prohibiting and/or discouraging Aboriginal enrolments discontinuous. Burgoyne recounts:

> We moved back and forth from Koonibba to Ceduna. I went to school there for three months before my parents pulled me out. The board didn't like Aboriginal students because they thought we were diseased.[21]

The camps on Koonibba then were home, especially in the early years, to those who refused the Lutherans' message. Fringe camps of 'Koonibba people' across the Eyre Peninsula also existed as spaces beyond or outside of the Lutherans' reach. Eckermann imagines them as the locus of sex, gambling and drinking, interpreting a return to Koonibba after a period in a fringe camp as an embrace of the mission's elevated Christian moral universe.

As Koonibba families spread out to towns and rural localities, the missionaries were also forced to become mobile: Koonibba missionaries began travelling 'up the road' (along the West Coast) and 'down the line' (the southern Eyre Peninsula) holding services for its 'dispersed congregation' in woolsheds and churches dotted along the way.[22] As social scientist Fay Gale noted, 'Only one third of the so-called "Koonibba people" still live on the mission; the others are scattered across Eyre Peninsula.'[23] Even when the majority then lived away from Koonibba, it was a shared connection to the mission that bound these people to each other and provided them with an identifying label, 'Koonibba people' or 'mission mob'.

Maintaining relations with country

Aboriginal people draw on the mission past today in ways that deepen our understanding of present Aboriginal identities. As highlighted earlier, certain Ceduna Nungas assert that to experience the world of the mission was to experience and be immersed in a world belonging to Aboriginal people, despite this world being so fundamentally organised by white outsiders in ways that both reflected and imposed their structures of thought. Memories of the 'old people' and the 'old ways', the determined maintenance of certain cultural practices as well as secret ceremonies, and the speaking of Kokatha are all stressed today.

Memories of material deprivation, which pivot on hunger, are recounted less with bitterness than pride in the fact that Aboriginal people continued to travel regularly, on foot and in horse-drawn sulkies, out the back of the mission, to hunt and provide for their less able kin. Mission mob maintained a relationship with their country via these frequent expeditions, visiting and drinking from the rockholes around which Rockhole Recovery itineraries are organised.

More complex still is the experience of Aunty Sue and her siblings. As earlier noted, they grew up on the mission in the 1940s and 1950s categorised as 'half-caste', and were conscious of their difference from most of the other mission children who had two Aboriginal parents, even if these parents were themselves of mixed descent. Kokatha academic and writer Dylan Coleman provides a moving fictional account of her mother's experience of this in her award-winning 2012 novel *Mazin Grace.*

In order to escape the reach of Welfare, Aunty Sue and Aunty Vera regularly went out bush. Aunty Vera talks of eating both galahs and eggs found in birds' nests, and Aunty Sue of hiding out bush for days with the mission's fairer-skinned children. She told Anderson and Walshe:

> I remember those tracks through the night and it was real dark and it was all half-caste kids, the older ones carrying the little ones and with the Grandparents—one up the front, one at the back and a couple down each side, keep us in line—and we'd go to Koonibba siding to my uncle's place and he'd feed us there and—wouldn't stay any longer than it took time to eat—and then we'd be off back through the scrub again. And the old people had to catch us food, even wild cat. But we would be out for three days sometimes.

'The bush', in these memories, is a hospitable place that is credited with sheltering, feeding and nourishing fair-skinned mission kids, in the process ensuring that they maintained their ability to locate themselves within the local Aboriginal world. In effect, those whose Aboriginality was regarded as most malleable by state government policies in the past were afforded an opportunity to experience something that is prized as central to Aboriginality in the present: relatively continuous, comfortable and dependent relations with country.

The presence of the 'old ways' on Koonibba was a central theme stressed by all of my interviewees. The Lutheran missionaries, as a matter of course, tried to discourage ceremonies on Koonibba, says Auny Vera, 'but Koonibba is a big traditional area'. She says:

> I can remember going down halfway between Koonibba and what we called three-mile gate, that's the entrance to the community now and inma, corroborees. Mama threw a blanket over our heads and every time we'd peep she'd whack us on the back of the head—well not whack but tap us on the back of the head, cover us over. So we pushed a hole in the

> blanket, so we could see. And I'd be looking and [my sister] would say 'my turn now, my turn now'. So, yeah, we saw what those corroborees are about.

Witnessing is not the same thing as embodied participation in ritual life, but a proximity to these inmas is prized, as high-stakes contests about legitimacy and cultural differentiation have escalated since 'native title started up'. Aunty Vera's memories of this scene segued into boiling anger at being called a 'Johnny-come-lately' by other Aboriginal people. She told me, 'A lot of people now say that we don't know anything about tradition. Sadly those people never ever attended a traditional ceremony.'

For Aunty Vera, growing up on Koonibba was equated with a certain level of exposure and access to traditional cultural knowledge: experiences that are highly valued in the contemporary context. In my interviews the detail of these experiences was not stressed so much as the significance of having grown up in a setting where 'the old ways' remained an ongoing part of one's life. Nungas who grew up on the mission also remember observing protocols regarding strangers entering the country: Aboriginal visitors waited on the rise above the mission to talk to the appropriate people before they stepped on to the mission.

Aunty Sue offered instances of the eruption of 'old tribal' ways into everyday life in her interview with Anderson and Walshe, identifying these as making a strong impression:

> There used to be fights out there. Like my Uncles would be fighting with some people and then next thing, you know the Grandmothers would be in it and they were real like tribal fights, they were.

This fighting once involved her grandmother 'belting another lady with a crowbar'. Aunty Sue clarified, 'They weren't very often and it was only mainly between two families.' She also told Anderson and Walshe:

> I can remember when one Uncle died and his whole family, his wife and his kids, had to go from house to house wailing, you know, really tribal, wailing and then everyone had to

> join them as they went—his family came to our house and then our family had to join them and go on to the next house and everybody finished up together somehow. All wailing and all. That was one that stuck in my mind, it was so loud.

Keen wailing by certain categories of kin is detailed in Ronald Berndt's account of the burial practices of Ooldea in the early 1940s. Here, a deceased wife commenced a grief-fuelled, 'heart-felt' wailing, before affinal relatives and friends took up the widow's 'first cry of sorrow'.[24]

Aunty Vera talked to me at length about learning Kokatha while growing up on the mission. The Lutherans 'would have preferred us to speak pure English,' she says. However, she mused, 'I think the beauty of growing up the way we grew up is the ability that we develop to jump from one culture immediately into another without taking a breath.'

Cultural, in this case, linguistic fluidity, rather than domination or assimilation characterised her account of life on Koonibba:

> See, if I had somebody here that I had to speak to in language it would be nothing to just leave you sitting there and let you listen. It's not the rudeness of the thing: it's how we spoke at Koonibba when I was growing up.

Aunty Vera's grandmother, however, spoke another form of Kokatha. The language spoken at the mission was not static. 'I used to say, "Mama whatta you talkin? Whatta you sayin? Tell me!"' Her grandmother would reply, 'I'm talking deep Kokatha.' Deep Kokatha, Aunty Vera told me, was 'the old Kokatha', only spoken by people who didn't speak English at all. Aunty Vera then said, 'Her deep Kokatha could also have been Pitjantjatjara … Mama was multilingual, speaking Mirning, Kokatha, Pitjantjatjara, whatever, whatever.'

Kokatha wasn't spoken in front of white people on the mission. But, I was told, 'as soon as the non-Aboriginal people would turn around and walk away—back to language!' Aunty Sue emphasises that her mother's generation faced great pressure and scrutiny from the missionaries. While they 'stood up front', her grandparents concentrated on teaching the kids 'behind the missionaries' backs'.

Hunting while hungry

By far the strongest theme of my interviews was food and the constant battle to have enough to eat on Koonibba, the mission having long ago abandoned any efforts at food production. From the Anderson and Walshe transcripts I learned that the government ration comprised flour, tea, sugar, potatoes and onions. And quince. Aunty Sue says:

> Quince was always *the* fruit. It was part of the rations. And we'd do odd jobs for the older people and they'd give us their quince. But I can't stand it now! That's probably why.

Rations were supplemented with kangaroo and possum meat and wild fruits: burrah, the wild peach or quandong, which is native; and wulga, the prickly wild tomato, an introduced species. Women went for rabbits using crowbars, while men sometimes hunted rabbits with spears and waddies. Nearby farmers sometimes came to the mission to sell eggs and fat, but the milk procured from the mission's cows went to the Children's Home and to white mission staff. Water was carted from an underground tank at the blacksmith's shop; the well at Koonibba rockhole was too far to walk to for drinking water, but was a popular swimming spot for the children in summer. A small shop sold tobacco, biscuits, jam and lollies. Aunty Vera recalled:

> [The shop] sold fruit and vegetables that were brought in. The farm [which was being share-farmed], as far as I can remember, didn't actually produce fruit and vegetables for the community. Sheep and wheat farming was the go there, but once a week they used to kill so many sheep and then sell it in the morning at the meathouse, but us all kids would line up around the slaughter yard to get the offings, because nurrundjerrie—sheep's stomach—that's good meat.

Aunty Vera remembers eating rabbits and also galahs. Whitefella judgments sometimes made their presence powerfully felt in these exchanges. Aunty Vera continued, anticipating recoil from the idea of eating galahs, 'Some people would screw their nose up at it but it's poultry. They eat quail, so they shouldn't screw their nose up at that.'

Both the memories of hunting while hungry, and of eating bush foods while hiding from Welfare are stressed as openings onto a way of being Aboriginal that the missionaries were intent on foreclosing. Aunty Sue talks about 'learning how to survive by our own wits'. The mission kids routinely spent their days catching gulda (sleepy lizard) and playing in the scrub. She told Anderson and Walshe, 'And when we would wander off for a full day, just kids, we'd come back full, we weren't hungry.' Guldas were cooked on little fires built out in the scrub, or brought home. Aunty Sue reflects that sometimes she would accompany the men from the mission for days, ostensibly to hunt kangaroos, but, as she told Anderson, 'it was something else'. These treks involved visiting rockholes out the back, and sourcing ochre for ceremonies.

It is this never-quite-defined but ever-present 'something else' that has come to be identified as the significant feature of this time spent out bush. Koonibba people, it is emphasised, remained a people who found opportunities to move about their country and hunt on it. They also had opportunity to visit its sites, maintaining ongoing relationships with the rockholes. The missionaries could not stop mission residents from hunting, as they were unable to feed them adequately. And so Nungas worked against the forces that were trying to cleave them from another way of life, remaining oriented to a relationship with country as well as to the weekly devotion suppers and Sunday church services.

Ripping down the gates: the end of the mission

During the late 1950s and early 1960s, Lutheran missionaries sent Koonibba students who showed academic potential to Adelaide to complete their education at a Lutheran private college. Aunty Vera, for instance, was already boarding at this school when the state government took over the mission in 1963.

By this time, the mission's housing stock was in a state of disrepair. Aunty Sue remembers one house collapsing completely as a group of adults sat playing cards in the kitchen. There was also a huge hole in the roof of her childhood home. Gale comments that stone houses on

Aboriginal reserves and stations across South Australia at the time were 'damp, badly fretted, or in danger of collapsing'.[25] There was intense overcrowding. According to Eckermann, the church envisaged the Department of Aboriginal Affairs taking over the mission to 'provide housing, employment, vocational training, and the like in a way that the Church could not hope to match financially'.[26]

In the early 1960s, the church was experimenting with self-determination and self-governance structures. The community met on a Monday night to 'discuss issues affecting the common good, and make decisions'. While a Superintendent implemented these decisions, Eckermann laid all credit at the feet of Koonibba residents:

> They carried out cottage repainting and repairs, repainted the hall and school, built stone tank-stands for the new cottages, surveyed and graded a street system for the village, built a community laundromat, re-roofed underground tanks, put down new tennis courts ... The Department of Aboriginal Affairs at long last came to light with modest grants [of two thousand pounds a year] for housing, and it was a source of pride that from foundation to ridge cap these cottages were built by Aboriginal labour under Aboriginal foremen.[27]

South Australia's policy of assimilation by means of relocating Aboriginal families from reserves and mission stations into the general community was in its death throes.[28] This, however, was what the Department planned for Koonibba:

> The Department made a takeover offer that clearly announced the aim of dispersing the people, and eventually wiping the Koonibba community off the map. It set a timetable of two years for the dispersal, with or without the consent of the people affected ...[29]

Negotiations involving proposals and counter-offers followed, with the Koonibba mission staff and community continuing to outline their vision for a self-governing community. However, in May 1962, Koonibba residents were shocked to hear the church had accepted the Department's offer. Koonibba's pastor and teaching staff immediately resigned in protest, and a petition against the terms of the takeover quickly raised eighty signatures.[30] The church and Department were unmoved, and from July 1963 'the government came in', as Aunty Sue puts it.

After the mission's closure, many Koonibba Nungas began moving into Ceduna. Sue's family also left Koonibba soon after this but went instead to Port Lincoln where Sue's mother's sister was living. While a general exodus from Koonibba ensued, the state's planned 'dispersal' never eventuated. Aunty Sue muses, 'I mean it is home, and you're always dribbling back to home again.' The mission's end coincided with the nascent self-determination policy period, the former mission becoming a reserve, and eventually the Koonibba Aboriginal Community.

In the years following the mission's end, Aunty Sue's mother was forced to relinquish her children, who were split up: some joined Aunty Vera to board at school in Adelaide and others were sent to live with various family members. Aunty Sue remembers that 'the government' convinced her mother to give up her youngest, newborn baby for adoption, telling her that only this way would she be able to keep her other children in her care. The whole family lost contact with this person for thirty years. As to the promise regarding the rest of her children, 'That was just a big, big con-artist job, big con job, because they got us afterwards.' Aunty Sue says:

> So you wonder why I don't trust governments. And people have asked me whether I was part of the Stolen Generation? I don't know whether that's classed as stolen or not, but I always say 'no', because they couldn't steal me, I kept running away. I kept running away back to the mission, so I don't see that as being stolen I just see it as a bit of fight between me and the government, and in the finish I won that fight. When I turned fourteen they left me alone.

For Aunty Sue, Koonibba remained home, and those who had stayed welcomed her. At Koonibba, her old aunties would tell her, 'We want you to stay with us but we're scared, we're scared the policeman will come, Welfare will come.' Aunty Sue would leave again for a time.

Remembering the mission

As is to be expected, Ceduna Nungas do not hold a uniform perspective about the process and legacy of the missionary experience. Some Ceduna Nungas perceive that the missionaries 'made us hate ourselves'. Others see it that the mission's objective was to physically contain Aboriginal people, and that Aboriginal people were patronised and also starved. To others, like Aunty Vera, Koonibba was, and remains, home: many West Coast Nungas continue to express a durable bond with Koonibba. Many Aboriginal people also hold certain Lutheran missionaries and other mission staff such as teachers dear in their hearts, and maintain ongoing relationships with them. Affection for individuals is sometimes expressed by those people who express bitterness about the mission experience overall.

In all cases, the mission experience remains a kind of touchstone for Aboriginal people of Sue's generation. Some see the mission as providing access to a high quality formal education, as well as a sense of belonging that ties them to other Aboriginal people in Ceduna. Yet others mourn the loss of a whole way of being that missionaries' efforts irrevocably refigured over the course of the twentieth century, and are vitally interested in its retrieval.

In emphasising the centrality of the mission experiences to Aboriginal collective identity on the West Coast, I echo others' words. In the early 1980s Jane M. Jacobs stated, 'The West Coast Kokatha identity is linked essentially to their Koonibba experience.'[31] A decade later Brock noted, 'People who came from Koonibba are likely to claim it as an identifying label, rather than use pre-existing language groups such as Kokatha or Wirangu as communal identities.'[32] This situation has changed.

The concept of 'mission mob' has been superseded by 'tribal' identifications. A fulsome understanding of the Koonibba experience brings home the point that the self-understandings that currently have purchase have reemerged, taken root and been nurtured relatively recently, and under specific political and social conditions. More broadly, this shift underlines again the instability of Aboriginal identity formations over time. The suddenness and profundity of these shifts give rise to complex contests over the substance and value of various ways of being Aboriginal and expressing an Aboriginal identity, bringing to light the constant interplay of others' desires and agendas, such as the missionaries' and that of 'Welfare', as well as native title.

Chapter 6

'We know who we are': the impact of native title on local identities

The unfairness of the thing

'There is no native title and I don't care what they say,' reckons Aunty Sue. According to her:

> Native title throughout the years has been a really shocking experience. First we had to choose one tribe, and we know that most of us come from two … We were demanded to prove to the government our continual existence to the land for the past 200 years. All these demands came on to us through the native title system, and the government bullying to try and get the land from us.

Sue once stood up in a native title meeting and challenged a lawyer representing the South Australian government to prove 'the government's connection to the land for the last 200 years'. Apparently, 'He nearly choked!' He said, 'You can't do that.'

Sue struck back, 'Why not? You're doing it to us.'

Eventually she became overwhelmed with 'the unfairness of the whole thing': 'Once we realised what native title was up to, we backed out of there.'

The impact of native title on local identities

In Ceduna processes associated with the preparation of a native title claim have disturbed Aboriginal people's understandings of themselves, occasioned intense interpersonal conflict and dramatically altered everyday social realities. The situation is not unique to this place. Glimpses of the kinds of intra-Aboriginal conflicts generated through involvement in native title related processes are sometimes afforded in the public record.

Consider the following examples. In Sydney, Dennis Foley, a descendant of the Gai-mariagal people of the Sydney basin and a well-known professor of Indigenous Studies, accuses those Kooris who hail from elsewhere but have long lived in Sydney of being usurpers, who have 'black-washed' traditional owners from the historical landscape.[1] His account of the Sydney situation provides an insight into the morally charged distinctions that have increasingly calcified since the early 1990s. Foley represents those Aboriginal people whose relatives moved to Sydney for economic opportunities throughout the twentieth century as failing to respect and acknowledge the traditional owner status of the descendants of Aboriginal clan groups who occupied the area in 1788 (but who have been disappointed in their efforts to have their native title rights recognised).

Patti Miller's 2012 memoir *The Mind of a Thief* deals sensitively with a major dispute about who could claim traditional owner status in the Wellington Valley in central NSW. Miller is a non-Indigenous writer who grew up in Wiradjuri Country. While the area Miller explores lies incontrovertibly within Wiradjuri Country, two local descent groups claimed a more specific connection to the Wellington Valley, one family group believing they had been deliberately sidelined throughout the claims process. A fierce intra-Aboriginal contest erupted, especially over the Wellington Common, which was eventually transferred to Aboriginal ownership in 2007.

Writing of the Kimberley region of Western Australian, geographer and native title expert Jessica Weir posits that issues of 'difference and equity' within heterogeneous Aboriginal communities can be highlighted *after* a native title determination, as traditional owners are formally consulted over proposed developments that will affect the broader Aboriginal community.[2] And finally, as part of a larger discussion, Alan Burns, whose 'blood ties' are to Yorta Yorta Country in northern

Victoria, tells of his changed social place in the community of Horsham in north-western Victoria after the native title claim of Wergaia people was resolved. Burns lost his role as a Cultural Heritage Protection Officer in Horsham, after twenty dedicated years in it, because local Weirgaia descendants began to say 'anyone who doesn't belong to country should have no rights to the country and have any say'.[3] His hurt is palpable. There are other stories of this kind, but these four sobering examples serve to illustrate the point: 'traditional owner' status has been elevated, and is fought over, impacting on those Indigenous people whose life stories render them unable to assume that mantle.

'Native title,' it was explained to me in Ceduna, 'attacks a person's identity and the very essence of who they are.' The situation is highly complex but basically unfolded as follows. Since the mid-1990s, many Ceduna Nungas have drawn on historical records to revive an identity as 'Wirangu', an appellation which had largely fallen into disuse by the mid twentieth century. The native title process here, as elsewhere, stimulated the resurgence of 'tribal' identities rooted in historical knowledge, and the documentation of their separate languages. However, Aunty Sue Mob see themselves as Nungas who also 'always knew' themselves to be Kokatha people, living out their lives on Kokatha Country and speaking the Kokatha language. They have some Mirning thrown in, but native title has forced them to foreground their Kokatha-ness as heated arguments about identity flared and Ceduna Nungas increasingly feel obliged to 'choose one tribe'. As anthropologist Ben Scambary notes of the Pilbara, 'Relatively few people emphasise multiple lines of descent when describing their language group and country interests'.[4] Asserting an unambiguous identity became crucial amidst years of turmoil.

Those people Aunty Sue Mob call the 'native title mob' are viewed as drawing on the historical sources in ways that contradict, 'correct' and supersede Aunty Sue Mob's previously held terms of self-identification. As more and more Ceduna Nungas have (re)discovered their Wirangu-ness, they have attained a kind of local moral and practical authority as traditional owners of the coastal area where Ceduna is located. Other Ceduna Nungas, whose histories, families and genealogies are intimately bound up with those people who now identify as Wirangu, have found themselves recast as people who *lack* traditional connections to the coast and to many specific places, including where they were born and brought up, and specific sites to which they express deep attachments and of which they have hold cultural knowledge.

As a consequence, Sue came to see native title as a cruel state intervention into her self-understanding. This is not the first time, she points out, that others have 'dictated who they said I was'. This point is crucial. It underlines Aunty Sue's cynicism about the discontinuous definitions of Aboriginality with which she has been forced to enact a dialogue over the course of her life. As I described earlier, Sue's generation keenly remember being categorised as 'half-caste'. They spent their childhoods under the threat of being removed from Koonibba because of the state government's definitional regime which underpinned child removal and assimilation policies: these policies believed that Aboriginal people were changeable and should be changed.

Sue often relayed an anecdote about first arriving at her Lutheran boarding school in Adelaide in the early 1960s. When she told the school principal she was Aboriginal, he said, 'I'll put you down as European.' 'You will not!' came her response.

Sue continues to refuse to accept that her own identity be determined, distorted or set down by others.

My analysis of the latest incarnation of this refusal was initially forged out of Aunty Sue Mob's cogent criticisms of the claims process and the category of recognition it establishes, a critique also found in other writing about both the *Native Title Act* and the *Land Rights Act (Northern Territory) 1976*.[5]

At stake in this particular case is the relationship between archival materials—which *some* locals *sometimes* affirm as authoritative guides to contemporary identity categories—and lived experiences. Aunty Sue Mob attribute a kind of rigidity to the colonial record, finding it unyielding to their desires. Yet the archive is not one thing, and is not necessarily as dogmatic and unrewarding as Aunty Sue Mob have found to be: it may well prove multi-vocal. Anthropologist Cameo Dalley puts this nicely when she observes that while some Aboriginal people hear primarily the inquisitorial voice of a distant anthropologist belonging to a bygone era, others hear and treasure 'the voices of their forebears'.[6] But in the case I describe, the archival record doesn't offer Aunty Sue Mob anything, whereas scorning it returns to them a sense of their own authority and agency.

Aunty Sue Mob's experiences occur at some distance from the legal process undertaken by claimants—this is about what happens around street corners and kitchen tables, rather than in meetings. My analysis of the interplay between contemporary identities and the return to archival records tries to simultaneously keep in view the impact native title has had on people's everyday lives.

Land rights on the Far West Coast

When the missionaries left Koonibba in 1963, and the mission gates were torn down, sweeping social changes were afoot. Soon after, South Australia became the first state to introduce land rights legislation with the passage of the *Aboriginal Lands Trust Act 1966*.[7] Under this act, the state government is able to transfer Crown Lands to the trust, which is made up of Aboriginal members appointed by the governor on the recommendation of people living on trust-owned land.[8] Initially the trust transferred unoccupied Aboriginal reserves that were the vestiges of the early colonial period. It now holds freehold title to a number of Aboriginal communities located on former Aboriginal reserves, leasing these to the relevant Aboriginal council for ninety-nine years.[9] In 1975, 890 hectares of land was leased back to the Koonibba Community Council on a ninety-nine year lease.[10]

Political historian Tim Rowse's analysis of the 1966 Act enables clearer understanding of later legislative epochs. Rowse shows that the South Australian discourse surrounding the Lands Trust Act 'did not evoke Aborigines ethnographically—as bearers of an ancient law—but historically and governmentally'.[11] Evocations of traditional custom and law were not the basis of this early land rights legislation, which instead stressed that these were a people 'understandably aggrieved and alienated by colonial dispossession'.[12] Rowse notes that Aboriginal people were understood in several ways: firstly, as wronged and alienated historical subjects; secondly, as putative political subjects whose coming into a political subjectivity needed careful supervision; thirdly, as economic subjects who needed a land base to practise and develop old and new skills; and finally, as 'a people', 'communal in their customs of property, with limited aspirations as individuals'.[13] Rowse is pointing out that at this stage rights in land did not arise from Aboriginal people's status as bearers of distinctive Indigenous cultural difference. Other ways of thinking about the land rights question were to emerge in Australia soon after this period.

In the 1980s, South Australia legislated for two more specific Land Rights Acts, which in both cases granted inalienable freehold title over enormous stretches of desert: the *A<u>n</u>angu Pitjantjatjara Yankunytjatjara Land Rights Act 1981* and the *Maralinga Tjarutja Land Rights Act 1984*.[14] The second act awards rights in land to southern Pitjantjatjara people, who were cut off from swathes of their ancestral country in the 1950s by the Maralinga atomic testing program.[15] These two acts come after the *Aboriginal Land Rights (Northern Territory) Act 1976*. The latter act certainly instituted the assumption that Aboriginal people's rights in land rested 'on the successful assertion of Indigenous difference', and the presentation of cases in ahistorical and religious terms.[16] Reflexive orientations to one's cultural past, as well as colonial entanglements must be minimised in the making of a successful cases. 'Acknowledgement of multiple or divided engagement is not helpful in demonstrating traditionality, since what is continuous between past and present must be assessable as Indigenous'.[17]

The passage of the latter two South Australian land rights acts sowed the seeds for new intra-Aboriginal tensions within the state. The geographer Jane M. Jacobs has persuasively argued that the *Pitjantjatjara Land Rights Act*, and the high profile political campaigns of desert communities leading up to it, put pressure on south-eastern South Australian Aboriginal groups to cast their own land rights aspirations in the terms modelled by the tradition-oriented Pitjantjatjara.[18]

Jacobs closely analysed the way Kokatha land rights aspirations were articulated in the 1980s in Port Augusta. 'The process has involved Aboriginal groups deliberately selecting aspects of their cultural inheritance which they know have become acceptable to external agents as proof of their unique and special interest in land.'[19] For example, Kokatha people adopted the Pitjantjatjara strategy for dealing with mining companies, which involved *not* disclosing the location of cultural sites, and instead marking out areas where mining could occur. When the Kokatha attempted this as Roxby Downs was being proposed, the approach proved unacceptable for the mining company for a number of reasons. Jacobs concluded that while the Pitjantjatjara identity was recognised, and its validity secured on the basis that it was 'traditional', the Kokatha group in Port Augusta needed to 'prove their Aboriginality' by the disclosure rather than withholding of 'traditional information'.[20]

These kinds of tensions are ongoing, despite their longevity. One Nunga in Ceduna complained to me that Maralinga Tjarutja people 'get recognition from the government ... the rest of us, we're invisible ... yet we're the people who were imposed upon'. Another joked, 'If the Pitjantjatjara head any further south, they'll claim Antarctica.'

As Jacobs summarises, 'success in gaining control over land is dependent upon the willingness of Aboriginal groups to articulate their Aboriginality, using procedures and symbols which are acceptable to those controlling access to land'.[21] Animating the complaints I heard was an acute awareness, sometimes explicitly expressed, that when it came to convincing the Australian public of the legitimacy of Aboriginal claims to land, factors such as skin colour matter; this immediately locates someone closer to the 'pole of mythic authenticity' that historian Patrick Wolfe described.[22] In the early 1980s Jacobs stated that, '"non-traditional" Aboriginals ... are deprived of specialised consideration in relation to land rights because of their lack of an overtly traditional life-style'. Ceduna Nungas still perceive this to be true.[23]

Homelands and the breaking up of the Nunga identity

In Ceduna, it is common to hear lamentations such as 'we were all just Nungas' before native title came along.[24] Similarly, in the western

Queensland town of Charters Towers, anthropologist Sally Babidge was told repeatedly, 'we was all together, all one mob, before all this land claim business'. This reflection, Babidge states, is 'not only a simple expression of nostalgia' but also an assessment about the effects of native title, which is seen to deliberately fracture broader-based Aboriginal groups. Native title, explains Babidge, was seen as 'just another piece of legislation to make us Murris fight amongst ourselves'.[25]

All this is true of my experience and, as Babidge suggests, there is an *element* of nostalgia at work. In Ceduna, however, the disaggregation, or separation of the term 'Nunga' into its component parts, which are expressed in terms of 'tribal' affiliation, seems to have begun in an earlier period. Many of my interviewees say that this process has its origins in local political developments: the 'homelands movement' of the early to mid 1990s. This first period of fragmentation was then intensified by people's involvement in the first wave of native title claims emanating from Ceduna throughout the late 1990s.

The establishment of communal land holdings called homelands in the early 1990s involved the purchase of local properties through the Aboriginal and Torres Strait Islander Commission (ATSIC) Land Acquisition Fund.[26] The local ATSIC office oversaw and engineered the purchase of these properties for incorporated bodies formed by the descendants of various sets of locally prominent ancestors.

Each day I drove past the Yarilena homeland, frequently giving lifts to its residents and visitors who fanned out across the Denial Bay road, walking slowly in the full sun. This eponymous homeland belongs to the descendants of Yari and Lena Miller, a Koonibba couple who moved from the mission to Ceduna in 1942, where Yari Miller carted night soil for the council, a degraded form of work befitting the racial hierarchy of the period. The Millers faced intense scrutiny, hostility and complaint from white residents, but they persevered in town until the mid 1950s before moving to a reserve on the outskirts of Ceduna.[27] This former reserve became the Yarilena homeland.[28] Homelands vary greatly in size, in terms of population and the amount of land owned: some host a settlement, services and small businesses; some run operational farms. Others are periodically occupied parcels of land, and do not boast much infrastructure. I know of nine such homelands in the vicinity of Ceduna but have been unable to find any publicly available documentation relating to their establishment, justification and constitution. From an interview with a former ATSIC employee I gleaned that ATSIC intended them to provide an economic base for their residents, as well as representing a concerted attempt to break up the social life of 'the Bronx', the notorious housing trust area of Ceduna that lies inland of the gypsum train line, beyond the reach of the sea breeze. Many housing trust houses were physically moved on the backs of trucks out to homelands, leaving the Bronx today dotted with overgrown vacant blocks, and its reputation for rowdiness intact.

Jo Jo, born in Ceduna in the early 1980s, was certain that the advent of the homelands ushered in a period of unprecedented conflict:

> Back when I was little, everyone basically lived in the housing trust area and just all got along great, didn't matter what family [or what] last name you were or anything, we just all lived together. Then they put homelands together, and put them all in their own little family groups and then it just started all this bickering.

She pointed out that many of these arguments centered, not just on inequitable resource allocation to the various family groupings as homelands were gradually established, but on people's decisions about what family group to orient themselves towards, in cases where they could claim a genealogical relationship with more than one antecedent. For Jo Jo, homeland groups remain the basis of social tensions. She was convinced that Nunga kids, who saw themselves as part of exclusive family-based groups, had banded together to target her young, fair-skinned son at primary school. 'Kids are more closer to their own little cousins now coz they all sort of live together in little groups,' she told me.

When I asked Jo Jo her views on the Wirangu/Kokatha distinction, which emerged later, through involvement in the native title claims process, she continued to foreground the distinctions that existed *within* the 'tribal' categories, based on 'little family groups':

> Things didn't seem so tense back then, it seemed like all the family was sort of together, and now it's all kind of broken into different little groups within Kokatha, it's like all these different little family groups now, instead of just the one big group, and, yeah, everyone seems to be arguing, wherever you are [about] what sort of group you're in ... we're all bit of each other anyway now, we're all, you know, half this, half that ... Because it's caused so much friction it doesn't really bother me, I'll tell anyone that I'm Kokatha but, you know, that's what I am, but it doesn't really faze me.

The demands of native title

As noted in opening, the 1992 Mabo decision found that native title still exists in Australia, the High Court 'giving belated recognition of original Aboriginal title to the country'.[29] In progressive quarters Mabo was celebrated and is still commemorated as a moral triumph. At the time a 'vicious and vehement' debate ensued, with organised farmers' groups and the mining industry mounting public campaigns, and hysterically proclaiming threats to suburban backyards.[30] The federal Labor government moved quickly to develop a legal framework for the realisation of native title. Aboriginal leaders such as Marcia Langton, Noel Pearson and Michael Dodson negotiated the terms of the *Native Title Act*, while opposing interests sought to influence the drafting of the legislation.

Despite the earlier developments outlined, native title has emerged as a more radically disturbing social force, partly for the reasons anthropologist Elizabeth Povinelli has described. Povinelli understands native title to place an 'impossible demand' on contemporary Indigenous subjects, who are compelled to identify with a lost, indeterminable object, that is forms of social organisation and laws and customs that predate colonisation, and which must be sufficiently intact and still observed by claimants today.[31] Note that things have come full circle since Aunty Sue's childhood—not having changed too much is the thing that is most desired.

Importantly, in the case I describe it is not so much the opaque object called 'traditional culture' that must be retrieved but the *names* previously given to collective identities. Native title claimant groups must constitute themselves and make themselves 'legible' by defining themselves in terms set out by the native title legislative framework.[32] Native title expert Tim Dauth proposes that 'group names should not be examined as discrete, fixed and discoverable artefacts or entities, but rather as complex, historically shifting, and highly contextual'.[33] Within the claims process, however, as Dauth concedes, 'much becomes invested in asserting the unique "authenticity" of such labels as unchanged pre-sovereignty entities', and the historical record is turned to as if these group names might indeed to be excavated from the recesses of the archives and traced into the present.[34]

John Howard's Coalition government amended the *Native Title Act* in 1998, in the process introducing Indigenous Land Use Agreements (ILUAs), which provide for legally binding agreements between a native title claimant group and another party. Soon after the 1998 amendments, negotiated outcomes emerged as the South Australian state government's 'preferred option' for the resolution of claims; the cost of litigation being a key factor.[35] A more general transition towards negotiated outcomes and agreement-making processes followed across the continent. Some native title experts argue that a significant result of this is that 'a much reduced level of documentation' and a 'far lower threshold of proof' are required within a consent determination process.[36] However, legal scholars caution against 'simplifications about the desirability of one mode over the others'.[37] For barrister Brett Walker the expectation that native title claimants negotiate over their native title rights is manifestly unjust, whereas litigation offers the 'just vindication' of this legal right by the party claiming it.[38] Walker is effectively asking what other property right 'is governed by legislation that, from the outset, encourages its erosion by compromise'?[39]

In Ceduna, the first native title claim for the region (a Mirning claim) was lodged in 1995. In early 2006, five partially overlapping claims were absorbed into the amalgamated Far West Coast claim, which was resolved in late 2013.

The political crisis produced by native title in Ceduna

For Aunty Sue Mob, the early stages of native title precipitated a kind of crisis about the nature of their own identities. This crisis led to Aunty Sue Mob rejecting the promise of native title on a number of grounds. Let me be clear: this is *not* an existential crisis, whereby Aunty Sue Mob find themselves experiencing doubts about who or what it is they 'really' are—although this is an accusation levelled at them by other Aboriginal groupings they are in conflict with[40] and a barbed charge they direct at those same others in turn.

'Our background is well known to us,' insists Aunty Vera. Aunty Sue Mob members told me many times, 'We know who we are.' I refer here to a political crisis, generated by an urgent imperative to respond to conditions that have proved profoundly destabilising, and by Aunty Sue Mob's felt desire to express and affirm their own identity as Kokatha people.

From Aunty Sue Mob's perspective, the native title claims process served to produce distortions that then acquired a forceful reality as a newly emerged group of people, as they saw it, were 'recognised', and their existence concretised: a move that carried a curious effect. Aunty Sue Mob see the Wirangu as a *creation* of recent times. Yet in local discussions, the native title process is credited with *apprehending* the latent presence of Wirangu people and the Wirangu language on the West Coast, affording it due if belated recognition and, in doing so, obscuring the conditions that underwrote its recent re-emergence, and the role of state processes in it. As this highly charged situation has evolved, Aunty Sue Mob's self-understanding and terms of self-definition initially emerged as a major casualty of the whole process. However, their response to the situation has seen only an enhanced awareness and import attached to their specific identity as Kokatha people, and to their efforts to maintain ongoing relationships to country they understand as their own. While other native title groups might well 'struggle for recognition' through the native title claims process,[41] Aunty Sue Mob struggle for self-definition *against* the native title claims process.

Recognition emerges as a central concept within the native title literature, but I suggest it is inadequate to the task.[42] The rise of a broader politics of recognition, emanating within the new social movements of the early 1970s, has been widely analysed.[43] Put simply, these emancipatory movements 'no longer struggle mainly for economic equality or material redistribution, but for respect for the characteristics by which they seem themselves culturally bound together'.[44] As the philosopher Charles Taylor points out in an influential essay, this demand for recognition, which remains characteristic of many contemporary political struggles, confirms the fundamentally inter-subjective nature of human life.[45] Taylor gave due attention to the damage of 'misrecognition', writing that nonrecognition or misrecognition' can inflict harm, can be a form of oppression, imprisoning one in a false, distorted and reduced mode of being'.[46] A more recent body of international Indigenous Studies literature casts serious doubt on the goal of recognition. For example, Yellowknives Dene political theorist Glen Coulthard argues that Canadian developments advanced under the banner of recognition serve to conceal the fundamental similarity of present state objectives to the more overtly dominant forms of colonial governance enacted in the past. For Coulthard, Indigenous peoples are still being dispossessed of their lands and self-determining authority.[47]

To return to Taylor's earlier point about inter-subjective conditions: being recognised depends on being seen by another; it is based on a relationship. If colonised subjects are to be recognised by a gesture of the nation-state, then the crucial question pertains to the nature of the relationship. Coulthard would characterise it as 'profoundly asymmetrical' and 'nonreciprocal'.[48] The precise question becomes, 'Recognition on whose terms?' The answer, of course, is 'the state's'. This reality is not unique to native title but it is starkly apparent in this case, as Sue is pointing out.

In Ceduna, as it was narrated to me, the moment when 'native title started up' stimulated a frenzied process of differentiation, realised through engaging genealogical records. Throughout the 1990s Ceduna Nungas became, primarily, 'the Wirangu', 'the Kokatha' and 'the Mirning'. In an illuminating discussion, native title anthropologists Simon Correy, Anthony Redmond and Diana McCarthy have theorised the destablilising effects of involvement with the native title claims process, describing a similar process. Correy et al say they

> have been struck by the powerful social effects of identifying, describing and maintaining these [intra-Aboriginal] differences and by the rapidity with which particular differences become ossified and transformed into enduring social distinctions.

Speaking with extensive experience of claims in New South Wales and also more remote areas, they

> have observed the alacrity with which the various claimant groups with which we have worked ... have reinscribed distinctions, generated by the native title process, between persons and the groups, locating these distinctions within a highly charged moral order. [49]

In the case I describe, the Wirangu/Kokatha distinction, *in its present form*, was certainly 'generated by the native title process'. It is located within a moral order that rewards 'traditionality', to deploy Merlan's term.[50] To be Wirangu over the time period I analyse here was to be morally ascendant in Ceduna, because it represented a greater degree of fulfillment of criteria specified under the *Native Title Act*. More concretely, Wirangu people have attracted federal government funding through the Maintenance of Indigenous Languages and Records (MILR) program for the purpose of documenting and reviving their language, which is regarded as 'critically endangered'.[51] Kokatha ('Gugada') language reconstruction projects have also been funded, but Wirangu has a special prestige in the town owing to its 'original' status. As Monaghan notes, MILR funding unintentionally promotes social divisions.[52]

Senior Wirangu figures have also been contracted to run cultural awareness training for 'mining companies and government agencies operating in the region'.[53] Wirangu people are acknowledged as 'traditional owners' by well-meaning local entities such as conservation groups as well as local bureaucracies and institutions which routinely program 'Welcome to Country' as part of their public events.[54] The distinction and energies directed toward the maintenance and elaboration of this distinction saw it transform, over the course of a decade, into an 'enduring social distinction', although just how enduring remains to be seen as hyphenated identities, which join together the various 'tribal' terms, seem to be gaining ground in the present.

The content of the contemporary cultural differences between Wirangu- and Kokatha-identifying people are, however, negligible. Anthropologist Simon Harrison's argument is highly relevant: in some cases distinctive ethnic identities arise through a process of denying or disguising resemblances. 'Shared features of identity,' writes Harrison, are 'disavowed, censored, or systematically forgotten'.[55] The term 'censored' is too strong in this case; more subtle processes of de-emphasis have served to enhance the uniqueness of these identity categories, and their separate languages.

Correy et al's explanation is slightly different: they use the Freudian notion of 'the narcissism of minor difference' to account for the ways in which a group identity may be forged by focusing on minor differences with significant social others, with which there is an overwhelming sense of similarity and a concomitant need to define oneself clearly.[56] The pressure to produce and then sustain clearly defined claimant groups creates an environment 'in which small differences between people and groups become suffused with very powerful emotions'.[57]

What is especially striking about this case is that after state processes succeeded in seeking out and generating 'iconic differences' between Ceduna's Indigenous groups, and after these groups were sufficiently differentiated into 'clearly bounded units',[58] then these distinct groups underwent years of mediation before being joined together in an amalgamated native title claim in 2006, which was resolved in late 2013.

In the process, a new (and to my mind promising) category of identity was instituted—Far West Coast People. However, this merging took place by stages, and Aunty Sue Mob members' everyday lives, identities and relations had already come to revolve around their refusal to participate in this process or even to accept its legitimacy. Aunty Sue Mob felt that they had, in effect, been told they were mistaken about the nature of their own existence. Further backtracking in time is required to grasp how such a painful and somewhat absurd situation came about.

The persistence of records

In 2003 the anthropologist and linguist Peter Sutton noted that native title has given rise to several succession cases

> where physical and cultural occupation of lands whose former occupants had shifted elsewhere, and/or became locally depleted, have turned into controversial bases for legal claims by members of the historically incoming groups.[59]

Sutton wrote about a Kokatha claim from Ceduna as an example of this more widely spread phenomena. However, he went on, 'the persistence of records plays a powerful role in preventing the ready extinguishment of consciousness of how things were before'.[60] As is now established, many Ceduna Nungas have indeed drawn on historical records to revivify their identity as Wirangu people, reminding Kokatha people 'of how things were before'. Precisely how has this reemergence of the category of Wirangu come about?

Linguist Paul Monaghan has conducted research on the Far West Coast for over a decade, working closely with a number of senior community members, mostly women, on Wirangu language and cultural revitalisation projects, as well as work on Gugada (Kokatha). The process has involved disentangling these two languages, which Monaghan understands mixed to form 'Mission Talk' at Koonibba throughout the twentieth century, with borrowings from English.[61] The reconstructed Wirangu language, Monaghan explains, 'is based on the colonial records of missionaries, police officers, anthropologists, linguists and the memories of a small group of senior women'.[62] Indeed the role historic records have assumed in this region has become so contentious that Monaghan describes every effort being made 'to be transparent in the use of archival materials'.[63]

A key text used in this process is a wordlist Daisy Bates recorded in writing at Yuria Rockhole, about 100 kilometres west of Ceduna.[64] At Yuria, Bates recorded Minjia, or Lucy Washington, the grandmother of the two elderly sisters who, throughout the claim period, were the last remaining fluent speakers of Wirangu.[65]

Daisy Bates is a mythical figure in the annals of Australian historiography. Born in Ireland in 1863, Bates arrived in Perth in 1899 and established herself as a keen amateur expert on Aboriginal culture in north-west Western Australia. From 1919 to 1935 she camped at Ooldea. Here, biographer Elizabeth Salter concludes in *Daisy Bates*, ethnology came second to martyrdom: Bates shared food with her companions, and tended to illnesses. She sought but never secured a salaried post befitting her status as a self-appointed 'protector'.

In 1938 Bates wrote an elegiac description of Yuria Gabbi (water), saying the 'walja—eagle-hawk—have now entire possession of Yuria Gabbi, for its owners and their relations have long since gone ... '. Standing near the granite outcrop, she observed 'an old dead tree, shaped like a rough cross, and upon its branches a walja is always to be seen sitting in the early morning'. She continued:

> The rabbit has come to Yuria, and dug burrows close by the water, and three of these burrows are near the dead sandalwood so walja waxes fat and lazy since food is now to be got without hunting. And only the cutting flints are there to tell of the old-time residents or those who passed.[66]

Bates believed the Aboriginal people she lived alongside were the residuals of a 'dying race', in the process of 'vanishing'. She could not have imagined the ways in which sites such as Yuria Rockhole have today been repossessed as rightfully belonging and of spiritual significance to contemporary Aboriginal peoples.

With Aunty Sue Mob, I once visited Yuria, an outcrop that erupts on the rise of an open plain of rippling grey-golden grasses. The occasion brought home to me that it is regarded as significant by *both* Wirangu- and Kokatha-identifying peoples today, as Aunty Sue Mob members respectfully wandered around a site strewn with flints perhaps handled by their own ancestors.

I wish to set aside the *content* of the early historical records for now. What I am trying to understand is the impact of a certain *process*—by which the accounts of early observers such as missionaries, anthropologists and Daisy Bates come to be privileged as authoritative sources on the subject of contemporary identities and group names—on Aboriginal people secure in their self-understanding. Native title anthropologist Tim Pilbrow calls this 'the power of the documentary record', wherein records are, paradoxically, at once relied upon for their facticity, as well as read cautiously with an awareness of the context of their creation.[67] Pilbrow is highlighting the involvement of contemporary claim anthropologists, who have a crucial part to play in interpreting the historical record for the purpose of the claim. This whole process, which unfolded slowly (and before I turned up), has embittered the people I know. Aunty Sue perceives that the native title process revolves around an acceptance of the fact that archival sources can legitimise contemporary identity formations, a supposition that undermines the authority and explanatory power of local sources, such as the understanding of their identity that 'the old people passed on' and the things that people say they 'always knew'.

Anthropologists who act as experts for native title claimants are sometimes highly alert to this dynamic: a land council anthropologist told Babidge that it seems 'wrong to be standing out the front of a meeting telling [Aboriginal] people about their history',[68] while Pilbrow writes that 'it is supremely difficult to negotiate such a dialogue without appearing condescending toward Aboriginal people's sense of expertise about their own culture'.[69] More pointedly, Aboriginal people are themselves highly attuned to the colonial overtures in such exchanges and express cynicism about the fact that their own self-understandings are accorded secondary status by native title related processes, while those things that can be verified through archival research are accorded primacy.

The 'earliest sources are best,' summarises anthropologist Basil Sansom controversially.[70] The potential problem that reliance on early colonial sources poses for those experts working on native title claims has certainly been considered.[71] But what kind of problems does the use of such sources pose for contemporary politicised Aboriginal subjects?

The very moment native title 'recognises' it simultaneously undermines, recognising ultimately that a greater authority, veracity and truth-effect inheres in the colonial record than in contemporary Aboriginal people's self-understandings. Here the terms of recognition are crudely exposed. Once they were laid bare, Aunty Sue Mob faced a decision to accept or refuse them.

Chapter 7

Engaging the historical record

'What about Tindale?'

In 2008 I raised with Aunty Sue that I would like to contribute to some kind of community-directed project, entirely separate from my research. Our conversation reflected changing conventions, as I sought an equitable relationship between researcher and researched—one that would result in tangible 'community benefits', rather than me extracting knowledge solely for my own reward. 'What about Tindale?' Sue asked me uncertainly. 'It would be really good if someone could do something about Tindale.'

I was at loss as to what to 'do' about Tindale, and instead happily collaborated on a small book documenting Aunty Sue Mob's bushfood knowledge.[1]

From 1928 to 1965, Norman Tindale was the ethnologist and curator of anthropology at the South Australian Museum.[2] With American physical anthropologist J. B. Birdsell, and at the request of the South Australian government, Tindale undertook 'what has been called the greatest systematic genealogical survey conducted on any indigenous population anywhere in the world'.[3] This genealogical information, collected between 1938 and the 1960s, together with photos, has been used for purposes radically counter-posed to the purpose for which they were collected. For example, in 2012 the State Library of Queensland mounted a poignant exhibition called *Transforming Tindale*, which included large charcoal and conte drawings by artist Vernon Ah Kee, based on photographs of his family members collected as part of the survey.[4]

Tindale and Birdsell's survey, underwritten by government interest in the 'half-caste problem',

> was hailed at the time as a major population genetics study on the effects of miscegenation ... Now, over 50 years later, this information is being used in a very different and innovative way to assist people trace their family trees and establish their Aboriginal identity.[5]

Neva Wilson, then an Aboriginal employee of the South Australian Museum's Family History Project, with extensive family connections on the West Coast, recounts travelling out there in 1992 and 1993 to inform people about the existence of the Museum's Tindale material, and seek permission for the publication of selected genealogies:

> The people were very responsive to the many questions I asked and were very excited and thrilled by the recordings of their family trees and photographs that were done so many years ago by Tindale and Birdsell; it gave them a sense of continuity.[6]

The situation however is more complex than this narrative of reclamation conveys. Tindale's findings have been taken to undermine, rather than fill out, some Aboriginal people's understanding of their Aboriginal identity: the information might not deliver a sense of continuity but instead highlight a discontinuity between what is socially known and significant about the local past, and what was written down in 1938–1939.

Furthermore, Tindale's 1974 map of tribal boundaries is a different matter entirely from the genealogies. The map has been critiqued for the firm boundaries it created, and the essentially monolingual model of social organisation it deployed.[7] Aunty Sue Mob resent the map, not just for Tindale getting it 'wrong' (as they perceived it), but for the aura of authority it has seemed to acquire over the past fifteen to twenty years. The lines on Tindale's maps had acquired a troubling fixity, effectively cutting Kokatha people off from what they understood as their country, and leaving them stranded on the map just north of places they know and care about.

British-Canadian anthropologist Robert Paine, writing about the 1997 Gitksan-Wet'suwet'en land claim case in Canada pointed out that the Canadian state demanded, in this case, 'that a claim to Aboriginality be demonstrated historically, from before contact. That is to say, before there were written records'. And yet, Paine noted, 'the State—as part of its own social construction—insists that historical truth is best found *in* the written' (emphasis in the original).[8] These comments are pertinent to the Australian situation. And here arises a dilemma: I find myself *always* tempted by a turn to the written, in order to test these many claims and counter-claims, believing, as part of my own social-constructedness, that historical truth is best found in the written. But to do so would be to enact what it is I seek to critique: the native title legal regime's demand that the substance of people's contemporary identities be brought in line with that which was set down in the past.

At the risk of repeating myself, this book is dedicated to capturing the everyday and lived effects of involvement in a native title claim, as they were described to me by a particular group of people in the present. I am an ethnographer and not a native title anthropologist; my approach and perspective reflect my interest in people, experiences and perception, over native title jurisprudence. The engrossing daily dramas that consumed Aunty Sue Mob members throughout 2008 and 2009 were defined by them as being about native title.

I also stress again that many Ceduna Nungas involved in the Wirangu renaissance have found the return to the historical record revelatory as they engage with processes of self-discovery in the native title era; by no means do I wish to discount the exciting possibilities that arise when new models of self-understanding are opened up. This period has been generative in a more literal sense, too. Three informative works are sold at the Tjutjuna (Ceduna) Aboriginal Arts and Culture Centre. A 'Wirangu storybook' tells of hunting for wardu (wombat), describing the eating of liver and fat cooked on a small fire, and the slow roasting of the rest in a ground oven as stories are told.[9] Two other works reconstruct the Wirangu language.[10] The reformulation of local Aboriginal identities since the mid-1990s, however, has also generated the deeply felt schisms I describe, and these cannot be ignored.

It is not possible to proceed with this story without providing some historical background. The historical material is by no means conclusive; I use it here to help explain how this situation came about rather than definitively solve any 'problem'. I have very deliberately not availed myself of the archival material stored in the South Australian Museum. I chose to follow Aunty Sue out bush rather than follow a line of inquiry that would have been interpreted as an expression of faith in the authority of these accounts, and made my relationship with Aunty Sue Mob tense.

The Wirangu renaissance

The treachery, as Aunty Sue Mob portray it, of those who have more recently begun to identify as Wirangu, was always illustrated to me by way of the following example. In 1974, Ceduna Nungas established an organisation known as the Far West Aboriginal Progress Association (FWAPA).[11] The organisation chanelled state and federal government funds, made available throughout the nascent self-determination era, for the provision of Aboriginal housing, health and employment services. FWAPA also organised social events, such as dances, a festival and a choir, for the Aboriginal community who, after the government takeover of Koonibba, were increasingly living 'in town'. FWAPA's newsletter was called *Kukatja Wangka*. Kukatja here is a version of Kokatha; the newsletter's name meant 'the Kokatha talking'.

Several people who went on to become prominent Wirangu-identifying figures in Ceduna were heavily associated with FWAPA and at that point of time, it is alleged, *never* asserted a distinct identity or raised any objection to the whole-of-community's aspirations being represented under the banner of *Kukatja Wangka*. This fact is consistently wielded to underline the claim that the reassertion of a distinct identity as Wirangu is both recent and opportunistic.[12]

I have been unsuccessful in my attempts to locate copies of *Kukatja Wangka*. But in the early 1980s, geographer Jane M. Jacobs quoted from the FWAPA newsletter, simply to point out that the other major population centre of Kokatha people was in Ceduna, while Jacobs herself worked with an eastern group of Kokatha people in the town of Port Augusta. Jacobs calls the following a 'public statement of identity'. I reproduce the original reference and citation, as they appear in Jacobs' MA thesis, in full:

> World renown[ed] linguist Professor John Platt, who has done many years research into the languages of this general area, agrees that while there were several groups of population which traditionally lived in the area (for example the coastal Wirungu [sic] group), the group from whom most of our members are descendants are the Kuktja [Kokatha] group who mainly occupied the lower fringes of the Western Desert (Ooldea and Westward) and who were subsequently dispersed into other areas (Koonibba, Yalata). (*Kukutja Wangka*, Official Newsletter of the Far West Aboriginal Progress Association, vol. 1, no. 2, Feb 1981.)[13]

Aboriginal people in Ceduna might tell me, on the one hand, that they were previously 'all Nungas' before the advent of native title. However, the quote above suggests that by the early 1980s there also existed a more specific consciousness that Koonibba was the site, primarily but not exclusively, of a Kokatha regeneration. Indeed, this is something that people consistently represented to me as something they knew while growing up on Koonibba—something they were taught by 'the old people'. In the newsletter Platt, an expert and outsider, is invoked to lend weight to these identity claims.

I have never heard any member of Aunty Sue Mob counter the authoritative opinion of one scholar or observer by providing an alternative expert citation from another. Instead, it is the significance and centrality of Aboriginal *self-accounts* that Aunty Sue Mob insist upon. They regard it as unproblematic that Nungas on the Far West Coast in the 1980s were largely, but not exclusively, descended from Kokatha antecedents (the newsletter says *most* of our members). This was a social fact but did not grant Kokatha-ness any special quality as against the qualities of Nungas who were descended from non-Kokatha peoples. As Monaghan summarises, 'There is some evidence to suggest Gugada [(Kokatha)] was the dominant tribal term operating in the wider Ceduna region in the 1950s, the time in which the older generation was growing up.'[14] Members of this generation went on to assume organisational roles in the self-determination era, and were involved in the publication of *Kukutja Wangka*.

The Kokatha ascendancy

Some historical accounts suggest Kokatha descendants greatly outnumbered Wirangu descendants well before the 1950s. Brock says that by the late nineteenth century Wirangu and Kokatha peoples were holding joint ceremonies on 'the west coast, in the Gawler Ranges, and to the north'. Brock continues, 'This suggests that the Wirangu under pressure had adapted their cultural and ceremonial life to that of the Kokatha.' While this observation renders the Kokatha ascendant, Koonibba's first pastor, Wiebusch, says Brock, 'ascertained that there were three or four languages spoken by visitors to the mission, but he identified Wirangu as the primary one and attempted to learn it'. Brock follows this detail with the following one: 'By the 1920s Kokatha had become the predominant Aboriginal language; the missionary at that time considered Wirangu almost extinct.'[15] It seems Brock understands that Pastor Hoff, who arrived in 1920 and left in 1930, learned Kokatha. However, Pastor Eckermann wrote:

> Pastor Hoff had abilities that made him a good missionary. This period [the 1920s] was probably the best in Koonibba's history in regard to the use of the Wirongu [sic] language. Both Pastor Hoff and his assistant, Pastor Juers, spoke the language fluently... [16]

When anthropologist Ronald Berndt corresponded with Hoff in 1939 he learned that 'the Kokata and Wirangu tribes have moved down to Koonibba', but also that: 'the Wirangu, which to-day [sic] is almost extinct, formerly resided near the coast'.[17]

In 1966 and 1967, John Platt recorded Gugada (Kokatha) speakers on the West Coast. Platt also made some recordings of Wirangu speakers, noting, 'The dialect is now almost extinct in that very few speakers remain and these are mostly so scattered that they have little opportunity for communication in Wirangu.'[18] When, in 1970, Aboriginal activists and their supporters gathered at La Perouse to mark the obliteration of Aboriginal language groups and people as part of the destruction wrought by colonisation, Wirangu was mourned as one of those languages thought to be utterly lost.[19]

For the sake of argument I will take up Eckermann's perspective on Hoff's effective use of Wirangu at Koonibba in the 1920s, as against Brock's. This is in the knowledge that Aunty Sue's generation grew up on Koonibba in the 1950s, and say they had 'never heard of Wirangu', confirming Monaghan's point, cited earlier, that Kokatha was 'the dominant tribal term operating in the wider Ceduna region in the 1950s'.

What happened between the 1920s and 1950s? Brock describes the major population shifts occurring in north-western South Australia in the first half of the twentieth century:

> [T]here was a movement south to Ooldea and the transcontinental railway line from 1917 to the 1940s; Ngaanyatjara speakers in the late 1920s moved from the Warburton Ranges and the Gibson Desert in Western Australia to Laverton, Mount Margaret, Kalgoorlie and Wiluna; by 1921 Antikirinya were moving east from Granite Downs to the Oodnadatta area, and Yankunytjatjara from the Everards were also moving east; and into the area they previously occupied came the Pitjantjatjara from the Mann and Tonkinson Ranges.[20]

In terms of the specific, empirical detail, it is the first phase of population movement that especially concerns me: this detail explicates the general point that 'during the twentieth century people from the north, who used Ooldea as a staging post, moved south'.[21] This in turn impacted Kokatha people, who previously predominated at Ooldea, but who were 'displaced by Antikarinja [sic] and later Pitjantjatjara'.[22] And so Koonibba, rather than Ooldea, became the central locality at which West Coast Kokatha people congregated.

It is useful then to briefly survey what was happening at Ooldea in the late 1930s and early 1940s. In August 1939, Ronald Berndt conducted research at Ooldea soak, a ceremony ground and meeting place, and the site of permanent water near the Ooldea siding on the transcontinental railway line, approximately 300 kilometres north-west of Ceduna.[23] Between June and December, 1941, Ronald and Catherine Berndt, both anthropologists, carried out a longer period of fieldwork at Ooldea, establishing a static camp in 'the main pathway to the Soak and within easy distance of the main camp at any time'.[24] Their heavy equipment made establishment of a permanent camp desirable, and it quickly acquired a name as 'the place of the currants'.[25]

However, around the Berndts' camp, those who congregated at Ooldea made thirteen moves for a range of reasons: because firewood was exhausted in one area, for example, because of a death, and to shift further away from the mission in order to conduct ceremonies. The population itself fluctuated; it stood at 200 persons at their arrival, and shrunk to eighty once the waterholes filled and groups headed north and north-west into 'the Spinifex'. At the height of the ceremonial season, the population reached a maximum of about 400 or 500.[26]

Ronald Berndt earlier told his reader that at Ooldea gathered members of the 'Anta'kirinja [Antikarinya] tribe, although representatives of the Pitjandjara [Pitjantjatjara], Murintja and Wirangu were present, members of these tribes having congregated here on the fringes of white occupation and away from their rightful countries'.[27] In fact, he gives biographical details for one Wirangu man, strongly implying that he lived at Ooldea without Wirangu companions. 'Kwana,' Ronald Berndt explained, 'spoke his own southern coastal language, which is dissimilar to that of the Desert dialects. He also frequently used the foreign language, as he lived among those who spoke it.'[28]

In a footnote, Ronald Berndt noted that Pastor Hoff at Koonibba had informed him in 1939 that, 'The Wirangu, which to-day [sic] is almost extinct, formerly resided near the coast …'[29] In another dramatic footnote, Ronald Berndt describes a 'fear' in the Ooldea camp of 'Kokata [Kokatha] men', who were said to be wild and to live in the east, but who never materialised when it was rumoured they would soon approach with 'spears that fell like rain'.[30] At this stage, then, it seems Ooldea was not frequented by people giving their 'tribal' affiliation or language as Kokatha. Indeed, the Berndts did not define their informants with primary regards to their 'tribal' identities, listing instead twenty-seven individuals by name and thanking them for their 'help, tolerance and patience'.[31]

Brock's summary of the large-scale movements underway in the twentieth century brings to light the fact that 'non-Aboriginal intrusion had indirect as well as direct impacts on Aboriginal people'.[32] One of the major impacts of colonisation was to alter the crosscutting territorial associations of various 'tribes' or groups of language speakers. Aboriginal people in the north-west of South Australia were moving even *before* many of them had encountered white people, sometimes because of the effects of colonial settlement experienced elsewhere, as pastoralists usurped hunting grounds, forcing Aboriginal people to share smaller areas with neighbouring people. Aboriginal people moved for reasons of ceremony and because of droughts, but they also moved out of areas where food was becoming scarcer because of pastoralism, and for reasons of curiosity, towards European population centres and novel attractions, such as the Trans-Australian railway line proximate to Ooldea.

Furthermore, there is evidence to suggest that *at the time of first contact*, the coastal groups were *already* under pressure from Kokatha groups moving out of the Western Desert. For his part, Aunty Sue Mob's foe Tindale surmised:

> At the time of first white settlement [of South Australia] in 1836, the coastal tribes of Eyre Peninsula were on the defensive against people moving south from the Lake Eyre region and south-east from the Western Desert, the most insistent being the Pangkala and the Kokata [Kokatha].[33]

Tindale suggests that this pressure was to do with the relative abundance of food on the coast, compared to the semi-arid inland. Significantly, Tindale speculates that Wirangu is a 'very old' language and its 'users may have shifted west earlier from the Flinders ranges'.[34] What is to be made of this picture of movement?

Captured in the colonial record

For the late historian Patrick Wolfe, writing in the early days of native title, the legislation's beneficiaries promised to be 'those could meet certain criteria for *un*invadedness'. He summed this up as a redoubling of this history of oppression since, '*the more you have lost, the less you stand to gain*' (emphasis in the original). Wolfe continued, formulating that, 'To fall within native-title criteria, it is necessary to fall outside history.'[35] Wolfe's oeuvre rewards readers with keen insight into the settler colonial condition, but I think this last comment misrepresents the situation. As Indian-born cultural theorist Arjun Appadurai has suggested, 'natives are not only persons who are from certain places, and belong to those places, but they are also those who are somehow *incarcerated*, or confined in those places'.[36] Appadurai's point needs finessing in this case: here, Aboriginal people are also held incarcerated within, or held captive to, a particular moment in time. Earlier, I cited Sutton's observation that Wirangu-identifying people are empowered to use the archival record to remind Kokatha-identifying people 'of how things were before'. Before? Before what, exactly?

The answer to this question should hopefully be becoming clearer. It is not simply 'before colonial invasion'. Instead, it is 'before Aboriginal people were first contacted by and their existence documented by settler observers'. The moment of first contact is firmly located *within* colonial history, rather than 'outside history'. It is this particular moment in time that is arrested, notwithstanding the fact that this moment is one moment among a bigger moment in flux. Tindale's speculation about the Wirangu language becomes highly suggestive. Aboriginal groups are recognised as the traditional owners of an area they were present in at a particular point of time. There is limited capacity here to grasp the ways in which Aboriginal people might 'creatively transform the experience of dislocation'.[37]

Aunty Sue Mob rail against 'the unfairness of the whole thing'; they rightly perceive that native title recognises and valorises the authority of the colonising order, rather than that of the Aboriginal figure, who is described and set down in the record. In this frozen moment in time colonialism's 'other' is apprehended by the coloniser. The native title claims process seeks to substantiate Aboriginal people's self-understanding by demanding that their own self-accounts are confirmed by, and are consistent with, outsiders' accounts of that frozen moment. As earlier stated, native title legislation moves to redress fundamental injustices of the colonial era, acknowledging Indigenous rights and interests in land, which were previously denied. But by this *very same process* it reinstates colonial relations between the nation-state and Aboriginal people.

Wirangu-identifying people do not, to my knowledge, dispute the fact that the Kokatha tribal identity and language had achieved predominance by the mid-twentieth century. In fact, it has been suggested that the reemerging Wirangu have suffered under a lifetime of being suppressed and isolated by the usurping Kokatha. A documentary about the then last two remaining fluent speakers of Wirangu makes this claim in its promotional material. The film's synopsis states: 'No one speaks to them in Wirrangul [sic] anymore. Everyone speaks the dominant language of Pitjantjatjara and Gokatha [sic]. To speak the language, they can only talk to one and other [sic].'[38]

What of Kokatha-identifying people? In effect those Nungas who, like Aunty Sue Mob, self-identify as Kokatha and who have grown up and lived on or around Koonibba mission-cum-community, and/or in Ceduna have, in recent decades, been cast as part of a 'historically incoming group', to use Sutton's seemingly innocuous phrase,[39] as descendants of 'Western Desert migrants' as Monaghan[40] would have it—or to put it more bluntly, as interlopers. Through their experience of the native title process, Kokatha people are rendered, by this new designation, as living in country that they do not rightfully belong to 'traditional way'. The basis of their relationship, and therefore the substance of this relationship, to the country in which they were born and brought up, country that they have intimate knowledge of, and a strong attachment to, and in which they have lived out their whole lives, are thus undermined. As earlier stated, not one Kokatha person I know in Ceduna has moved more than about 50 kilometres from the birthplace of their grandparents. And yet over the past two decades, these Kokatha people have been repositioned in the literature and in local discourse as a kind of migrant people, with the inference that they are out of place. In an everyday sense they have experienced a strange *affective* dispossession. That is, they have been made to *feel* less secure in their sense of being at home, rather than being dispossessed of land in any material sense.

At this juncture, I feel compelled to highlight the unsatisfactory terminology used in dealing with such scenarios in the anthropological literature, and increasingly within Aboriginal settings. The terms 'traditional' and 'historical' people are employed to differentiate between those Aboriginal people who reside in the same area where the genealogical record indicates their ancestors resided, first, and those people whose ancestors lived in country other than that where subsequent generations settled or were forcibly moved, second.[41]

If these two categories were to be applied to differentiate between Kokatha- and Wirangu-identifying Nungas, then they would be applied to people who have lived, and whose recent ancestors lived, through the same set of experiences. These terms might serve analytical ends, when used carefully, to explain the way the distinctions between two varieties of colonial experiences were politicised by developments beginning in the earlier land rights era. But they have come to act as descriptive terms, as if they accurately refer to categories with naturalised content. Here anthropology's problem with time can be seen to persist.[42] These terms obscure the fact that every other person with whom we share the world is our 'coeval' or contemporary. We are all in fact 'historical persons': no-one has lived through any more or any less history than anyone else. By that I mean that we are all contemporary people whose shared present in Australia is produced by the course of colonial history. 'Traditional people' were no less swept up in the forces of colonialism than 'historical people'. An intense moral and political charge courses through this distinction, and it cannot be put to use innocently of its effect; 'traditional people' are rendered as more properly Aboriginal, and more deserving of rights in land.

Chapter 8

Fighting about native title

Forced coherence

In my fieldnotes and interview transcripts, 'native title' seems both everywhere and nowhere as an effect of its everydayness. When I asked questions about it in casual conversations, I was rarely supplied with answers made sensible via narrative. The 'force of feelings'[1] consistently diverted any attempts on my part to hear narrative-based accounts of what has happened 'since native title came in'.

French sociologist Pierre Bourdieu argued that the seemingly innocent question of 'What comes next?' is designed to elicit an ordered sequence of events; the question, however, 'imposes an attitude to temporality … opposite of the attitude involved practically in the ordinary use of temporal terms'.[2] Bourdieu criticised social scientists for this technique which, among others, represents an attempt to 'force coherence' onto social phenomena, experience and forms.[3]

My own attempts to force coherence onto the phenomenon of native title failed miserably. Conversations out bush and around the kitchen table all seemed to veer and break off, punctuated—out bush—by kids nagging, babies crying and cups of tea being made, and—at the farm—by the phone ringing, cars pulling up and people heading out to the verandah for buyu (a smoke).

One evening I wrote fieldnotes in which I tried to recall and list the things that a conversation out at the farm that afternoon had zigzagged between. Gary sat at one end of the kitchen table, Rhiannon and I around the table, and Sue moved restlessly between dinner preparations, the sink, the stove and the phone in the hallway. We talked of: a $700 phone bill recently received by a family member, and the unsympathetic response from the phone company when they pleaded they had kids to feed and couldn't pay ('tough shit,' the company said); plans to contact the *West Coast Sentinel* with an exposé about this phone company's unfeeling and unjust operations; preparations for an upcoming 21st birthday and the ordering of cakes; forceful advice offered to me about giving Ned a wombat bone to cut his baby teeth on (a niece who did so 'has the best teeth in the family'); an overview of the names certain family members had been given at birth but don't use, going by nicknames or middle names instead; and ideas for fundraising for an upcoming Rockhole Recovery trip, the ostensible topic of our 'meeting'. At one point Gary's phone rang, and he answered it with a bright, 'Hello son,' while the phone in the hallway rang repeatedly and Sue went in and out to pick it up and give a hoarse, quick, 'Hullo!' Rhi and I sat bemused while Gary and Sue nattered away on their phones, either side of where we sat silently.

And yet all of the above was also shot through with a series of jagged, brief and utterly unforgiving comments about someone who was known to be Kokatha, but was currently 'sitting with the Wirangu'. We seemed to spend hours fulminating on this person, whom I had never met, but without them ever being the topic of conversation. About this same person it was sometimes said with passion, 'We know whose womb [they] came out of.' This person's own efforts to reposition themselves as Wirangu would never convince Aunty Sue Mob members that this person was not Kokatha, as the person in question had previously understood and, it was alleged, publicly proclaimed themselves to be.

On another occasion I was driving a cousin of Aunty Sue's somewhere when she burst out, 'Liar, liar, liar, liar!' at the casual mention of someone's name. 'I'd like to rip the curly hair from [their] head!' she said.

The subject of her rage, I later established, was accused of having appropriated this cousin's own childhood stories and memories of Koonibba so as to secure her legitimacy on a native title related committee. In truth, it was said, this woman had been removed from her family and missed out on an upbringing at Koonibba. This last example brings home the cruel burden Aboriginal people bear as the late liberal multicultural state rewards those Aboriginal people who were most successful in evading state-organised efforts to assimilate them in a not too distant past.

Eventually I abandoned altogether lines of questioning aimed at gathering an account that made use of 'continuous time'.[4] Instead I amassed discontinuous fragments: muttered utterances, caustic close-lipped pronouncements, gestures that seemed to condense fury into infinitesimal actions, such as the sudden flick of a cigarette into the dust. Conversations came to abrupt ends with dramatic, finalising condemnations: 'big shots'; 'liars'; 'sell outs'; 'that little bitch'; 'fucking cunts'.

These seemed like dead-ends but their accumulation also represented openings onto other kinds of narratives and experiences about native title, out of which this messy picture emerges. In the gaps between things said and not said, in the pauses between glances, gestures and words, I have tried to pry open 'a space for these stories' about native title.[5]

Kokatha-Wirangu relations today

Aunty Sue Mob members exhibit a range of responses to the phenomena of 'the Wirangu'. Some maintain that the Wirangu identity and language has no basis in any kind of historic or contemporary reality, whatsoever. They dismiss the sources from which Wirangu identity and language have been reconstructed, and see them as lacking all credibility and truth-value. Others are more accepting of the legitimacy of the Wirangu as a distinct 'group', and presumably accept the veracity of these sources. But they do not accept that Wirangu descendants should be seen as the rightful 'traditional owners' over the coastal region, the site of Ceduna and Koonibba mission. This is seen as an opportunistic and unfair repositioning on the part of some local Aboriginal people, who have sneakily outmanoeuvred other local Aboriginal people with whom they share a history. Many assert that the Wirangu language has been 'reconstructed' by plundering from Kokatha: Aunty Sue Mob members allege that Wirangu people are 'stealing' from Kokatha in order to bolster their own claims to traditionality, credibility and an intact language, faced with evidence that Kokatha enjoys greater strength today than Wirangu. Others suggest that the Wirangu were always a minor entity, dwarfed numerically, culturally and linguistically in pre-contact times by the Kokatha, a fierce 'tribe' of meat-eating warriors. ('Guga' means meat, from here: Gugada/Kokatha.) It is seen as grimly ironic that the Wirangu today could assume superior social status.

For example, Jamie, whose maternal grandmother is Sue's mother's sister, saw the Wirangu identity as a recent phenomenon. 'All I know is the Wirangu … they only just come in not very long ago. There's Wirangu and there's Mirning and all that stuff, just because of the native title.' He continued:

> Ages ago we can just walk up there to [a homeland associated with Wirangu-identifying people] and just sit down and have a drink, fire going, talk about the old days. Now you go out there and you start a big fight if you even say 'native title'.

I knew, however, that Jamie was still welcomed at this particular homeland, even while most members of Aunty Sue Mob regarded it as enemy territory and refused to step foot there. His generally vague answers to my questions reflected an attitude of disengagement with native title, which meant that it was possible for him to maintain pre-existing social relationships potentially interrupted by the conflict:

> [W]hen I go there I just go and see my uncles down there, I don't worry about anyone else. And we just sit down, have music going, fire going. Just sit down, talk about old days, you know. They talk about hunting tomorrow or the next day, and nothing about native title. Nothing.

Years ago, Jamie did attend a native title meeting, but he quickly walked away from the process after this experience. He told me he sat 'on the Kokatha side' (he was 'grown up' by a senior Kokatha-identifying community member). He was shocked to realise, 'The Wirangu didn't even want to talk to me.' Furthermore, someone from Yalata approached him to remind him of his genealogical links through his father to the Pitjantjatjara: 'They said, "Oooh, you should be on this side."' He told me, 'Well I'm not going to spilt myself into two pieces, and go sit there on my [paternal] grandma's side as well!'

In short, some Aunty Sue Mob members certainly accept that 'the Wirangu' have a reality. Others cock an eyebrow and quickly snort 'so-called' when the very word is mentioned. But some Aunty Sue Mob members fall silent and stiff at even the mention of the word 'Wirangu', becoming near paralysed with anger.

'Sister against sister': the everyday effects of native title

In 2008, I was visiting Sue at the farm as she busily opened the mail. She slid a butter knife along the inner edge of an A4-sized envelope addressed to her, pulling out a copy of *Aboriginal Way*, the publication of the Aboriginal Legal Rights Movement's Native Title Unit. This edition advertised a 'fancy' dinner in Adelaide celebrating fifteen years of native title: the ticket price included dinner and entertainment. 'Well, if they want entertainment, I'll give them entertainment for free!' promised Aunty Sue, in a darkly humorous mood, tossing the newsletter to one side.

Things-to-do-with-native title saturated everyday life in this outback town while I lived there, giving it a presence in settings and scenarios quite seemingly unrelated to the procedural vicissitudes of this drawn-out process. As native title anthropologist Katie Glaskin notes, native title related issues have 'spilled over into every-day talk'.[6] This seepage continues into other areas of life, in all sorts of untidy ways. As the claims process reshapes social relations, the tenor of everyday life also shifts.

In Ceduna, 'native title' might be given as an explanation for avoiding eye contact with someone in the supermarket aisle. 'Native title' is cited as the reason behind dirty fist fights, out the back of the pub, and other threats—explicit, rumoured and imputed—of violence. A muttered 'native title' is proffered to explain, in part, why half of a gathered group files into the old church at Koonibba for a funeral, while the other half mourns outside. 'Native title' might prompt someone to leave an event abruptly after recognising that a 4WD belonging to 'Wirangu mob' is slowing down, indicating and pulling in to the same event.

'Native title' is the reason a Nunga friend, around at my house for a game of cards, jokingly threatened over the course of the evening to redraw the boundaries of the map of 'Aboriginal Australia' we had Blu Tack-ed to the kitchen wall, so as to extend Kokatha territory all the way to the coast. This map is a copy of the wall map created by David Horton in 2000 and partially based on Tindale's map. We hung it as an acknowledgement of Aboriginal ownership of the continent. Yet to my Kokatha-identifying friend it was part of the arsenal of erasure of his own particular place in Aboriginal Australia.

'Aboriginal people are split,' says Aunty Sue. 'It's sister against sister on these issues.'

At another time, she elaborated:

> The conflict of, between native title, the people that want native title, that want mining, and the people that don't—well, they're not even talking to each other … It's really sad. Once upon a time I could walk down the street and say, 'Hey brother!' And now I don't say anything, he doesn't say anything. And the same with the sisters, you know, 'Hey sister!' None of that's there anymore; it's gone.

She quickly clarified, 'It's still there, but as far as native title mob, people that want native title, they've lost it. The ones that are on the outside still got it.'

Sue is adamant that educated Nungas stood to extract more benefits from the native title claims process, understanding the possibilities and 'milking them for what they were worth'. Meetings, she explains, can be daunting, and 'a lot of people don't understand all the big words … so they sit back quietly, they just don't know how to react'. She laments, 'Before native title came on board, everybody was happy, same with homelands. Everybody was just happy in their housing trust homes, and going to the beach, and going to the bush and being a big happy family.' Then, the broader polity was reorganised, first along lines of 'tribal' identification, but also, crucially, according to social standing. '[A]ll of a sudden the poor people weren't good enough anymore, both in native title and homelands. The poor people were only just there to use for votes.'

The conflict I examine in this book was represented to me in absolute terms in many interviews and conversations. In reality, social practices were more fluid, and relationships contingent on specific circumstances. Aboriginal people on either side of the 'split' did sometimes still associate in certain contexts, young kids were at school together and teenagers went to the same parties. There were, however, some implacable enemies who cut across the street in preference to passing each other by.

The consequences of the reformulation of Aboriginal identities are omnipresent in everyday life. As those people now recognised as Wirangu traditional owners have gained local prestige, the status of Kokatha, as a category of existence, has been adjusted and overall diminished since the mid 1990s. People who do not identify as Wirangu and instead retain identities as Kokatha have not necessarily *lost* prestige as individuals, but they resent the rise of locally prominent Wirangu figures, perceiving that their recognition and valorisation occurs at their own expense. It is significant that the authority to 'welcome' people to country—to effectively act as hosts, and to treat others as guests—belongs now to the Wirangu. The conflict I describe is locally well known and event organisers are usually cognisant of its rough outline, carefully acknowledging the presence of Wirangu, Kokatha, Mirning and Pitjantjatjara people in Ceduna today before any official Welcome to Country takes place. But the association of the coast and the site of Ceduna with the Wirangu, however understated, is always noticed and keenly resented by the people I know.

Writing about anger

As flagged in opening, I sometimes felt I could never get a handle on native title, or sustain a focused conversation about it. I was grumpy when one morning my partner Shane went to the farm to help fix something and later complained in frustration that instead of attending to the task at hand everyone 'sat around the kitchen table talking about native title for hours'. Over the course of an interview with Sue I thought I was perhaps, at last, going to establish something chronological about the native title claim process, along the lines of 'what comes next', as Bourdieu put it. Aunty Sue told me, 'Everything we've talked about [in terms of their genealogical and cultural knowledge] is now used against us … so we've clammed up. It's all there, to help native title to get through court.' Seizing on this, I said eagerly, 'When is it [the claim] going to court?' Aunty Sue replied:

> I don't know, I guess it'll have to, but I mean this one alone is a big pot bubbling over, you know, it's gonna bubble over, it's a witches' court. I can't see how six claimant groups can get native title over the same land, and then … we're probably classed as the seventh, outside of native title, saying, 'You can do what you want, this is not your land, you can go to the government, you can fight … you can negotiate with the miners and the government, but you're not touching this land and that's it: it's not the government's land.' And there's no way in the world they can claim it …

Sue was referring here to her perception that the distinct groups whose claims had been absorbed into the amalgamated claim were claiming the same land against each other (which was not the case). Native title is seen to have unleashed a kind of monster as it bubbles over: these are images of toxicity and excess. Most pointedly, Sue understands that she has created a new identity out of this process: Aunty Sue Mob become a kind of 'seventh tribe', a group of Kokatha who are disillusioned with native title, and whose disillusionment is so foundational to their identity in the present, it constitutes them as a distinct social group.

Not all people who identify as Kokatha broke with the native title process, of course, and this became part of the problem from Aunty Sue Mob's point of view. Because these close relations remained active participants in the claim, genealogical material relating to Aunty Sue

Mob's antecedents formed part of the claim material—even after Aunty Sue Mob members withdrew interviews earlier given about cultural knowledge (oral testimony also forms an important part of claim materials). Aunty Sue Mob experienced themselves as ensnared. They might have backed away from native title, but when they tried to 'pull out' altogether they found that 'native title is keeping us there'.

I have tried here to convey something of the emotional tenor of local life, rent as it is with expressions of fury, bitterness, cynicism, suspicion and betrayal. Sue says she used to cry in meetings. 'But all my life, when I'm angry, I used to cry first.' After the tears stopped, she was ready to fight. 'Okay miners and government: you watch out.'

These feelings about native title are inextricable from all I have outlined earlier in the book using cooler, analytical terms: Aunty Sue Mob's experience of native title as an alien thing, imposed on them by the outside, and something that has resulted in a strange sense of being dispossessed, as they are told that they are apparently not the rightful ('traditional') owners of country they have always regarded as their own. Native title forms part of the political recognition increasingly extended to Indigenous Australians from the late 1960s onwards, yet a sense of profound loss has in this case been an unintended consequence of these gains.

Coming at this conflict ethnographically involves hearing Aboriginal people expressing their anger at and about other Aboriginal people. It is not easy to hear or write about heated intra-Aboriginal disputes. While state effects and imaginings are the object of my critique, and Aunty Sue Mob certainly rail against native title as an institution, ultimately Aunty Sue Mob take as their most resented enemies not 'the government', not native title, and not mining companies, but other Aboriginal people, many of whom are intimately known and related to them.[7] They allege they are the victims of the wrongdoing of these Aboriginal people, and represent them as deceitful, self-interested, as imposters and conniving thieves.

I have made difficult decisions as to the material I include and exclude here, and am plagued by worries that I will expose Aunty Sue Mob to more pain. And while I worry about others I own that I also worry about myself: I risk becoming the object of some people's anger. While writing about these experiences might be criticised as inappropriate, to avoid them would equally represent an act of bad faith. I am helped here by anthropologist John Morton's reflections on his involvement in several disputes emanating from land claims in Central Australia:

> I would say that one of the things which characterises my experience of Aboriginal disputes is that they can appear (to 'us') to have a certain 'raw' quality: they seem 'uncivilised'—definitely not bourgeois.[8]

Morton, using the work of innovative anthropologist and artist John von Sturmer, sees this 'as both a lack and a possession'. While the Arrernte people he writes about may fail to adhere to notions of good behaviour, Morton perceives that 'there is also a kind of directness involved which is often muted under so-called "civilized" conditions', continuing:

> While such behaviour might be registered [by the whitefellas in attendance] simply through a general sense of embarrassment, there may also be feeling among those representing the case that the Aboriginal cause is almost certainly harmed by any such exhibition of 'poor form'.[9]

Morton wonders if anthropologists are in effect 'in the business of "refining" Aboriginality'.[10] To gloss the nature of this conflict would make me a party, I think, to a process of 'refining Aboriginality'. Of this I want no part. Instead, I've endeavoured to capture the 'raw quality' of this particular dispute and to bring to life Aunty Joan Mob's everyday experience of native title.

There is no ignoring a conflict of this kind. This conflict, and the destruction of social relationships it has entailed became a defining feature of Aboriginal life in this outback town. But it is not just destructive, it is productive: this is a conflict about who people are, or who they are not, and as such is part of what gives life its substance. Fighting with others sharpens the contours of the self. Among my amassed fragments are plenty of snippets about the ways a speaker's eyes might flash and their nostrils flare, as in anger they became animated, energised and excited. While this is a story, certainly, of unpredictable forces that have wreaked havoc, and which threatened to destroy both particular relationships and the 'unity' of the Aboriginal community supposedly enjoyed in times past, Aunty Sue Mob are also creating something new out of all of this. Sue may have imagined disrupting the celebratory dinner in Adelaide with her antics, but her thrust is not obstructionist.

Chapter 9

Tending to rockholes

Rockhole trips

If Aunty Sue Mob have experienced native title as an attack on their self-understanding and the claims process has frayed established social relationships, then what happens next? What is Aunty Sue Mob's rejoinder to these distressing developments? These conflicts have in turn fuelled creative ventures. As earlier stated, Sue directs her prodigious energies into organising and executing a twice-yearly event, Rockhole Recovery.

Recall that every September, as the Seven Sisters first blink in the southern sky, and again in March, before they slide beyond view, she leads a camping trip 'out the back'. In reality, the March trip is often pushed back to April so as to coincide with school holidays: seasonal rhythms and contemporary cycles are both to be taken account of.

'Rockhole Recovery'—or 'rockhole trips'—entail six, sometimes seven days of 4WD travel and involve visiting a series of rockhole sites, strewn across the Yumbarra Conservation Park, Yellabinna Regional Reserve and the more distant Yellabinna Wilderness Area.

Aunty Sue Mob jointly undertake these rockhole trips with urban-based greenies. Many participants come to these trips in the same way I did: I heard of them through Rhiannon, who piqued my interest about these creative ventures after she partook of the second trip Aunty Sue organised, in September 2006.

'I used to always go out the back and clean rockholes as we could,' says Sue. Once greenies became involved in 2006, 'We started the rockhole cleaning and maintenance in earnest then.' Here I describe my experience of these trips in more detail.

Water sources in arid country

Aunty Sue wants to 'carry on looking after the country like the old people used to, even though we don't live out there anymore'. This commitment, which was humbly stated, finds its focus in the care Aunty Sue Mob dedicate to rockhole sites. But what role did water sources play in the lives of 'the old people' who still lived 'out there'?

While it is inadvisable to attempt to reconstruct a pristine version of pre-contact Aboriginal life in this area, the work of the Berndts, introduced in previous chapters, gives valuable insight into the importance of rockholes to Aboriginal groups across the whole region prior to colonisation. The Berndts noted that in 'pre-European times routes existed throughout the [Western] Desert region along which passed articles of trade'.[1] These trade routes were tied to known rockholes. Parties came down from the north along the 'water-hole routes', bringing pearl shell from the north-west and native tobacco, which grew in the Everard ranges, to trade for wombat fur used in making twine. Red and yellow ochres were also traded. The Berndts also used the present tense, explaining, 'Water-hole routes cross and re-cross the whole Western Desert region … From an early age youths become familiar with all the water-holes of the area in which they were born, and this knowledge is broadened considerably when they accompany their fathers on long treks.' Groups travelling across this region must sometimes 'cross waterless stretches of country', but knowledge of soaks, rockholes, and water-holding plants meant they 'need never die of thirst'.[2]

Extensive knowledge of water sources was not just a matter of practical necessity. The routes followed were not the shortest possible but followed ancestral tracks. 'From time to time parties, particularly of novices before initiation or of initiated men for increase ritual, go out on a pilgrimage visiting the water-holes intimately associated with the ancestral beings'.[3] In the Dreaming, the major 'culture heroes' in this region travelled from the north or north-west, creating certain physiographical features of the country[4] and making the waterholes along which they travelled.[5] These culture heroes also instituted rites and

A wire clothesline stretches across the dusty yard at Aunty Sue and Uncle Gary's farm.
Photograph: Jessie Boylan

Aunty Sue out the back, collecting jungoo jungoo—a water storing plant.
Photograph: Breony Carbines

Rockhole site after heavy December rain.
Photograph: Eve Vincent

Car convoy, September 2008.
Photograph: Eve Vincent

Shovels at rest after a day spent uncovering the partially obscured rockhole site.
Photograph: Jessie Boylan

Memorial to Goog.
Photograph: Eve Vincent

ceremonies at the waterholes,[6] and at Ooldea the Berndts learned that ceremonies were conducted 'in water-hole sequence'.[7]

The Berndts also concluded that water sources were central to the model of social organisation in place here. A totemic affiliation was acquired with the ancestral gubbie (as Aunty Sue spells 'water') site at which one was born. They noted a tendency for people to return to the rockhole with which a child's father was affiliated when birth was impending. Of this waterhole/rockhole birthplace, a person would say 'that's my [gubbie]'. One's gubbie and a number of surrounding water sources comprised what the Berndts termed 'horde country', and which today would be called a clan's estate. Of this, it was said, 'that's my country'.[8]

Rockholes today

The rockholes then are all interconnected Dreaming sites. Sue explains that the rockholes 'are to be looked after at all times': 'Some of those rockholes start filling up from underneath and the rains will come and help fill them up properly.' In the 'old days', someone would have been designated the role of remaining with this precious source of water, 'keeping it clean'. Rockholes, she is explaining, were (and are) looked after to renew the productivity of the area, increasing animal and bird life.

She comments:

> And if an animal fell in, that was a bonus! Because they pull the animal out straightaway and that was their feed, without damaging the water supply.

One rockhole is a dramatic formation that rises steeply out of the scrub and can be climbed up and wandered over. Its blotchy brownish, orangey, greenish surface resembles the pockmarked skin of a wizened reptile, with folds and wrinkles. Deep green pools are found on its hide.

This largest outcrop can be glimpsed from afar—on rockhole trips Sue draws visitors' attention to a sliver of rock on the shimmering horizon, coming in and out of view as the convoy of 4WDs makes its way up the track towards it. Aunty Sue is thrilled by this tendency of the rockhole to conceal and reveal itself, as if it conspires to sometimes hide and at other times pop out, teasing and beckoning those who approach it. From atop this rockhole, a sweeping 360-degrees view of the dark green mallee scrub spreads out below; from high above, the dramatic rises and steep descents appears as gentle undulations. The country stretches out as an unruffled surface of the sea, undifferentiated and dark green, in every direction to the horizon. Aunty Sue Mob members, however, orient themselves to known features that are not necessarily visible: the direction in which they lie and their approximate location is always known and noted.

In September 2013, I travelled with two of Sue's mother's sister's daughter's adult sons, who classify Sue as 'mother', and Ned, by then five years old and bouncing around gleefully with his can of 'cool drink' on the back seat: I belted along with Aunty Sue my co-pilot in a battered, trusty six-cylinder workhorse. Way out the back, striated dunes shimmered raw pink and peeled, and the charcoal remains of mallee scrub sprouted shiny verdant leaves. Fire had swept through here, and in the gullies the undergrowth exploded into difference: a profusion of wildflowers had us picking and identifying clusters of petals, sometimes silky, sometimes brittle—everlasting daisies, billy buttons, bush peas, the desert rice flower, parakeelya, wiry podolepis, among many more. We stopped frequently to rest, collecting the yellow, lilac, vermillion and crimson blooms nestled in among the spiky spinifex.

Another rockhole does not rise from the landscape, seeming instead to form a depression that has settled into the sand. Its hard, orange circular rockface spreads out, and is slightly sunken, sand skittering across it in the wind. Another site features a scattering of rust-red rocks, one of them cleaved in two by the father of the seven sisters as he threw a boomerang at the 'dirty old man' who chased the sisters into the sky. Another is a slight rise marked with the imprints of ancestral beings and with shallow pools scooped out of its surface.

This last rockhole's character morphs and changes, according to drastically different seasons and lights. In the filthy, searing heat, bush flies collected on our bodies, crowding into the shallow depressions where our eye sockets and nasal bridges met and cloaking our sweaty backs in patches of vibrating black insects. On these days, the rockface seemed a hard, grey tablet ringed with tough, stubbled grasses. In March 2006, dark water, thick sludge and the remains of a partially decomposed emu and wild dog were bucketed out of its deep well. A putrid stench hung in the thick, hot air. This was designated men's work, as it followed the cleaning out of the most sacred women's site, where only women were allowed to view the rockhole empty of water. I huddled nearby in patchy shade with a miserable baby—11-week-old Ned—in my arms, waving the flies from his face.

In the winter of that same year, rain fell lightly, revealing the distinct and subtle shapes of its grooves and crevices, casting the whole lichen-covered rockface in soft, green hues. Small bright green and turquoise-coloured finches, with wet, shiny backs, flitted through the trees and flew low across the rockhole. A naturally occurring soak by its edge was choked with thick onion weed. Another time, after days of summer storms and heavy rain, the sky silver and sun pouring through dense clouds, the earth seemed rich, red and muddy, and the rockhole's pools teemed with warm water. The ongoing importance of rockholes as water sources for species such as emus, wedge-tailed eagles, kangaroos and dingoes has since been revealed. In collaboration with Natural Resource Management authorities, Aunty Sue Mob have made use of sensor cameras at this particular rockhole site, and thrilling black-and-white footage captures the traffic of stripy emu chicks and others.

Today's rockhole pilgrimages see parties ranging across the Yumbarra and Pureba conservation parks and the Yellabinna Regional Reserve.

A pamphlet devoted to promoting the 'Parks of the Far West' describes the rockholes that dot the wild scrub north of the dog fence:

> Within this parallel dune system are small islands where granite outcrops (inselbergs) trap water after rain. These are extremely important to local wildlife and have significant Aboriginal cultural associations.[9]

What is technically described in the pamphlet as a 'parallel dune system' entails a series of undulating sand dunes that run east to west.

In order to better grasp and then convey the thoroughly corporeal experience of travelling across this country, on the March/early April 2012 rockhole trip, I marked down each time we rose to the crest of one of these rises and went bumping and crashing down the other side, recording each east–west ridge. Strokes were made on the instruction manual for our car stereo, which I found after scrabbling through the glove box for something to write on. The trip was so jarring, it became difficult to form each dash in what eventually resembled a wobbly row of fence posts. At some stage water or perhaps lemonade was spilled on this record. I also jotted down the times and reasons for us stopping on the way: I noted that we stopped at 4:30 pm to re-tie the load on the trailer, as it had bounced loose; we stopped at 4:40 pm for a cigarette break, at 5:05 pm for someone to vomit and again at 5:45 pm to re-tie the load on the trailer. My scrawled 'fieldnotes' from this day, in some sense, playfully parody positivist social scientific research methods; the imperfect imprint of this experience and others makes clear the messy and bodily reality of fieldwork, and the constant improvisations and responsiveness it demands.

My record of 99 dunes is a very rough approximation and was dismissed by Sue as uninteresting 'trivia'. The shape of the country, as well its significance, is subject to interpretation. Some dunes present as dramatic steep inclines of deep, soft sand: a 4WD driver can take several attempts at their ascent, before slowly churning their way over the peak in low gear. Others are smaller undulations, rising and tailing off, following each other in quick succession: it is not always clear where one begins and ends.

Organising and executing rockhole trips

The first rockhole trip took place in March 2006. I interviewed one greenie, Clare, who went along on this first and most chaotic trip. Clare told me:

> There was a total sense of danger. Yeah, it was pretty intense. We were all out there, and Aunty Sue was really stressed out. It was just her and the ten greenies. And I've since come to

> see that Aunty Sue gets stressed out anyway, with those sorts of trips, but I think she was extra stressed out coz it was just her having responsibility for all of us who were clueless out there. So there was this total sense of danger the whole time—we were freaked out about scorpions and snakes and wild dogs ... when we were out at [a named rockhole, which is a powerful women's site] which was the furthest away site, it was all just really charged, I guess, coz we knew we were at this most sacred of all the sites and it was clearly a really significant place.

Aunty Sue found some fresh camel tracks and concluded a large young male camel was tracking a female with a baby:

> So she was like, 'He'll be totally aggressive. These camels can kill you, they'll attack you.' So we had to park the cars in a circle all around the fire and all sleep within this circle of cars. She was like, 'Everyone be on the lookout all the time. Be prepared to make a run for the cars.' And also freaking out about the wild dogs. She was like, 'If you need to do a wee, just do one right next to [where you are camped]'... People stayed up on watch all night. It was full-on.

Clare and I agreed that Aunty Sue has relaxed into her role as host over the years, and bears less responsibility as the lone guardian of numerous 'clueless' innocents now that her family is also heavily involved in Rockhole Recovery.

Since 2006 a handful of greenies have formed long-term and close relationships with Aunty Sue Mob: these greenies help organise Rockhole Recovery, publicising the dates and details to their activist networks, and keeping Aunty Sue informed of any emails they receive from potential participants. They arrive for rockhole trips with three, four or five 4WD carloads jammed full of people and a trailer loaded with bulk organic foods, donated by a supporter in Adelaide. Other greenies hear about upcoming trips through friends or on interest-based email lists that they subscribe to. They come along for 'the experience' or 'the adventure,' perhaps only once. They willingly volunteer for cooking duties, help pack and unpack cars, put up and take down tents and, of course, clean out rockholes, but are less proactive participants in the trips overall.

Aunty Sue plans Rockhole Recovery itineraries in advance and sets the departure date at least a month ahead of time. The itineraries themselves are liable to change up to the day before setting off, but the departure dates remain fixed. An itinerary usually involves a day of travel to the first site then a second day of work cleaning the rockhole. The third day might be spent travelling to another site, and the fourth day cleaning it. Another site might be visited on the following day, after travelling for the morning, and then be cleaned that afternoon or on the morning of the sixth day. Or the sixth day is spent packing up camp and slowly heading back into town. Alternatively, the convoy might travel a short distance from one rockhole and down to an ochre site, Paint Lakes, to spend the sixth night, before heading back into town on the seventh day.

In March 2009 I was involved in helping Aunty Sue and Rhiannon organise the upcoming trip, handling the email correspondence with greenies. In the few weeks leading up to the trip I formed a habit of dropping little Neddy off at the Minya Bunhii childcare centre (where I also worked as a casual employee) for a few hours each morning before driving to the farm, having a cup of tea and looking over the list of things to do, which Aunty Sue had neatly printed in biro and kept in her spiral-bound notebook. There was always something new to be added, usually thought of as we looked over the existing list and slowly worked our way through it.

Often we repaired damaged equipment. On one such day we realised both that new batteries were needed for all the lanterns and torches and that some of the lanterns needed replacing, as they'd been smashed beyond repair. It took us several days to complete this seemingly simple, single task as we: figured out exactly which lanterns to buy as replacements; compared the prices of camping gear in various stores, weighing this up against everyone's feelings and extended commentary about each of the local personalities employed in each of the stores, and lengthy accounts of the social role of their families in local history; agreed how much of an extremely limited budget to spend on new lanterns. Only then did Aunty Sue, Uncle Gary, Rhiannon and I make a time to meet up together 'in town' for the express purpose of purchasing two lanterns and several packets of batteries. In sum: organisation of rockhole trips was always characterised by a combination of collaboration and negotiation, fluidity and spontaneity, and a kind of infuriating inaction: endless delays in realising even simple-seeming tasks because toing and froing, lengthy discussions and ruminations, and a dispersal of the authority to make decisions were commonplace.

In March 2009 we held several working bees out at the farm, sorting through camping and kitchen gear stored on the verandah accumulating a thick layer of dust since the last rockhole trip. One afternoon, we worked in the heat of a pulsing overhead sun. Gary sat on the side of the trailer, carefully sifting through the rubble we were hurling into it, picking out useful bits and pieces to be hoarded for future use. We sent half a trailer load of ripped, trashed, dust-encrusted junk off to the tip, as well as sorting through all that remained: stacking the swags onto old metal bed frames, piling all the jumbled tent skins, poles and pegs together to be gone through 'another day', organising boxes of kitchen gear—tin plates, tin mugs, cutlery and huge cast-iron cooking pots which rattled around in sturdy metal chests, and sweeping clean and then folding tarps. Black beetles scuttled out from under everything as we dragged around old shelves and tackled the swags, sifting our way through mismatched camping accruements. Ned, who was by this stage one, plunged his fat little hand into corners thick with spider webs before pouring a bottle of water over himself and then crawling, drenched, through a layer of soft dust. I had long since given up getting dirt stains out of his baby clothes.

Consumed by these organisational tasks in the busy weeks leading up to Rockhole Recovery, Aunty Sue was in her element. She would sit at the kitchen table with her glasses on, poring over the 'to do' list as well as the list of participants, organising 'bums on seats', allocating people to cars, mulling over the mix of personalities and possible tensions, leaving space for gear, ensuring there were enough confident drivers and enough reliable vehicles to take those people who had expressed an interest. She would pick up the phone to hassle Aunty Sue Mob members to commit to coming, if they were prevaricating or still in the process of sorting out other claims on their time—namely work and school. There were always last minute additions and cancellations, on the part of both greenies and Aunty Sue Mob members. And there were always, always problems with cars.

Rockhole Recovery departures were generally delayed for a minimum of four hours. Among the reasons recorded in my fieldnotes for us running late were: innumerable runs into town to pick up last minute supplies at the supermarket, such as drinking cups for babies, or diabetes medication; two greenies driving a 200-kilometre round trip down to Streaky Bay to drop off assorted dogs at a kennel—arriving at the pound they found no-one there, so had to put the dogs into their kennels and secure them themselves; the complicated task of deciding which eskies would hold what cold-stuffs and many attempts at repacking meat and cheeses so as to keep it all cool; Aunty Vera disappearing altogether and none of us being able to reach her by phone—she was to surface hours later with very little explanation of where she had been; I was commissioned to head into town to drop off a pot of soup to someone, left-over foods from home were not be wasted, and there were kin to care for; last minute repairs to car fridge cables, car engines, radiators, a trailer and the back door to our car, which was busted and had a slide bolt pop-riveted to it to keep it closed; repacking bags to squeeze them into small spaces; the making of stove-top pots of espresso coffees for the greenies and cups of teas for Aunty Sue Mob members as the waiting dragged on; filling 20-litre water drums from the farm's rainwater tank, then stacking these into the trailer and tying them down; checking and re-checking the fuel capacity of all the cars travelling and working out how many jerry cans to fill with diesel and how many with petrol, then taking a whiff of the assorted cans in order to ascertain which had previously been filled with which fuel, before heading into town to fill these jerry cans. Once the collected greenies realised that we were not about to leave just yet, they decided to drive into town and pick up take-away cappuccinos from the pizza shop, or remembered that they needed to go to the post office or to Centrelink or to run an errand.

And so the delays accumulated. On the March 2008 trip, prior to departure, food had be located, unpacked, then the remainder repacked, in order to make lunch for the twenty-five people gathered around the yard, most of whom lay on whorled swags in the sun or sat in the shade of the verandah talking and smoking rolled cigarettes.

Greenies *wanted* to be of use, but mostly hovered at the edges of activity waiting to be allocating a task, while those who'd had an active role in organising the trip rushed around purposefully. Greenies were enthusiastic about any opportunity to contribute, quickly forming a human chain that stretched from the yard to the verandah one morning, as we unpacked the trailer load of organic vegies in foam boxes when it arrived from Adelaide. Similarly, out bush, as camp was being packed up, some people hovered while others worked. There were always bodies kneeling on the ground rolling bedding tighly into swags, and letting tents down, their billowing, cloud-like forms collapsing before they were stuffed back into bags. The kitchen had to be packed away: compost dug into the ground, fold-out tables' legs kicked in, cardboard boxes burnt on the morning camp fire. And still some people drifted around asking, 'What can I do?' while others kicked a soccer ball through the scrub.

After crossing the dog fence, that is, having finally made it out the back, car tyre pressures were released for driving on the sand and nervous greenies asked Uncle Gary and male members of Aunty Sue Mob for some advice as to how to 4WD up the steep dunes.

'Give it to er,' was what Uncle Gary told Shane on our first rockhole trip in March 2008, before roaring with laughter. Sometimes he replied, 'Stick it to er' or 'Gun it'. In all cases he meant something along the lines of, 'Put the car in a low 4WD gear and give the accelerator your all.' It sometimes took three or four attempts for inexperienced 4WD drivers, or for the cars pulling heavy trailers, to make it over the steepest dunes. A whole lot of glass beer bottles were once smashed through the back of our car, and often our bums lifted clear off our seats and into the air while we came flying over the dunes.

Along the way the convoy frequently stopped for a range of reasons: to fix flat tyres; because things fell off the trailer; because the trailer itself fell off the tow ball; because the pop-riveted slide bolt affixed to our back door rattled off and we had to tie our car together with a piece of rope; for travelling mothers to breastfeed babies.

After departure, then, it could take anywhere between two and a half to six hours to travel 80 to 100 kilometres and finally find ourselves, stiff legged and dehydrated, 'out the back'.

Chapter 10

Making assertions

Sweaty work

Rockhole trips are a means to make assertions. This is not all that they are, of course, but Rockhole Recovery can productively be understood as expressing, dramatising and symbolising three specific yet interlaced assertions.

First, Aunty Sue Mob undertake trips out on country to signal their rejection of what they see as the passive, even submissive, role of 'claimant'. Aunty Sue Mob defiantly assume that they are entitled to enjoy and express their relationship to country, refusing to wait to be authorised to do so. Second, Rockhole Recovery involves Aunty Sue Mob realising that relationship via sweaty, smelly physical activity. This sensory, deeply physical experience stresses a contrast between the process of outlining people–country relationships to satisfy the state's requirements, in words, and the process of expressing and living this relationship, with bodies. Finally, the tasks undertaken over the course of Rockhole Recovery are highly symbolic. Rockhole trip participants clean out permanent water sources, maintaining the ecological health of significant cultural sites they see as neglected by other Aboriginal people who assert a privileged ('traditional owner') relationship with these places.

More pointedly still, trip participants' efforts are also directed at rehabilitating one particular outcrop that has become covered with sand over the years. In digging out this specific site, Aunty Sue Mob hope to symbolise a more general condition, which underlines their opposition to mining. The country that sustained and was sustained by 'the old ways' is still there—it lies submerged rather than lost.

The refusal to 'claim'

Rockhole Recovery expresses a critique of the state–claimant power relations that underpin the native title process. 'Native title,' perceives Aunty Sue, 'means admitting the government owns the land. And I hate that.' Sue frequently says she refuses to 'go under government's thumb'. Whatever its status in Australian law, the land 'belongs to us and it's still part of us'. 'I don't have to prove nothing to them [the government],' says Sue. Prioritising heading out bush over claiming the right to country through formal mechanisms expresses this refusal to prove anything to the state.

'We have all forgotten,' anthropologist Patrick Sullivan observes, that what the term 'claimants' refers to is 'claimants to registration of existing title'. Instead, as Sullivan says, native title claimants 'have been reduced to claimants for a land grant', a position Indigenous people find 'immensely demeaning'.[1] Smith and Morphy also note, 'to enter into a native title claim, no matter what reservations are voiced by the claimants, is to submit to the state's authority over the contemporary existence of Indigenous property rights'.[2] Aunty Sue Mob refused to accept this submissive role, as it confers on Aboriginal people a passivity that is anathema, especially to Aunty Sue whose restlessness always lay tightly coiled, ready to convert into action.

Rockhole Recovery then is an example of Aunty Sue Mob's efforts to maintain an ongoing relationship to their country—to spend time with it and maintain a physical presence on it—without submitting to the state's authority by having to 'claim' their right to do so. Instead they do so, *and are conscious of doing so*, with flagrant disregard for legal processes that originate from the federal government and which seek to make a determination around a contention taken to be self-evident. That is, firstly, that Aboriginal people own the land. Secondly, and more controversially, that they are *the* Aboriginal people who can claim legitimate ownership over the land. Related to this first critique is the second assertion of a superior mode of stating and enjoying this relationship to country: an embodied mode rather than a bureaucratic one.

A word of caution is due. It may seem that I am presenting a binary opposition between claimants and rebels here, as if I am *documenting* an existing dualism between the first group's condition of passivity and the second group's capacity for proactivity. In fact, Sue effectively *generates these binaries* in the same moment that she animates, or makes use of them, to underline her political point. Sue's activities, which are designed to be noticed by others, render stark the decisions local Indigenous people face: in or out of the claim process; spend the day in town or head out bush; accept incorporation, however reluctantly, into an objectionable process or embrace absolute refusal.

Indigenous people might, of course, pursue other political strategies *within* the claims process. Anthropologist Frances Morphy, for example, provides a vivid sketch of the way Yolgnu people inserted their own discourse about the sovereignty of rom (Yolgnu 'laws and customs') into the courtroom during the Blue Mud Bay hearing, a complex case which eventually found that Yolgnu traditional owners' rights extend into the intertidal zone, according to the *Aboriginal Land Rights (Northern Territory) Act 1976*. Yolgnu, writes Morphy:

> see and understand the power relations that allow the Australian state to assert its sovereignty over them. But they also consider that this sovereignty was imposed without their consent, and that there was never an act of conquest … In their view the native title process was as much about the issue of sovereignty—at least in the sense of the recognition of the jurisdiction of Yolgnu 'law'—as about 'rights', and their participation in the process must partly be understood as a political act.[3]

The Yolgnu claimants proceeded to ensure rom momentarily 'displaced Australian law in its own space', reorganising the courtroom as it filled with a ceremonial performance and sacred objects.[4]

A further project illustrates Sue's rejection of the condition of passivity, and her impulse to act without waiting. In 2015, Sue described to me re-routing a road through one of the conservation parks in 2009: 'That came about because the miners drove their big machinery over the rocks [at a particular rockhole site].' Sue had seen the identifiable tracks of an exploration party's vehicle, on the actual rockhole itself, which cracked the surrounding rockface. 'We wrote to [the Department of] Heritage with photos but we hadn't heard anything back from them. So we said, "Okay, we will just re-route the road. Away from the rockhole." Which is what we did.'

Visiting greenies assisted Aunty Sue Mob members to drag fallen tree limbs, sticks and stumps across the old road and create a detour in a sparse area, so that no trees needed to be felled. The new route was not respected until the local National Parks and Wildlife office, whose staff were extremely supportive of the project, supplied 'Revegetation Area' signs. The new road is now always used by members of the public travelling through this park, and the old has overgrown.

The significance of a sensory physicality to Rockhole Recovery

The native title lawyer David Ritter comments wryly, 'more than one native title lawyer has the dispiriting experience of convincing people to stay in town when they would rather be hunting and fishing, in order to prove their traditional relationship to the land'.[5] Aunty Sue Mob are well aware of this paradox and have worked it to their own end. On days that the native title representative committee and community members gathered in Ceduna for day-long, indoor meetings, Aunty Sue was *especially* keen to head out the back on spontaneous day trips. And so too was Rockhole Recovery, although much more carefully planned in advance, part of a tactical assertion of a relationship with country that was realised by being on, spending time with, and working on, country—a practice intended to highlight the contradiction between those who, it was alleged, would claim a relationship to country by 'reading about it in a book', attending meetings or by 'doing dot paintings in the hall'.

Native title involves articulating a relationship with land through formal legal mechanisms, authored by the Australian state, and involves putting that relationship into words on paper as the first step in making a claim. By contrast, Rockhole Recovery involves putting the relationship with country into action. Rockhole trips can feel shambolic, haphazard and pretty crazy at times, however underlined they are by passionate commitments. These characteristics should not be regarded as deficiencies that impede the experience of rockhole trips: they are positive attributes of them. This project is born of Aunty Sue's resourcefulness and ingenuity. Furthermore, they speak to the nature of Aunty Sue Mob members' relationships to their country—country they are familiar with and comfortable in, as well as determined to visit and spend time on despite resource constraints.

Most crucially, rockhole trips involve participants getting filthy. Wearing only thin rubber gloves, we have plunged hands into thick, foul-smelling gloppy sludge at the bottom of rockholes in order to tug out sticks, whole bones and feathers. Sweeping stubborn red sand off the edges of a rockface, our limbs dried out, becoming coated in fine red particles, which clung to arm and leg hairs and smudged limbs in dirt brown hues. Aunty Sue Mob assert that *this* is precisely what having a living, ongoing relationship with country entails.

At a 'debriefing meeting' following the March 2008 trip, some greenies tentatively raised the point that they would have valued, in effect, more talking about the issue of mining: they wanted the political framework around the trips to be better explained, made more explicit and to be presented to them in words. It was clear, however, that Aunty Sue wanted greenies to experience being on country. After a greenie suggested, 'Maybe a half-day meeting, before the trip?', Sue jumped in. 'Half a day!? Half an hour.'

In fact, the alliance between greenies and Aunty Sue Mob is an extremely effective one precisely because greenies are also habituated to disorder, improvised methods, resourcefulness, running late and getting dirty. Sue obsessively and deliberately makes use of scraps, avidly collecting discarded glass and plastic bottles and aluminum cans to cash in through the South Australian container deposit scheme. She receives 10 cents per deposit, and once made $400 on a single drop-off. Known spots where A<u>n</u>angu have been drinking discretely in the scrub can yield a significant haul of empty bottles and crumpled cans. Gary has crafted steel pickets into claws with which to go razor fishing on the mudflats. Greenies had, at some point, collected Iluka Resources mineral sample bags made out of thick, filmy plastic. We staple-gunned these to the bottom of the verandah at Rhiannon's house, fashioning a barrier to stop snakes slithering onto the verandah from under the house, as greenies slept outside in swags the night before a rockhole trip.

Resourcefulness may well be endemic to isolated rural areas, and is also attributable to historical and ongoing experiences of poverty. There are certainly echoes here of former times: out at Koonibba mission, pannikins (mugs) were made out of old sweetened condensed milk tins. And recall Iris Burgoyne's description of mattresses fashioned from seaweed. Today, shredded paper is used to make dense paper bricks, which are burnt in winter, especially by elderly people who cannot collect firewood.

But Aunty Sue was intent on making a more significant point by her committed resourcefulness: she stressed that she saw herself as 'the bottle-o woman' who would fill her car with fuel paid for with the proceeds of recycling, rather than accept mining royalties. Greenies then happily aligned themselves with Aunty Sue Mob, not just because of shared conservation values, but because this mode of living resonated. Some of the greenies involved in rockhole trips, for example, are surreptitious foragers of discarded but perfectly good food out of supermarket bins.[6] Aunty Sue relishes the fact that she once shared such a salvaged meal with greenies.

American anthropologist Paul Stoller urges ethnographers to 'describe the sensual aspects of the field'.[7] Further, Rockhole Recovery *as an experience* simultaneously asserts and enacts that a whole-of-body experience—seeing, tasting, smelling, listening and especially touching—is integral to Aunty Sue Mob's relationship with their country. Under Aunty Sue Mob's direction, as Stoller urged, I also tried to 'let the sights, sounds, smells, and tastes' of rockhole trips 'flow into me'.[8]

The taste of rockhole trips involves mouths thick and tongues slow with thirst, slaked sometimes with warm, sweet fizzy lemonade. Rockhole trips tasted to me like greasy, slippery eggs for breakfast, and buttery soft white toast cooked on the fire and absorbing the sweetish scent and taste of smoke and burning cinder-dry mallee stumps and sandalwood burned on the shoreline of Googs Lake. For others, it tasted of tender wild meats and juicy, fatty kangaroo tails. On one occasion we ran so low on drinking water we decided to forgo washing dishes, travelling with smeared dinner plates from the previous night stacked messily into the back of one car, and eating fried eggs for breakfast with slices of toast substituting for plates. Aunty Sue and Uncle Gary chugged back into town with empty drums bouncing around their trailer and returned in the evening with it weighed down with containers heavy and deliciously full of clear rainwater.

The touch of rockhole trips is dry skin and scaly limbs, sunburned and peeling noses, and jeans stiff with dried sweat and dust, sticking tight to legs, which ached from the days of car travel and nights sleeping in the swag. Men grew stubble, becoming prickly and then hairy. Rockfaces were warm and smooth under foot and beneath supine bodies resting in the sun. The thick sludge at the bottom of a rockhole squelched between fingers. This mud smelt rich, pungent and earthy, sometimes foul. A decaying emu and wild dog once seemed to us partially suspended in flight, the dog pursing the bird into a pool and both drowning as they struggled. The scene of the pursuit was partially frozen, but their flesh slowly disintegrated into the foamy greenish, blackish water. On human bodies, acrid sweaty smells mixed with the strong, beach-y fragrance of sunscreen. Decomposing food stunk out the camp kitchen, a whole esky full of uncooked meat once went off, discovered too late, while bread frequently grew mould and lettuces sweated in foam boxes.

Night falls quickly out bush. The heat evaporates, the sun sliding behind the low tree line and the scrub suddenly suffused with rich, sticky colours—buttery yellow, then sienna, rust and sometimes a lurid flamingo pink. The trees became stark black outlines before merging with the night, compelling all in camp to retract to the fire. One's capacity for listening seemed in this period heightened, as sounds carried and could be picked out clearly: the tinkling of cutlery and the clinking of metal plates as dinner was prepared, the bird calls in the mallee scrub, the cracking of wood as flames consumed twigs and branches. Frogs sometimes started up their low bobbing in the rockpools. In the still early mornings sounds were also distinct and separate: someone's thongs slapping against their soles as they moved about making tea, a steady stream of piss expelled behind the bushes rimming the camp.

The country lies submerged rather than lost

Aunty Sue Mob members repeatedly stated that the local native title representative committee had determined that mineral exploration teams observe a 200-metre buffer around rockhole sites. In Ceduna, Aboriginal people involved with native title over this period of time stated that rockholes are not threatened by exploration out the back because of this buffer. But as Sue explains, a mine at a rockhole site would amount to 'total desecration'.

In the kinds of resource frontiers described by anthropologist and environmental humanities scholar Anna Tsing, new ways of looking at things are produced. Tsing, writing of Indonesia, tells how Japanese trading companies joined with Suharto's New Order regime in the 1970s to begin exploiting the archipelago's heterogeneous tropical rainforests. 'Instead of biodiversity, loggers now only saw one family of trees'—the towering dipterocarps. Dipterocarps were re-made as 'disposable plywood for the Japanese construction industry',' and other species of trees, fungi and fauna came to be seen as 'waste products'.[9] Further, the forests were reimagined as uninhabited because the human-tended plants of forest dwellers had become waste.

Aunty Sue Mob also seem to me to perceive that mining companies have helped foster a new way of seeing the rockholes: as individuated entities, whereby each site might be treated in isolation of each other. Aunty Sue Mob persist in seeing the country as a 'continuous entity'.[10] The rockhole sites all connect to each other and can be seen to manifest an underlying story: Aunty Sue Mob advocate protection of the whole country as the only option for ensuring perpetuation of their cultural inheritance.

In a more day-to-day way, Aunty Sue Mob members counter this talk of buffers by pointing out that the outer edge of each rockhole is difficult to determine, as sand has blown across these sites over the years. The relationship between being in possession of cultural knowledge about sites and opposition to mining is by no means clear cut. Knowing the stories associated with particular rockhole sites could form the basis of an opposition to mining, and those Aboriginal people in Ceduna who embrace mining are criticised for not adequately knowing and understanding the country, and therefore not knowing what they were losing. However *not* knowing the bush could also form the basis of being uneasy about the idea of mining: if it wasn't known what was there, and what it all meant, then how could one definitively know that it wouldn't matter to interfere with it? Indeed some rockholes that exist in older people's memories can no longer be found at all. In August 2008 I accompanied Aunty Sue on an arduous yet fruitless search for one such rockhole. It is impossible to know if the site has since disappeared or if we picked our way carefully across the wrong tract of country.

The rehabilitation of another partly covered-over site, a task begun in September 2008 and not yet completed, has involved us witnessing a change to the very size and shape of the rockface each time more work is done. This unsettles any sense of certainty that the edges of this buffer zone can be reliably ascertained. When Aunty Sue decided to begin rehabilitating this partly submerged rockhole, she did so partly for its own sake but also to symbolise a more powerful, general point not specific to this particular site. That is, the country that sustained and was sustained by 'the old ways' is still there; it lies submerged rather than lost. Over the course of Aunty Sue's life she has seen this particular rockhole shrink. She has watched a line of trees come 'marching down the hill' and start encroaching on the rockface.

The September 2008 Rockhole Recovery venture was unusually large as it coincided with school holidays and was funded by a grant scheme dedicated to keeping Indigenous culture 'strong'. While Aunty Sue expressed ambivalence about accepting funding from 'government', it made it possible for poorer family members to participate in a rockhole trip: food and fuel were the major expenses covered by the modest grant. Aunty Sue Mob outnumbered greenies; our thirteen-car convoy carried around sixty people in total, about forty members of Aunty Sue Mob, including kids, and twenty greenies.

Aunty Sue set participants the task of uncovering the edges of this small, partially obscured rockface. This was intended to unsettle the confidence with which the native title clamaint group declared rockhole sites identifiable and protected. A ute loaded with shovels, brooms and kids in the tray trundled down the track from camp to the rockhole. The kids quickly set to work scooping the dirt out of what appeared to be shallow pools, but this was only because they were so filled in; they have since proved much deeper. The rehabilitation involved heavy, hard work because the red sand was so compacted. At first the greenies pulled out onion weed, by tugging near the roots, and then heaped it into a floppy pile. A few of us started work on the edges of the rock-face, scraping and digging away the layers of dirt, trying to trace its contours.

With brooms, trowels, shovels and even the jagged plastic remains of a broken bucket, trip participants scraped away layers of fine, red-brown dirt. Heavy mounds accumulated on tarps, which were spread out at the rockhole's edge. A team of four men repeatedly carried a side of the heavy tarp each, then dumped the dirt into a ute before the load was driven a short distance from the site. The men joked about being council workers as they leaned on shovels waiting for the tarps to be refilled. On another occasion, Aunty Sue paused in her sweeping of this site and shook her head, feigning exasperation, 'Housework!' Two long afternoons and then a full day, from sun up to sun down, were spent digging out the rockhole, gradually seeing a shallow pool emerge and the rockface spread and take form. At the time of writing, this immensely satisfying process is still underway.

To symbolise is to 'act politically', states anthropologist Allen Feldman. Feldman is intent on undoing the distinction between 'expressive activity in contrast to effective practice'. His insight is that symbol and action are neither opposed to each other, nor complement each other. In the H-Blocks of the English prison of which he wrote, Republican 'symbolization of the condition being protested transformed that very condition'.[11] Rockhole trips certainly involved generating symbols but, as Feldman teaches, these should not be understood simply as a means to a 'real' political end. Rockhole trips transform the condition of passivity and disempowerment that Aunty Sue Mob find themselves in, propelling them into a new space, and new condition.

The presence of greenies

What is the role of greenies in all of this? Greenies are organisors, helpers, friends both old and new, and have clearly been deployed to make more effective the assertions underpinning rockhole trips. But their presence on these trips, borne of their commitment to Aunty Sue Mob's vision, has a deeper significance still.

Greenies have a part to play in Rockhole Recovery not just because of the material resources and labour they contribute to the practical-cum-symbolic tasks at hand but also because they take up, reproduce and put into circulation Aunty Sue Mob's understanding of the terms of their identity. Aunty Sue Mob's struggle for self-definition necessarily involves a dialogue. To a satisfactory extent, although of course not ever fully, greenies see Aunty Sue's family in the terms they wish to be seen. First, greenies understand themselves as guests of Kokatha guides on Kokatha Country. Second, they see their hosts as possessing integrity as uncorrupted Aboriginal cultural subjects because of their opposition to mining.

Elsewhere, I have elaborated certain problems arising from this relationship, and I will touch on them again briefly here.[12] Non-Indigenous desires for contact with Aboriginal people, idealisation of cultural otherness, and postcolonial guilt combine to shape, constrain and sometimes wreck these relations. This is not to say that the greenies involved in rockhole trips are problematic individuals, but rather to suggest that unstable dynamics are always at work as environmentalists engage with Indigenous political agendas within a settler colonial setting. The task of critique might be construed as hurtful, but this is certainly not my intention. I am of the greenie world, and I am implicated in all I present here.

As explained in opening, Aunty Sue 'got up and asked for help' at the Kulini Kulini bush camp, having observing that the Kupa Piti Kungka Tjuta had formed productive working relationships with Melbourne-based, green non-government organisations (NGOs), as well as attracting the more specific support, between 2000 and 2004, of a small collective of activists called the 'Melbourne Kungkas'. I was a member of the Melbourne Kungkas for the five years of its existence but for various reasons did not make it to Kulini Kulini. A flyer promoting this bush camp stated, 'We are going to stand up and fight strong. And you fellas have got to help us.'[13] At Kulini Kulini, Aunty Sue observed greenies in this helping role: facilitating meetings, seeing to camp logistics, collecting firewood, making cups of tea for elders and much more. Sue was explicit in her hope, now realised, of building her own 'greenie network'.

Aunty Sue's request was met with a response, and in March 2006 she organised the first week-long peripatetic camping trip undertaken into the scrub affected by mineral exploration leases, in close collaboration with a dynamic greenie she had met at Kulini Kulini. On this first trip Aunty Sue travelled with ten greenies, all of them women, under—in effect—her guardianship. Later this project became known as Rockhole Recovery, and men were also invited to join the trips. Sue describes the greenies as her 'backbone' in those early years.

Greenies contribute, minimally, their labour and resources to the task of monitoring and cleaning rockhole sites. They 'chuck in' money to cover fuel and food, and if they possess suitable 4WD vehicles these are filled with trip participants, both Aboriginal and greenie. The idea is to stimulate in the greenies, over the course of the trip, an awareness of the presence of this non-iconic, pristine mallee scrubland, and the threats facing it, which are dramatised as imminent but start to seem amorphous on further investigation. Sue hopes greenies go beyond being better 'informed'; as stressed, the trips are sensual and experiential, and also are designed to awaken in greenies an affective response to being on country. If a viable mineral deposit was discovered and developed in the future, especially one proximate to a rockhole site, Sue hopes greenies could be called upon to act. She sums up this strategy by saying she was taught by others, including the Kungkas, that if you bring 'white people with you', then 'in years to come they're gonna help you fight for the land'.

Indeed, in March 2007, members of a rockhole trip stumbled across local contractors engaged in exploration work for Iluka. This was before Iluka had finalised the Indigenous Land Use Agreement for Jacinth-Ambrosia with native title claimants, which was signed in December 2007, and the company was sensitive to conflict with local Aboriginal figures. The greenies travelling with Aunty Sue on this particular rockhole trip established a spontaneous 'blockade', although this seemingly self-evident phrase gives me pause. Sue's social identity of course is not simply that of a politicised troublemaker, having lived a life entwined with known black and white locals.

On that March 2007 trip, two white contractors in a ute 'personified' Iluka, in anthropologist Alex Golub's terms.[14] In film footage of this particular mining company–Aboriginal protestor confrontation, Sue chats casually with the confused men. These are 'local boys' who call Aunty Sue by her first name. There is a familiarity in evidence, despite the greenies' construction of this event in terms of an ideological opposition. Exploration was temporarily halted after the contractors made radio contact with their supervisor. This moment confirmed Aunty Sue's faith in the greenies' capacity to respond effectively when called upon.

However, things get more complicated when the frame is broadened. In this book I interpret rockhole trips as undertakings inextricable from Aunty Sue Mob's daily creative/political struggle 'against native title'. Sue's family struggle for self-definition, reinvesting in the terms of their long-held self-understanding: as Kokatha people speaking the Kokatha language and living out their lives on Kokatha Country. In fact, the terms and basis of Aunty Sue Mob's self-understanding has not just remained intact in the face of the pressures exerted on it but has been bolstered and its import amplified.

Aunty Sue Mob may well reject the authority of outsiders, experts, whitefellas, historians, linguists, anthropologists and, ultimately, the nation-state, over the definition of who they are and where they fit into the local population. But if they are to express and affirm their own understanding of who they are, what bit of country they rightfully belong to and what bit of country rightfully belongs to them, how are these claims to do more than just be given voice? How are they to travel out and become lodged in the world? When Aunty Sue Mob seek to take back and direct the terms on which they are understood, they ask others to recognise them on these terms in order to stabilise and cement these terms as more valid than imposed terms. In sum, if Aunty Sue Mob are going to tell this old-but-new story of self, then they need listeners.

Greenies become involved in this existential-political struggle as they take up, reproduce and circulate Aunty Sue Mob's claim. They leave Ceduna understanding themselves to have travelled through Kokatha Country with Kokatha traditional owners, learning Kokatha words for things and helping in the maintenance of Kokatha cultural sites, often remaining unaware that this formulation is hotly contested in Ceduna.

American anthropologist Daniel Fisher describes an analogous process in Darwin. Fisher interprets the way the Larrakia Nation has joined with the Northern Territory Government to work on the 'long grasser' issue as representing, in part, an opportunity for the Larrakia to secure a form of 'nonlegislative recognition'.[15] In this moment the Larrakia are cast as the rightful and responsible hosts of those itinerant long grass campers who hail from elsewhere, whereas securing status as traditional owners, as defined through land rights and native title legislation, has proved an extremely vexed and disappointing undertaking. Aunty Sue Mob become, in the moment of a rockhole trip, the hosts of their greenie guests, whereas their experience of the native title claim saw them recast as living on another people's country.

Greenies' role in this conflict, however, could come under challenge from the outside and from within. In 2008, in a letter to the local paper, the *West Coast Sentinel*, an Aboriginal resident of Ceduna complained bitterly about the activities of people who they argued lacked local cultural authority and recognition, mocking Aunty Sue's following among the 'greenies you all seem to have latched on to'.[16] Greenies' visits are fleeting, and even those who make return visits have only a limited access to the bigger picture. Most people are not in a position to realise that another truth claim has overridden Aunty Sue Mob's understanding of Kokatha history and identity over recent years. It is left to the local letter writer to point, however implicitly, to a conflict intimately known to Aboriginal readers.

Two greenies did come in time to grasp the interconnected conflicts over mining and identity that they found themselves in the midst of, and grappled with their discomfort. Clare had a long-term involvement in rockhole trips and a young man named Bobby lived briefly in Ceduna, spending six months in the town after coming along on a trip. They were both unsettled by their perception that in order to achieve closeness with Aunty Sue Mob it was best to keep at a distance and objectify other Aboriginal people in Ceduna. In reality, their growing sensitivity may have heightened their perception of the stark terms of this conflict. I found that when I came into contact with a range of Nungas and whitefellas in Ceduna, especially through my work at the Minya Bunhhi childcare centre, Aunty Sue Mob were not perturbed by my casual contact with people they were in conflict with.

For both Clare and Bobby, however, this perception increasingly alienated them from other greenies, although interestingly not from Aunty Sue Mob. Bobby especially expressed deep cynicism about greenies' willingness to treat Aunty Sue's pro-mining enemies 'like these mysterious other Aboriginal people', about whom they showed little curiosity, despite their keen interest in 'Aboriginal issues' and 'Aboriginal culture'. As Clare expressed it:

> There's not a right and a wrong way to be Aboriginal, or to be more Aboriginal or less Aboriginal, you know. But greenies seemed to be saying, 'This is the real, proper way to be Aboriginal, and these [other Aboriginal] people [who welcomed mining] have sold out.'

Bobby greatly valued his connection with Aunty Sue Mob, enthusing to me that he 'really, really fucking liked them' but was also vitally interested in the contradiction between what he had previously believed about 'other Aboriginal people' and what he experienced when he got to know some of them. Bobby was also affronted by greenies' apparent disinterest in these other Aboriginal people. He told me:

> [Greenies] didn't know them, didn't have anything to do with them. But there was all this stuff about 'they were this' and 'they were that' ... They never meet any other Aboriginal people. It's almost like it doesn't matter to them ... Anyway, I was meeting these people as soon as I got here, and I was like, Fuck! They were really interesting, inspired people who were just as charismatic [as Aunty Sue Mob members] ... They struck me all the same way as the mob we know struck me. You know: interesting and lively and charismatic and engaged and benevolent and radical. They struck me in all the same ways. The language they used was the fucking same, 'We're fighting for our people' ... This one [Nunga] I became close to talked about how she was always 'fighting for her people' but she worked in child protection. She considered that to be fighting for her people. Being 'big, strong community people' ... That was fighting for their people, which is effectively the same as Aunty Sue, you know.

I emphasise that there is nothing duplicitous about Aunty Sue Mob's invitation to greenies. They reject native title wholesale, and talk freely of their experience of the claims process, revelations which can prove shocking to their supporters. Yet greenies persist in stating that they stand in solidarity with or in 'support of Aboriginal people', a phrase that serves to obscure, possibly unwittingly, a much more conflicted reality. In fact, they act in support of *particular* Aboriginal people, on the condition that they share their political goals, even if they oppose mining for different reasons. This pits greenies into a contest not just with mining companies and the state but also with other Aboriginal people who welcome mining and for reasons far more complex than greenies could be expected to learn of. This fact is as inescapable as it is unsettling and, as seen above, some greenies are willing to grapple with it.

Elsewhere I have urged environmentalists to reimagine Aboriginal people as political actors as much as bearers of Indigenous culture. Currently, what I see as a cultural determinism underpins greenies' imaginings and valorisation of a homogenised Aboriginal self-state, the truth of which remains either accessible to contemporary Aboriginal people who are 'naturally' environmentalist in their outlook, or inaccessible to them because they have become 'culture-less', which corrupts or confuses their position on environmental questions. Greenies are recruited as important interlocutors in the struggle for self-definition; however, their narratives about authentic and corrupted ways of being Aboriginal see Aunty Sue Mob members again having to chart a course between being-as-subject, in which case they are met as fellow political agents, and being-as-idealised-object, in which case they are met as representatives of Aboriginality.

Laying claim to contested country

Aunty Sue Mob set out in dust-coated cars on epic bush trips, entering their country along conservation park access tracks prohibited for public use. They establish camps and sink wombat carcasses into hot coals. Rockhole trip participants start the sludge pump and get to work cleaning rockholes with brooms and shovels.

Through all of these acts, by inserting their bodies into country that was at the centre of a conflict, Aunty Sue Mob lay claim to country by possessing it, being in it and expressing their relationship to it. Moreover, rockhole trips advance Aunty Sue Mob's struggle for self-definition as they recast and enact the following: that they are Kokatha people, living out their vitally alive and embodied relationship with Kokatha Country. This enactment is then taken up by greenies, visitors who absorb and reproduce the narrative authored by their gracious hosts, Aunty Sue Mob.

There are yet other actors in this scenario, and they too need to be taken account of. The bush is certainly a place that welcomes Indigenous people, nourishing Aunty Sue Mob, literally, spiritually and politically. This contrasts with town, which remains a place in which whitefellas attempt to assert and legitimise their dominance.

Chapter 11

Where dingoes howl

Out the back, again

'Did you see that eagle?' Aunty Sue asked after we stopped the vehicles and climbed out. It was early May 2008 and we were heading out the back. A dignified bird of prey with stiff, chocolate-brown feathers gripped a desolate branch. Sue relished retelling of her sighting, saying the eagle looked down its beak at her with a haughty expression before turning its head slowly and taking flight. Her imitation of its arrogance was effective: she lowered her eyelids, took a sharp breath in and then puffed out her nostrils.

Out the back, beyond the dog fence, Aunty Sue Mob make contact with awe- and fear-inspiring country. Here eagles hover, suspended high in a perfect blue sky. At night dingoes send up plaintive howls.

Geographically speaking, Aunty Sue Mob move through country that lies north-west of a stretch of the lengthy 'dog fence' that starts in western Queensland, turns south toward western New South Wales, tracks west across northern South Australia and then drops down to the coast, finishing at a point just west of Fowlers Bay.[1] Individual run-holders in South Australia first erected fences in order to protect stock from dingoes in the late 1880s. In 1946 the *South Australian Dog Fence Act* provided 'for an unbroken line of dog-proof fencing across the northern parts of the state'.[2] Between 1985 and 1987, a 120-kilometre section of the dog fence netting north of Ceduna was replaced with 91 kilometres of metre-high, seven-wire electric fence.[3] Sue and Gary worked as contractors on the dog fence over this time, camping out bush for short stretches of time, sometimes tugging their caravan behind a two-wheel drive Holden ute. Uncle Gary reminisced:

> We used to go there on school holidays ... I had all the family out here, the young boys, our lads, putting in dog fence posts, and we used to get a dollar a post. They used to earn good pocket money over the Christmas holidays.

Something else happens, something less practical and more profound, when Aunty Sue Mob cross beyond the dog fence. I came to understand the fence as marking a boundary between two zones, which can be seen in contrasting terms. On the town side of the fence lie agricultural districts, where land has been cleared, worked and its potential harnessed according to human plans: here a domesticated crop is grown—wheat. Beyond the dog fence stretches the bush. This zone acts as a repository for personal memories of the immediate past, recalling mission childhoods. And it also affords access to another way of being. Here the deep, shared Aboriginal past *felt* closer.

A grasp of the substance of ways of being Indigenous prior to colonisation have, of course, assumed ever more significance in the era of native title. Contemporary continuity with pre-colonial cultural traditions is drawn out, documented and legitimised through the claims process. Complicated problems arise as Aboriginal people respond to these demands and cast themselves in the state's terms, as I have emphasised so far.

However, this is certainly not all that is going on as Aunty Sue Mob passionately talk of drawing closer to the deep Aboriginal past as they head out the back. How to account for Aunty Sue Mob's own avid interest in the power of the 'primordial', that is their interest in the ancient Aboriginal past? Aunty Sue Mob's experience of and the meanings they attribute to being in the bush need to be taken seriously, on their own terms. The bush is a site of pleasure and of healing, of danger, and of sustenance.

The power of the primordial past

I see 'the state' as not simply external to and acting *on* Aunty Sue Mob. The subjectivities of Aunty Sue Mob members, like those of all contemporary people, are as much constituted *through* state effects, even in the very moment they articulate positions that are explicitly against this state. There is no outside of power, as Foucault established.[4] And so Aunty Sue Mob frequently reproduce certain of the tenets central to the native title system as they struggle 'against native title'. Anthropologist Benjamin Smith sums up the effects of native title on Aboriginal identity as follows:

> The appearance of language-named tribes to label 'groups' held to exist within the Aboriginal domain is … suggestive of ongoing transformations of Aboriginal subjectivities, generated through the state codification of the more indeterminate and fluid articulations of local Aboriginal attachments to country.[5]

What I am saying is this: Aunty Sue Mob's reassertion of and re-investment in their Kokatha-ness, in their explicit rejection of the logic of native title, can be understood as entirely consistent with this process of solidifying Indigenous identities, and as such is commensurate with the logic of native title. These theoretical points might seem obscure. They can also be grasped by turning to everyday occurrences. The map of Aboriginal Australia was not thrown out, even though its premise was rejected. Rather, my friend threatened in jest to re-draw its boundaries with texta in protest at where the neat lines currently run.

What is to be made of Aunty Sue Mob's invocation of familiar ideas as part of their rejection of native title? Like native title claimants, Aunty Sue Mob present and understand themselves as having a continuous connection to country and authentic relations with land. One possible response would be to call this 'strategic essentialism'.[6] This term is drawn from the work of Indian historians who formed the Subaltern Studies group. These scholars retrieved rebel forms of colonised consciousness, and in the process made use of 'positivist essentialism in a scrupulously visible political interest'.[7] That is, they seemed sometimes to accept that oppressed groups had intrinsic identities, but only on the condition that possessing this intrinsic identity advanced the interests of those people bearing those identities.

Or, this might be understood using a very similar notion, that of 'repressive authenticity'.[8] These are historian Patrick Wolfe's words. They emphasise the negative aspect of engaging with native title and the unrealistic expectations it places on colonised people: that they somehow have remained miraculously not-fully-colonised and their Indigenous culture remains intact. But Wolfe also acknowledged that Indigenous people can 'strategically acquiesce' to this requirement, in order to achieve local goals, although this carried with it the risk that the state that generated this resistance will also contain it.[9]

These analytical perspectives, which have obviously influenced me, do not seem to fully get at Aunty Sue Mob members' embrace of 'essentialist' aspects of their Aboriginality. What it means to be Aboriginal was certainly explained to me terms of an innate essence, and Aunty Sue Mob members draw on and identify with the image of a primordial land and body. I also sensed a liberating potential in doing so, which is lacking in the models of risky compromise.

In the early 1990s, anthropologist Andrew Lattas published some forceful criticisms of Australian intellectuals' perspectives on the perceived problem of essentialism. Lattas summed up:

> An enormous amount of intellectual energy is currently directed at establishing Aboriginality as something that is invented through European involvement. What is often ignored is the sense of autonomy from the control of the 'Other' conferred by images of the past and by images of primordiality and indeed the necessity to have an image of the past if one is to have a sense of ownership of oneself.[10]

Lattas was commenting on the turn taken in Aboriginal studies in the late 1980s. This was an important period, in which scholars shifted away from taken for granted notions of Aboriginality as a category based on biological descent and/or as bearers of the hallmarks of Indigenous culture. Instead, writers increasingly explored the ways in which Aboriginality, like all forms of identity, is 'the product of human imagination'.[11]

Lattas, however, identified a certain tendency within this body of literature. He criticised Australian intellectuals who cautioned against or rejected outright any kind of Aboriginal essentialism as a legitimate, 'productive' basis for individual identities or political consciousness. What Lattas particularly questioned was why a group of non-Indigenous scholars' were attempting to adjudicate as to the 'best' definitions of Aboriginality. What drove these authoritative interventions into 'the narratives which people employ to formulate themselves'?[12] Wolfe himself was very careful to make clear he would undertake no such as task, writing 'I have nothing to say about what makes Indigenous people Indigenous to themselves or to other Indigenous people'.[13]

According to Lattas, the political implications of Aboriginal interest in independence and autonomy are to some outsiders disturbing. Lattas interprets a 'fear of essentialism as a fear of difference and a fear of subordinate others producing and claiming some essential autonomous otherness'.[14] Michael Dodson has argued strongly for Aboriginal people's 'right to draw on all aspects of our Aboriginality,' including images of the primordial past. The past, Dodson says, 'is a source of freedom'.[15]

And so I came to see that heading out the back involves Aunty Sue Mob members connecting with an image of the past that recalls a time before and a place removed from colonisation. Aunty Sue Mob evince a keen interest in involved interactions with and use of the deep past when forming their contemporary Aboriginality, relishing an irreducible difference. Being out the back affords Aunty Sue Mob members access to a liberating sense of what it means to be Aboriginal, linking them with a way of being that predates white society.

The 'sense of autonomy' glimpsed out the back returns something else to Aunty Sue Mob: the sense of ownership over themselves that was lost through involvement in native title is restored. This is part of what gives the experience of being in the bush its profundity. Further, and more specifically, heading out the back involves Aunty Sue Mob members connecting with an image of the past that recalls a time before and a place removed from the sometimes-tense reality of contemporary race relations in Ceduna. Getting 'out' of town involves getting *away* from town. A brief account of some of the race-based dynamics of town life can make clearer the further significance Aunty Sue Mob accord to be in the bush.

'The dogs' and Ceduna's race-based social hierarchies

In opening, I touched on the fact that the relationship between Aboriginal people and whitefellas in Ceduna is characterised by a central contradiction: between lived intimacy, on the one hand, and social distance and separateness on the other. Furthermore, this first and readily apparent contradiction—intimate, interpersonal entanglements coexisting with a gulf between black and white—obscures more complex co-dependencies, which sustain life in this place.

Aboriginal public drinkers and campers are especially represented as a grave problem in local and national forums. In Ceduna, the tenuous and unpredictable agricultural economy is supplemented with a large number of jobs in welfare provision to address social issues such as alcoholism and family violence. Without this service sector, the town's economic fortunes would be drastically altered: in effect, that which is taken to threaten the social life of this small town ensures its very viability.[16]

Indigenous cultural critic Aileen Moreton-Robinson argues that it takes a 'great deal of work' to maintain the Australian nation as a 'white possession', an insight which also applies to Ceduna.[17] Moreton-Robinson explores the ways in which the formal acquisition of territory, through which the British Empire acquired Indigenous peoples' land and dispossessed sovereign peoples, articulates with more personal sentiments: 'the right to be here'.[18] Controversial local policies and debates do some of this work. Certain of Ceduna's respectable civic realms remain, in effect, whitefellas' places. Both innocuous seeming signs and controversial local policies seek to contain radical forms of cultural difference, targeting bodily schemas and practices that are regarded as disgusting, such as bare feet and spitting. Daily discussion of these questions absorbs many of the town's Indigenous and white residents, as well as inches of column space in the local paper each week.

More specifically, the local council makes use of a private security firm with dogs to patrol Ceduna's streets and parklands in order to enforce council by-laws that prohibit loitering, littering, public drinking and camping in public places, an initiative that underscores the racial order of the town. Dingoes and wild dogs may reign out the back, their soulful night-time howls setting our hairs on end. But 'in town' muzzled domesticated dogs serve to police social transgressions and stabilise the always contested racial hierarchy of this place.

The story of *these* dogs was precipitated by a riotous event. The 2007–2008 summer holiday period witnessed an influx of (Anangu) 'visitors' from Yalata into Ceduna.[19] An incident that occurred at a New Year's Eve party was, from the perspective of the local white social elite, the proverbial last straw, after weeks of mounting tensions in high temperatures. At 3:00 am on New Year's Day 2008 two police officers were called to a 'disturbance'. A group of thirty to forty revellers abused and assaulted the officers, before one Aboriginal man helped the police back into their car. The officers were treated for minor injuries at the hospital and 'returned to their duties'.[20]

The council called for an injection of funds into policing efforts and also announced a decision to restrict access to the foreshore public toilets.[21] The state government quickly seconded a team of militarised police ('Starforce officers') from Adelaide to Ceduna the following weekend[22] but the council also decided to pursue what it saw as a more long-term solution. In March 2008, regular foot patrols by two men, authorised as council officers, and two guard dogs began. The men were principals of a security firm based in Port Lincoln.[23] The team is known as 'the K9 Unit', or colloquially as 'the dog unit' or 'the dogs'.

The dogs' introduction was precipitated by a crisis and was intended to be a short-term measure. Influential Italian theorist Giorgio Agamben famously developed the idea that the 'state of emergency' has become the rule. In the state of emergency Agamben describes, an expansion of sovereign or state power sees special laws enacted, which suspend the operation of normal law.[24] This is not the case here as *seemingly* trivial and effectively dormant bylaws, such as 'no littering', made at the lowest level of governance, the municipal council, are revivified in a muscular attempt to regain control over public space. These laws may be minor, this initiative warns, but they enshrine 'civilised' norms. Instead of establishing a space of exception to law, it's the perceived exceptionalism of Indigenous offenders in the eyes of the too-sympathetic law that the initiative sought to end.

In their first four days on the job, the K9 Unit issued fines totalling $2000 for by-laws offences.[25] The mayor wrote, 'If the court dismisses the fine—as sometimes happens—then we will send the bill to the attorney general'.[26] Here the mayor was anticipating that Indigenous offenders might be spared the full force of the law, in keeping with the 1991 Royal Commission into Aboriginal Deaths in Custody's recommendation that prison be a last resort for Aboriginal offenders. Agamben's thinking is helpful nonetheless for his emphasis on the way extraordinary measures become routine. The dogs, which seemed so shocking at first, have become an ongoing feature of Ceduna life, and continue to patrol the streets.

Anthropologist Tess Lea and others have examined the practice of 'moving on' Aboriginal people from the commercial zones of Darwin and Alice Springs. They conclude that this practice represents expelling those who don't spend and consume from sites of profit making.[27] Another way of seeing this is that those who persist in 'being otherwise' are removed from 'hostile zones', to adopt anthropologist Elizabeth Povinelli's vocabulary.[28] This holds true of the situation in Ceduna, in terms of the pressing fear that tourists will recoil from these scenes. The town's parks and especially the pretty strip of coastal foreshore were to be expunged of the presence of visiting A<u>n</u>angu. (One letter writer thanked the council for 'enhancing our living environment', predicting 'we will soon be SA's top tourist destination through your positive attitudes'.)[29] The K9 Unit was charged with shifting this highly visible and, importantly, noisy way of living from public view. (A resident who did not wish to be named told the *Sentinel,* 'They would yell at you in the foulest language.')[30]

This objective is not necessarily as sinister as it sounds. The men working for the security firm reiterated that they saw their role as an extension of existing social services in Ceduna; they often drove Anangu to town camp or called ambulances, taxis or the sobering-up facility to a person's assistance. This is a technique Lea et al call 'dispersal to zones of rehabilitation'.[31]

Sensory responses, such as disgust and complaints about noise, were central to local condemnations. For example, in the *West Coast Sentinel,* the mayor wrote:

> The standard of behaviour shown by some visitors to our town and some residents has been absolutely disgusting and unacceptable. We have see tidy streets turned into pigsties by idiots upturning rubbish bins, bottles broken on footpaths, drunken parties disturbing innocent neighbours, vandalism of property and generally disgraceful actions from a small minority of people who do not deserve to be a part of our community ... [32]

The theme of inversion suggested by the mayor's image of the 'upturned rubbish bin' was reiterated. The president of Ceduna's Business and Tourism Association stated, 'They come out at night when the rest of us are going to bed and they disappear in the morning when the rest of us are getting up to go to work'.[33] The dogs were to put right what was upturned, to bring aestheticised order to a state of social disorder. Local residents defending the dogs' introduction also emphasised the rubbish strewn along the foreshore and the repulsion that items such as discarded nappies engendered. (The anonymous resident quoted previously stated, 'Youl'd [sic] find some disgusting things left behind after they'd gone—like dirty nappies'.)[34]

Other themes beside rubbish recurred. Broken glass posed a danger to public safety, complainants stressed; residents and councillors also condemned people's rowdiness, 'foul language' and the disruption of residents' sleep. This is not the time to discuss the long history of colonial images of the degraded 'drunken Aborigine'[35] or of swearing as a form of subversion.[36] Here I highlight simply that the bodily grotesquery attributed to visiting A<u>n</u>angu *was further produced by the measures targeting them.* Recall that the council restricted access to the foreshore public toilets after the New Year's Day incident. This forced A<u>n</u>angu to keeping doing in public that which they were then derided for doing in public. A white farmer of my limited acquaintance mused, 'They are sort of like animals; they shit in the bushes.' This fact is entirely attributed to a kind of primitive instinct, which it is assumed 'they'—members of a race—share. Yet it is an outcome of local policy: the only toilet on the main street, co-located with the tourist centre, bars entry to those with bare feet.

Aunty Sue Mob member Jamie summed up, 'You've got Yalata people coming down and leaving their rubbish, you've got the council, and you've got the dog unit chasing people around … They ['Yalata people'] might be just walking down the street: dogs pull up. It really hurts.' That some Aboriginal people are subjected to scrutiny, even when they are simply 'walking down the street'—that is, when they are just being themselves—is experienced by Jamie as painful. Aunty Sue told me she saw the men from the K9 Unit kick the soles of the feet of a woman sleeping on the grass, in order to rouse her. As an observer of this scene, Aunty Sue felt utterly powerless to intervene, and was cast as unusually passive in bearing witness to this sleeping woman's degradation.

And so a sense of white 'possession' pervades Ceduna, and is guaranteed by many subtle means, including the more extreme measures described above. Out the back, however, it is Aboriginal people who assume an authoritative presence, inverting the race-based social order belonging to town.

Indeed, Aboriginal residents of Ceduna sense constantly that powerful forces surround them: they are especially present out the back but they are also sometimes evidenced from the vantage point of town—stormy skies, suddenly rough seas, gritty, swirling orange winds are all laden with the potential to mean *something*, and inspire speculation. These phenomena might emanate from the roughshod temporary scrub camps of A<u>n</u>angu, located beyond the confines of the town proper, and are seen to be an influence on daily events: supernatural phenomena and the skills of culturally knowledgeable men and women are respected and feared. Most Ceduna whitefellas know nothing of any of this, while many Nungas regard whitefellas' all too typical ignorance with some satisfaction—condemned as they are to live with limited means to understand, explain and sometimes even notice significance occurrences. Other Nungas resent the fact that whitefellas have failed to acknowledge that they live in the midst of so much 'culture'. This provides another example of the ways Aboriginal people and whitefellas continue to live separately, in some regards, while so many other aspects of their life experiences are shared.

It is in travelling through the dog fence and being out bush though that Aunty Sue Mob seize most fully the possibility to reimagine and invert the established social hierarchy that is worked at in town. It should now be clear that Aunty Sue Mob's struggle is an effort to create, dwell in and relish something beyond native title. Rockhole Recovery is central to their effort to forge, shape and inhabit this alternate reality. But being out the back offers something else: the bush also provides an escape from the scrutiny, stresses and pressures associated with town life, from racism and whitefella judgements. Out the back it is Aboriginal people who are assumed, both by themselves and by greenies, to belong more fully, rightly and deeply. The bush recognises Aboriginal people, greeting them and communicating with them through subtle signs such as the strange behaviour of birds. Being out the back is affirming and much more: the bush is seen to have the power to redeem and heal Aboriginal people.

'Wonder what the rich people are doing?': the bush as 'relaxing'

Aunty Sue mulled over a possible caption for a large-format image of the vast and sparkling salt bed, Googs Lake, which was to feature in an exhibition of photos of the landscapes traversed over the course of Rockhole Recovery. The exhibition, called *Ngaligu Munda—our land. Images from Kokatha Mula country* was mounted in Fitzroy, Melbourne and organised by greenies in order to raise funds for future rockhole trips and to bring attention to the mining issue on the West Coast. Sue settled on, 'When we sit here we say, "Wonder what the rich people are doing now?"'

Googs Lake, as well as Paint Lakes, are two sites regarded as especially accessible, restorative and peaceful places to spend a night camping, or have a fire and picnic on a day trip.

Paint Lakes is a wide, oval clay-pan, sticky under foot. Driving there, car passengers find themselves involuntarily ducking and weaving in an effort to avoid the low, overhanging branches, sticks and strips of bark that come swiping, flapping and thrashing at the car. On rockhole trips this same track has claimed a set of roof racks, a 4WD snorkel and a rear window, which was smashed to smithereens when Aunty Sue's sister, who had temporarily borrowed a greenie's vehicle, swerved to avoid one branch and another one came through the window from the opposite direction. The narrow, twisting strip of a track drops down a steep incline to arrive at the edges of a sweep of bare ground, rimmed with stunted mallee. The sky blazes above the open area. Out on the lakebed patches of grey, white, the purple of bruises, a golden yellow and rich brown swirl together. For the 'old people' this was a source of ochre and most probably a place for gatherings and ceremonies; less is known about the meanings associated with this site than others I visited with Aunty Sue Mob.

We enjoyed many simple picnics on the Paint Lakes shoreline; it was an easy two-hour drive from town, and a day trip was often called for if people were 'stressed'. We lit small fires, perhaps to grill a fish on or to bake potatoes in foil. We once cooked a snapper slowly in buried coals. We waited for it for hours but agreed it was 'a beautiful feed', the steaming white flesh falling off the bones. Tea was drunk from a thermos brought from town, and more made in the billy, while picnickers sat on a checked rug, on logs, or in foldout camping chairs. Commentary usually centred on how 'relaxing' it was to be somewhere quiet and still to enjoy a fire and a hot cup of tea. 'Every day feels like Sunday out here,' mused Gary once. But time itself was not forgotten: watches were not worn but some members of Aunty Sue Mob checked mobile phones to see if diabetic medicine was needed.

In the documentary film *Keeper*, Aunty Sue is depicted taking her then thirteen-year-old granddaughter to Paint Lakes. The teenager, in thongs, digs up some ochre, wielding a heavy shovel. Then she sits on the lake edge with her Nana and rubs the gold-flecked dirt into her skin. Aunty Sue does this as it makes the skin soft; the golden grains, she says, have relaxing qualities. 'Kind of like foundation?' the granddaughter asks. And then, applying it to her cheeks, 'Does this suit my complexion?' Aunty Sue grunts her assent as the two of them rub themselves, rhythmically, happily, with the earth.

Perhaps this activity of rubbing sutures contemporary people's bodies to the substance of the site, and also joins the present to the past. Sue's grandmother is said to have spent hours patiently chipping mica off the face of the Koonibba Rockhole. And the Berndts, those anthropologists who worked at Ooldea in the 1940s, recorded many instances of the rubbing of substances into skin: burial rites involved initiated men rubbing sand from the inside of graves into the back muscles of the boys' legs,[37] and prior to the time of the Berndts' fieldwork, the rubbing of putrefying matter over mourners' bodies was an act of veneration towards the deceased[38]; young women rubbed their growing breasts with red ochre to encourage their growth.[39] At Paint Lakes all visitors were encouraged to literally absorb the calming, healing and relaxing properties of the bush into their bodies. Golden dirt was crumbled between fingers and massaged into shins, forearms, necks and cheeks.

At rockholes, Nunga women who were in need of healing from abuse and damage were encouraged to lie in the grooves and hollows of rocks in the sun, in order to soak up the positive energies that lay latent in the country itself. These were sites where the ancestral beings had gone in, or had imprinted themselves on the landscape.[40] Draped on warm rocks—eyes closed, bodies soft—they melded their contemporary Aboriginal selves with the land and an ancient Aboriginal way of being. Their sense of self had, in various ways, been attacked or belittled through their experience of being in a sometimes violent present: in this moment it was enlarged and enriched as it fused with the Aboriginal past. Indigenous figures such as scholar Judy Atkinson stress the therapeutic potential from identifying with, contacting and drawing on an Aboriginality of this kind.[41]

The day trips devoted to recuperation and leisure often culminated in picking bush medicine—stuffing garbage bags with strong-smelling, spindly leaves. Bush medicine has itself inherently calming qualities and can be used to aid massage, as well as being used for chest congestion, aches and pains. Aunty Vera told me that one afternoon she was driving back into town after picking bush medicine and felt herself become drowsy; she realised the pungent aroma of the plants emitted in the confined space was making her sleepy. Bags were often filled for others who had been unable to make it bush that day: greenies would collect for some of the elderly women of Aunty Sue mother's generation, for example. Aunty Sue Mob members make bush medicine by boiling the plants down in a base; traditionally goanna fat was used but today it's most often margarine. The mixture congeals to form a thick yellow paste or may be bottled as a greener, runnier liquid, depending on the maker. 'Bush med' is for sale in the Ceduna craft shop and the Cultural Centre but also, via the relationship with greenies, in shops stocking 'eco-friendly' products in Melbourne.

The task of filling the bags out bush is therapeutic too, emphasises Aunty Sue. In *Nguly Gu Yadoo Mai*, she explains:

> When you're actually picking, there's a group of you, you're picking the bush medicine, you're yarning away. It's like a social thing ... So what people don't realise is just how much they're talking to each other while they're doing it. So it's sort of like a therapy, I guess. And they talk about anything and everything.[42]

Before stepping on to a rockhole, Aunty Sue instructs everyone present to choose a small stone, and then toss it gently on to the rockface, calling out to the old people in greeting. Visitors who were coming out on country for the first time were encouraged to introduce themselves, stating their name, provided they did not feel too self-conscious talking out loud to the spirit world, as some greenies tended to be. Aunty Sue's own addresses were always friendly and casual in tone.

In town Aunty Sue Mob watched and were watched by others. This involved being 'being dissected under white eyes',[43] as well as also constantly negotiating the wariness and antagonisms that marked many intra-Aboriginal relationships over this period. Out bush it was the kind, wise and attentive ancestors whose eyes were understood to be omnipresent, their spirit presence manifesting throughout their purview. Close attention was paid to the evening's frog calls or the movements of a strangely friendly bird, who hopped about close by, confident and seemingly familiar. Out bush the atmosphere of others' scrutiny lifts, and the presence of Aunty Sue Mob is legitimated though an entirely different system of signs, this one intelligible only to Nungas, who would then translate it for the benefit of their guests.

Sitting by the fire in the evening was also conducive to storytelling sessions ('yarns'). A volley of tales would pour forth, most of them involving minor illegalities, or at least human foibles, and featuring characters on the margins of life.

> A man (all characters were named in the original telling of the story) wanted cigarettes. He said, 'I'm going out for ciggies' and came back hours later, nonchalant. Everyone wondered where he'd been. Nowhere was open in Ceduna, so out he'd driven to Nundroo to buy a packet of cigarettes: that's a 300-kilometre return trip for buyu.
>
> Two girls decided to sleep in their broken down car, they 'crashed out' and woke in the morning to find it had been jacked up and all four tyres stolen without them stirring.
>
> Some 'Yalata Nungas' pushed their car down to the Yalata turn-off and waited for sympathetic whitefellas to tow them to the nearest garage, which was also where the nearest 'grog shop' was. Here they filled the boot with grog, then prevailed upon other whitefellas to tow their car back to Yalata. 'Well that car actually had no engine!'
>
> Two men were out fishing, and their fishing boat went down because of a 'freak wave'. Their bodies were trapped inside

> and their families desperately wanted to bury the bodies. The best 'abalone swiper' in Australia went down to get the bodies, even when the police refused to. It was 'that abalone poacher' who gave grief-stricken families 'what they wanted'.

In these stories, innovation, ingenuity, resourcefulness and generosity were celebrated, and the fickleness of life ruminated on. Many stories praised people who might otherwise have been understood by members of the moralising middle class as dodgy or as criminals. Crooked country cops, for example, who warned people when and where they were likely to be booked for drink driving, were talked about with enthusiasm.

Out the back then provides for relaxation, therapy, the joining of bodies with country, and conviviality. Yet amidst these experiences of pleasure and fulfillment, a sense of unease tugged. My fieldnotes record idle conversations over buttery potatoes, horoscopes being read out loud, hot water from the billy topping up cups of tea drunk out of oversized pannikins. But I also noted another thread: constant commentary, warnings, worries and stories, all of which underscored that the bush was as harsh as it was kind, and that it should be regarded as potentially unforgiving, powerful and dangerous. These presences and portents are quite different in type from the anxieties associated with town life.

Chapter 12

Where dogs reign

The bush as dangerous

'We're scared of our own country!' Aunty Sue commented cheerfully on my first trip to Ceduna, as we camped behind the dunes on the wild coast. She discouraged me from swimming because of the sharks. Recall the greenie Clare being 'freaked out by scorpions and snakes and wild dogs': this fear was instilled into greenies and shared by Aunty Sue Mob members.

Respect for the 'old ways' and the power of the life-sustaining ceremonies of the past can make some Nungas nervous about the bush. Anthropologist Jennifer Biddle describes that for Central Australian Warlpiri people not being able to look after country is anxiety-invoking: the potency of country, which once made people fearful about entering others' country, now makes people 'frightened of their so-called "own" country if it has not been inhabited for a long time'.[1] Similarly, for Aunty Sue Mob, out the back secretes latent powers, which are only partially understood today.

There is, of course, no way of escaping the historical and social conditions that shape all contemporary people. Aunty Sue Mob members do not live out everyday lives in which events are determined and interpreted in very specific ways by reference to the laws and transcendental powers left behind by ancestral beings. Understanding and belonging to the bush thus involves understanding that some things now lie beyond contemporary knowing and full reach. Non-human beings and forces reign in the bush, just as that aloof and majestic eagle looks down its hooked beak proudly, surveying the human presence beneath it. These non-human beings and forces are held at a respectful distance. Fear or awe of the bush enhances rather than detracts from its pleasures.

These fears of familiar territory found their apotheosis in warnings about wild dogs and dingoes out bush. While cultural studies scholar Fiona Probyn-Rapsey carefully analyses the cultural significance of maintaining a distinction between dingoes and wild dogs—the first pure category is understood to face extinction as a species as it becomes ever more genetically mixed with the hybrid category of 'wild dogs'—in Aunty Sue's usage, and hence mine, the two terms are often used interchangeably and 'dogs' is used to cover both.[2]

Heading out bush usually involved entering Yumbarra Conservation Park through an access gate prohibited from public use, which bore two signs: 'WARNING. NO PUBLIC THOROUGHFARE. FENCE MAINTENANCE TRACK ONLY. Poison baits and traps occur at regular intervals in the vicinity of the fence. Unauthorised persons using this track do so entirely at their own risk.' And: 'DANGER. DINGO TRAPS NEAR FENCE.'

On numerous occasions we found a residue of the electric current that surged through the dog fence also, strangely, running through the gate. Aunty Sue, who always led the way, would quickly pull the loop of the lock over its neck, incurring a mild electric shock as she did so. We always stopped at this spot for the first of many 'smokos' (cigarette breaks), pulling over just after entering the gate. We had crossed into another realm, and a stop marked the transition.

The other reason for stopping in this particular spot was to dig up a traditional water source, the plant called jungoo jungoo, which grew in thick clumps on the edge of the scrub. Jungoo jungoo, Aunty Sue, explains, is 'all part of the water supply in the desert'.

'Where did you learn about that one, Aunt?' I once asked, as I took close-up photographs for inclusion in the bush food book.

She replied simply, 'From the old people.'

Having passed through the dog fence, Aunty Sue would wander around, buyu in one hand, looking for jungoo jungoo and checking to see what kind of movement, of machinery and people, had recently occurred through this entrance to the park. The warning signs on the gate referred to the fact that people set lethal steel-jawed traps around the perimeter of the fence on the conservation park side as an additional precaution to stop any animals that were attempting to breach the fence and or gate at this point; on occasion dead dogs were found in the traps.[3]

These discoveries always make Sue 'wild'. She firmly believes that once we were out the back we had entered a realm where dogs, rather than humans, have the more legitimate claim to reign. The farmers have their land, she reasons: the clearing of the scrub in the late nineteenth and early twentieth centuries is accepted as an historical fact 'that's all done, over and done with now'. The fact that farmers had so thoroughly usurped and subdued these large tracts of territory only underlines the importance of the point that the dogs must have the integrity of *their* place respected: this was where dogs run. Yet at the same time she was vigilant, almost obsessive, in her warnings about the danger these animals posed.

On my first rockhole trip in March 2008, when I travelled with tiny Ned, Aunty Sue watched me like the crow she was often associated with, insisting my family camp close to the fire. When Shane and I went to unroll our swag she shook her head, laughing mysteriously and threateningly, 'Oh no, oh no. You won't be sleeping there.'

She seemed grimly satisfied in revealing to me how vulnerable she regarded tiny babies to attack.[4] On all rockhole trips and camping trips out the back, the parents and small children present are allocated a tent and forbidden to sleep under the stars in swags. Dogs, Aunty Sue was adamant, could smell a lactating mother. Indeed, after camping on a cold mid-winter night at Googs Lake in 2008, we woke to find several fresh sets of dog prints outside the tent where I had slept and breastfed throughout the night—one set of prints was 'big as a human hand', we agreed hyperbolically. Three dogs had circled the perimeter of the tent, before leaving camp without taking much interest in anything else.

This fear quickly seeped into me. Another night we were camping nearby a rockhole, I was walking Ned to sleep in the stroller along a dark track. The hairs on the back of my neck stood up and I had to force myself to put one heavy foot after the other. The thick, black night pushed forcefully against me. My movements tense and slow, I was compelled to turn back to camp and sit down at the fire. Aunty Sue seized on my description of the ill-feeling that flooded through me, affirming that my fears were well-founded.

Stories and warnings about dogs would often segue into stories about camping out bush with the old people, who were always quick to 'growl' (hush) crying babies in camp. From these stories, other stories about the old ways of being would flow. The fear of dingoes then opened a window onto another mode of existence and another time: that of the old people and the lives of mobile hunter-gatherers. The presence of dogs stimulated Aunty Sue mob to evoke the everyday of those pre-contact times when Aboriginal people's whole lives were lived out bush. Aunty Sue Mob relished being able to access and conjure up images of this time and their ancestors, who inhabited it.

One late evening, between 10:00 and 11:00 pm on the March 2012 rockhole trip, a magnificent, multilayered dingo howl seemed to encircle our camp. The chorus was distant but the sound also seemed to surround us, as the camp lay quiet under the stars and the fire burnt low. 'Why do dingoes howl?' asks anthropologist and environmental philosopher Deborah Bird Rose.[5] 'According to people who know them well, dingos howl with grief,' she replies. But also:

> Their primary motivations are to locate and communicate with other members of the group, and to announce their presence to other groups …. They howl in harmonies that increase the sound of their voices, and they tell each other who and where they are.[6]

The next morning, as eggs were fried for breakfast, Aunty Sue Mob discussed the dingoes' howl. It was understood that on this night, the dingoes howled in order to communicate with each in announcing *our* presence, out bush: our entry into their domain. Aunty Sue Mob's presence, and that of their guests, had been noticed and knowledge of it shared. Our presence was neither resented nor welcomed, as far as I could tell. But there was an implicit assumption, among these speculations, in which the dingoes were assumed to recognise the particular humans whom they howled of: Aunty Sue Mob belonged out here, they were familiar, indeed relatively frequent visitors, rather than strangers. The dingoes howled on our first night out bush, but we did not hear them again. This confirmed the agreed-upon interpretation: they had already noted and shared news of our presence.

Talk of dingoes then, and the ways in which dingoes were understood to talk about Aunty Sue Mob, suggested relations of familiarity, even though fear and respect was born of this familiarity. Dogs were respected bosses of a wild world that was the permanent home of Aunty Sue Mob's antecedents, but remained outside of the contemporary Aboriginal experience. And so this fear mixed with complicated pleasures: it was exciting to have access to and to enter a realm that lay beyond the agricultural districts, where traditional countries and all the meanings bound up in them had been sublimated to modern desires, where the land had been made productive and had fallen quiet, and from which dogs were barred.

Walking through 'killer country'

While the fear of dogs was both pervasive and suggestive, other fears came into focus out bush. On the September 2008 rockhole trip, greenies decided to spend a morning walking about 5 kilometres along the track from the rockhole where we were camped down to Paint Lakes. Some of the teenage Nunga boys walked with us but no adult members of Aunty Sue Mob evinced a desire to walk. Greenies, on the other hand, strongly associate being in the bush with walking, both to keep healthy by exercising, and for the purpose of immersing themselves in their surrounds, observing different plant communities, identifying plants and birds, experiencing and appreciating its sounds and smells.[7]

Our bodies bear the unequal conditions of our existence.[8] By that I mean greenies and Aunty Sue Mob members inhabited a range of different kinds of bodies upon which intersections of race and class were imprinted—health-conscious, middle-class greenies' self-disciplined bodies could generally handle walking distances that our adult

Aboriginal companions, the majority of whom smoked, could not. Aunty Sue asked me anxiously, as we were all filling water bottles and lathering on sunscreen, 'Are those old ladies coming?' I had no idea who she meant. Eventually I realised she referred to three bush-walking enthusiasts aged, at the time, in their late forties. Aunty Sue's niece ribbed her, 'They're fitter than you, Aunt.'

Aunty Sue was not amused. 'I'm not walking; that's the point.'

She shifted her worries onto the heat. We were trying to get going before 8:00 am, but didn't leave until 9:00; delays were as much a feature of time out bush as they were on the day of departure from town. Aunty Sue circled among us warning, 'You're walking into killer heat out there,' and also, 'That's killer country.'

Before we left camp Aunty Sue listed everyone walking. With her glasses perched on the end of her nose, pencil in hand, she assembled us, produced her checklist, ticked us off one by one, then counted heads. She ordered us to stick together, not to let anyone fall behind, and to all wait if someone needed a toilet stop. Finally she told us she'd send a car down the track to check on us if it heated up. As we set off a greenie commented, 'I have a feeling it won't be very long before we hear a car.'

Aunty Sue's instructions quickly fell by the wayside, greenies moving at their own pace, chatting in small groups, and diving off the track and into the bush for a piss on their own then catching up. Walkers spread out along the track and trudged through the hot morning.

Clare had stayed back but followed later in the car. She told me that back at camp Aunty Sue Mob members were evidently agitated, fretting about greenies walking through Kokatha Country without guidance or protection. Ostensibly, greenies are vitally interested in and sensitive to the spiritual potency of the places Aunty Sue Mob share with them. Yet on this morning they were unaware that the bush was filled with ancestral spirits, to whom our presence and purpose might need to be explained.

Greenies equate *driving* through the bush with being alienated from it. They complain about spending 'too much time in the car' over the course of Rockhole Recovery and seek to bridge that distance by moving through the country and 'connecting' with it. For Aunty Sue Mob, driving involves maintaining a stance of respectful remove.

Tess Lea notes that in remote Aboriginal communities both visitors and residents will expend considerable effort heaving themselves in and out of 4WD vehicles in order to drive a mere 50 metres.[9] Driving short distances was characteristic of Ceduna life, too. My partner found employment in the South Australian public service and one evening after work related in amazement the extensive process of booking a work car, picking up the keys, signing the car out and then back in—all to drive to a meeting that was a five- or perhaps ten-minute walk away.

There are, I think, two things enacted via the distinction between walking and driving. Firstly, driving provides a crucial vantage point from which to effectively scope a broad sweep of the social landscape. 'Cruising' the streets might involve passing a number of key locations, noting the whereabouts of instantly recognisable parked cars and assessing very quickly who is around and doing what, who is sitting down on the street with whom, who is standing on a corner, perhaps hanging around 'nuisance style'. Secondly, driving is prized as autonomy, either one drives or one walks and is ultimately dependent on lifts. The very poorest walk around town; driving thus expresses a social distinction. When greenies visited, Aunty Sue Mob members frequently teased them for their habit of walking from one end of town to the other. One Nunga friend playfully performed the difference between greenies and Aboriginal people one day in Port Augusta for the benefit of Rhiannon and I, circling the supermarket's carpark like a shark, insisting that he could not bear to walk even a few metres.

This was not the end of the intrigue surrounding the walk to Paint Lakes, however. At Paint Lakes we sat down in the shade waiting for more vehicles to arrive to carry our whole group back to camp. After a ute-full of Kokatha men arrived with spades, a few greenies went out onto the lakebed with them, the Kokatha men pointing out and helping dig up different colours of clay. Months later some members of Aunty Sue Mob were still trying to establish why it was that a bout of gastro passed through the camp in the following days. They were certain it had something to do with the morning of the walk, when a group of greenies moved through the country for hours unaccompanied, while greenies assumed that it was to do with the combination of an unusually large camp, the pit toilet and communal food preparation.

One theory put forth, but eventually disproved, was a fear that when the first walkers arrived at Paint Lakes they had perhaps disturbed the ochre and even painted it on inappropriately. I knew that no particular gravitas was attached to simply *being* at Paint Lakes, or to looking at the ochre. However, throughout this tense period of speculation, I realised that it was important to be in the presence of someone who belonged to the country. While greenies walked through the bush in order to 'bond' with it, in this case the presence of strangers in that country had produced only a profound sense of discord.

'Going out for gulda': the bush as a source of sustenance

Much more positive associations surrounded the bush when it was considered as a source of food. The bush is Aunty Sue's 'supermarket', she is fond of saying. Sue sometimes framed her anti-mining stance and determination to protect her country from exploitation by stating, 'What little bit of land we've got left out the back—that shows you there's bush tucker here—we need to keep.' She also often says, 'The grannies [grandchildren] need to learn how to survive out here'.[10]

As established, part of what being out the back represents is the possibility of imagining one's re-entry into a place and time in which it was, and Aunty Sue insists it still is, possible to survive without white people and, more specifically and demonstrably, white foodstuffs. I interpret this as an interest in the possibility for some kind of Aboriginal autonomy, as much existential as economic. Independence is an imagined ideal, and its practical impossibility is everywhere evidenced, acknowledged and accepted—Aboriginal and white lives are of course intertwined. Out bush lies a realm of exploration, not future plans or concrete aspirations. Collecting and eating bush foods allows people to experience, and literally embody, a sense of autochthonous otherness and autonomy.

Aunty Sue reflects on the land and sea as sources of plenty:

> Usually the ocean is full of food during the summer months. So that's what the old people used to do. They go out [inland] for

> winter, go back out bush wintertime, come down summertime.
>
> There's a smorgasbord out there when the tide's out. You get your fish that gets trapped in the shallow water, like flounder for instance. You've got cockles, periwinkles, razor fish, scallops, mussels, cockles, abalone, the crabs. It's just all there. So if anybody starves around this place here, they're either ignorant or they're lazy, because the food is there.

What's being valued here is, on one level, the intimate knowledge of 'living off the land' held by the old people, and there are very conscious efforts to transmit this cultural knowledge to children out bush. On another level, the 'starving' body is a synecdoche: Sue is talking here of a form of deprivation she fears the Aboriginal community enduring. Bush foods nourish the social body because they feed it with images of riches connected to, and reminders of, the experience of an independent, self-sufficient, pre-colonial Aboriginal selfhood. While eating bush foods, Aunty Joan Mob luxuriate in images of plenty enjoyed by Aboriginal people in times past, and potentially accessible to them today.

Australian-born public intellectual Germaine Greer has lamented:

> Everywhere in Australia bush tucker has become harder and harder to find; the valiant women who take their children bush have to resist their constant whinging for hamburgers and Coke.[11]

These kinds of simplistic binaries—between courageous, yet defeated, tradition-oriented elders and debased, pathetic moderns—recur in Australian conversations about Indigenous people. For Aunty Sue's family, a coherent and distinctly Aboriginal experience involved drinking a can of Coke while out collecting bush foods.

Indeed, the recordings done as part of our bush food project have produced sprawling, discontinuous and multilayered transcripts. In one, a football match featuring Port Adelaide plays at full ball on a battery-operated radio, nursed on an elderly woman's knee a short distance from where we cooked gulda on the fire. The teenagers and younger kids pass around a can of Coke ('here, hold this') while taking turns knocking gulda heads against the tow ball of parked 4WDs, until the lizards went limp.

We stuffed them with paper towel, as Aunty Sue declared herself 'too lazy' to find blue bush, which they were traditionally cooked with.

While we were collating the bush food book, *Nguly Gu Yadoo Mai*, Rhiannon and I recorded its authors, Sue and her aunt, Nana Marcina Richards, talking about their knowledge and memories relating to each item featured. On one occasion, Rhiannon questioned Aunty Sue about this tradition/modern dichotomy. Rhi asked Aunty Sue to respond to cynical comments made about Nungas using guns and cars on hunting expeditions.[12] Aunty Sue shrugged these off easily, stating:

> [Whitefellas] always liked saving their traditions, so why can't we share their traditions? I mean, they brought 'em here, and Nungas are smart enough to work out, 'This is a good thing, we'll do it.' … Same with the rabbits, you know, when they brought 'em over. The Nungas weren't backward in using that as a source of bush tucker.

Rhiannon agreed, 'Yeah, we don't go in horse and carts, us white people.'

Aunty Sue replied, 'No. Or tjina [by foot]. No, we've got cars that get us places a lot quicker, so why not?'

Sue included a section in the bush foods book entitled 'Ring-ins'. She describes eating rabbit, the box thorn berries (now regarded as a noxious weed), walga (wild bush tomatoes) and camel.

The bush is credited with *already* nourishing and ensuring the survival of Aunty Sue's generation *as Aboriginal people*. Recall that Aunty Sue, her sisters and other fair-skinned mission kids remember heading out into the bush north of Koonibba Mission, eating galahs, birds' eggs, guldas and even wild cat in order to escape 'Welfare'. The very survival of their Aboriginal identities depended on familiarity with the bush; their ability to 'live off the land' for days at a time is seen as fundamental to them having escaped the fate 'government' would have had them meet. Aunty Sue Mob see it that those Aboriginal people who were removed as children were 'lost'. That is, from the point of view of those who remained, their relatives were always searching for them (and in many cases eventually found them).

But they were also 'lost' to the world of kin relations, knowledge of their cultural traditions, and a relationship with the country of their ancestors. The bush is seen as a hospitable place that is credited with protecting, sheltering and nourishing fair-skinned mission kids, ensuring that they maintained their ability to locate themselves within the local Aboriginal world.

While the bush behind Koonibba is the place where Aunty Sue's generation hid from Welfare, and the very survival of their Aboriginal selves depended on this patch of bush, Aunty Sue insists that this was also an opportunity: 'During those trips too we learnt a lot; we had to survive in the bush.' Profound and disturbing ironies are at work here: forces aimed at the destruction of a particular way of being Aboriginal enabled the consolidation of a strong Aboriginal identity, expressed in terms of a connection with land-based knowledge and culture. The method of Aunty Sue's escape from the long reach of Welfare at this time of her life forms the basis for her familiarity with and felt attachment to the bush in the present moment. Furthermore, these childhood experiences of managing to stay on the mission laid the foundations for a confidence in her Aboriginality. Bush foods enabled both her survival, but also the sustenance of her Aboriginality.

Today, Aunty Sue Mob members make pronouncements about the validity of people's Aboriginality based on their knowledge of and the historical depth of their attachment to the land. That is, other local Aboriginal people are questioned and devalued if they are seen to have a superficial attachment to local places. While there is a degree of sympathy for those who were removed and returned to their families later in life, any of these Nungas' attempts to speak knowledgably about their traditional country are scorned. Aunty Sue's Aboriginality was once cast as malleable by state policies committed to its dissolution, and Herculean community efforts had to be undertaken to protect it. It has now acquired immutable and respected qualities, because of a childhood spent 'going bush', partly in order to escape Welfare.

The more general and everyday procuring of bush foods to supplement rations was also a strong theme of reminiscences about Koonibba, as I earlier explored. While feeding families whose basic rations were inadequate was a necessity, again this process nourished the social body. Aunty Sue tells a story in which the move off the mission and into town, a move that gathered momentum in the 1950s, precipitated a loss of traditional food knowledge, which was linked to their Europeanisation. She is saddened by thinking of a period in which those Aboriginal people slowly lost their 'hunting spirits'.

> When the people started coming, moving into town they were pretty well in town. They don't go out much at all. It was left up to, more or less, the Mission mob. Coz I suppose when they moved to town, they were getting educated and whatever in the Western system. Then they wouldn't have gone out for gulda.

Whitefellas' relationships with the bush

None of what I have explored above is to say that Ceduna whitefellas do not also have their own relationships with the bush. We often encountered groups of local white campers and day-trippers out the back. Aunty Sue would usually approach these groups to give tips as to good spots to camp, or to share information about the state of roads and tracks. Gary told me he had always loved the bush. As a teenager, 'we [a group of white mates] used to go out bush, we weren't interested in town at all, every chance we got … we went away'. Uncle Gary went out the back, 'beyond the dog fence … as far back as we could, sort of munch around roads with the old land rover'. 'We used to call it bush bashing, now we call it body bashing,' he liked to joke.

Megan Poore's unpublished anthropology PhD thesis about Ceduna whitefellas makes much of local whitefellas' relationships with the landscape. Poore summarises:

> Love for the landscape and fear of it do not necessarily cancel each other out; in fact Ceduna people live with this paradox every day, and much of the survival ethic as disseminated in town depends on it—we must survive in a hostile

> environment which we fear, but we also love this hostile environment.[13]

Poore shows that newcomers to Ceduna are guided to reshape their views of the landscape. At first, they might see the surrounding landscape as 'ugly, inhospitable, bleak, even intolerable and unknowable'. They are initiated into a process of reinterpretation, with the hope that they will come to 'appreciate the power and grandeur of the land', eventually come to extol its qualities as 'splendid, beautiful, magnificent, perhaps a little forbidding … certainly enigmatic'.[14]

On my first rockhole trip we paused at a monument to two whitefellas who had forged a road through the scrub. In 1973 the Denton family began clearing a way through sandhills and mallee and spinifex scrub north of their farmhouse using only a conventional, two-wheel drive utility and a tractor equipped with a front-end loader blade.[15] A bulldozer was used where the sandhills got too steep. 'After three years and with the support of locals in the form of fuel and supplies, the road was finished'.[16] The now deceased 'Goog' Denton and his son Dinger (also deceased) are remembered by way of a simple stone monument, into which are pressed mementos: handprints, stone artefacts, a photo, the key to Goog's bulldozer and a Carlton Draught beer can. The plaque commemorates the pushing of Googs Road from Lone Oak to Mount Fink. A second plaque is dedicated to Dinger Denton, who died at the age of twenty-seven.

Aunty Sue encouraged greenies to respect the association between Goog and his 'beloved outback'. She was distinctly unimpressed by local Nunga agitation, some years earlier, to change the name of Googs Lake to its Indigenous nomenclature. Goog loved the bush, she believed, and had made it possible for others to experience this particular place. It was not his race-based identity that should be considered; it was the life he lived and his actions. The Dentons, she told me, used to keep a visitors' book at their farm for people to fill in as they were heading out or back from camping at the lake. They often camped by the lake themselves and returned home with other campers' rubbish. The Kokatha name for it, Aunty Sue thought, was no longer known, so why not honour someone who had a love of the bush? From Aunty

Sue's confident perspective, whitefella relationships with the bush were no threat to her own sense of belonging to her country.

'Wild and free'

In June 2008, I travelled out bush for a week with a quiet cousin of Aunty Sue's, Laurel. She wasn't at all self-conscious about her limited knowledge of the country we drove through. Once I asked, 'Are we almost there?' and she replied mildly, 'Wouldn't have a clue.'

On another day on the same trip, Aunty Laurel mused while we were driving along, in a statement characteristically understated and expansive all at once, 'I like the bush. I'd just like to live out here somewhere. If I won the lottery I could build a house with glass all around. I'd be wild and free.'

Epilogue

Things changing shape

In the year I lived on the Far West Coast I rented a tin box of a house trucked from the Ooldea railway siding to the locality of Denial Bay, a settlement ten minutes from Ceduna and on the same bay. Each day, as I drove the road between Ceduna and Denial Bay, I passed a yellow sign: *Caution Sunglare.*

Aboriginal people often walked this road into town, sometimes flagging vehicles down for a lift. Walkers fanned out across the road and moved towards the edges unhurried, without turning to look at approaching cars. They walked in bare feet, women wearing skirts and big floppy t-shirts over soft, saggy mimis, men sporting flannies and faded jeans.

Debris in this bright landscape was especially mutable—a scrap of truck tyre appeared as a goanna, rusted coiled wire seemed a snake, sticks everywhere looked like lizards. A stump of wood might catch my eye—I'd see the turned head of an alert bird, an eye and beak in profile. One day I mistook a discarded gumboot for an echidna. I was getting my bearings, figuring out what was what, and where they lay.

As is often noted, social researchers are likely to find the shape of their study shift according to the way their research participants redirect their attention, through subtle or explicit means. The contours of this very study kept morphing. At first I intended to fix my analytical gaze on the familiar—on greenies. I had spent my twenties working in solidarity with grassroots Aboriginal political struggles and returned to university seeking to probe the environmentalist–Indigenous alliance. The question of native title soon forced its way into view, becoming central.

While this book has at its focus certain aspects of the life story of just one wise, steely and funny Aboriginal woman, I hope it has also served to shed critical insight into the native title claims process that consumed Aunty Sue's attention for many years, and of which she has developed a critique. For Aunty Sue, native title did not provide the means to address the history of colonial dispossession by affording her recognition. Instead it drew her into conversation with the colonial archive in ways that misrecognised her, threatening, initially, her sense of identity. Further, native title seemed only to provide for compensation for mining of her country. But she is adamant her ancestors handed her a responsibility to 'fight for the land'. She seeks to halt mining, to 'leave the land as it is' or 'munda yumadoo iliga'.

Her cynicism regarding native title processes draws attention to its resolutely colonial nature. The Mabo decision affirms the sovereignty of the Crown, and the *Native Title Act* 'explicitly guaranteed the validity of all existing property rights so, from the commencement of the Act's operation, non-Indigenous interests did not have to be concerned about actually being dispossessed of any valid existing interest'.[1]

Furthermore, native title legislation implicitly defined the legitimate rights-in-land-bearing Indigene as an essentially different cultural subject, conferring legitimacy on those Aboriginal people who can narrate a collective and individual story of cultural continuity in the midst of colonial experiences of dislocation and dispossession, which effected discontinuity. Colonial modes of knowing and recording Indigenous people become instrumental in that very process of successful narration, whereby contemporary people's claims might be substantiated by recourse to written historical sources.

Further still, the native title system accords claimants and native title-holders rights of negotiation over developments such as mining, which institute structurally inequitable processes that condition an embrace of corporate interests. Indigenous people might well wish to refuse others' designs on their country but the *Native Title Act* affords no right of veto.

Feeling the wind

General points aside, the particular shape of the specific native title-related conflict I have documented here is also ever changing. In closing, I note briefly some post-determination developments.

Native title claims require the establishment of a Prescribed Body Corporate (PBC), which represents native title-holders and manages their native title rights and interests in the event of a successful determination. Aunty Vera resumed friendly contact with those people involved in the relevant PBC, the Far West Coast Aboriginal Corporation, after the 2013 resolution of the claim. She reasoned that since 'they [Iluka Resources] are out there ripping up my bloody country' she should have access to the attendant benefits.

Aunty Sue was initially more circumspect. In 2014 she glossed the PBC as yet another new incorporated body in the dense organisational landscape that is 'meant to help Aboriginal people'. I sat on the verandah of the farm house with her, dunking biscuits in large mugs of tea made for us by one of Sue's granddaughters. When I asked her about her relationship with members of the PBC, she replied, 'Well, I wouldn't lower myself to go in there and ask for help.'

However, in early 2016, Sue accepted an invitation to join the board of the PBC. The intensity of the conflict had ebbed by this stage. Indeed, I had attended a flag-raising ceremony in the main street of Ceduna as part of NAIDOC Week in July 2015, and was struck by the charismatic host's emphasis on a hyphenated identity. He firmly introduced himself as a 'Mirning-Wirangu-Kokatha' man. This young man embraced with confidence an identity formation that seemed impossible for Aunty Sue's generation to articulate over the time of my fieldwork, perhaps signaling a relaxation of the emphasis on asserting unambiguous and differentiated identities I have described in this book.

Over recent years, Sue has also reflected soberly on the deaths of a number of senior community members. She felt she could not attend their funerals without seeming 'hypocritical'. But in death attention was refocused on these people's whole lives, prompting Aunty Sue to look past the last decade of conflict with these figures, and recall decades of shared experiences that had begun in childhood at Koonibba.

Sue's main reason for joining the board of the PBC, however, was to ensure she was privy to more detailed knowledge of the mineral exploration underway, and any proposed developments, in the region. How else was she to know 'what the hell was going on out there'? While she had effectively ghosted the claims process by her carefully designed activities undertaken outside of but with reference to it, once the claim was resolved she had to change political tack. Remaining wholly outside of this space now seemed to carry considerable risks—what if a new mine were proposed without her knowledge?—and offer few benefits.

Alongside this involvement, Sue has stepped up her commitment to other causes. She has fostered national and international relations with environmentalists as she becomes increasingly active in the campaign against South Australia's potential embrace of the nuclear industry. This has seen her travel to Vienna, the United States and also tour Australian east coast cities, talking about South Australia's nuclear history and its effect on Aboriginal peoples.

In October 2015 both Australian houses of federal parliament passed legislation to trial radical welfare reforms, which are designed to impede welfare recipients' capacity to spend unemployment benefits on alcohol or gambling. Ceduna was the first designated trial site for the cashless 'Healthy Welfare' card, with reforms taking effect in early 2016 and extended in 2017. Sue has keenly followed these developments and made an impassioned submission to the inquiry established prior to the passing of the relevant legislation, the *Social Security Legislation Amendment (Debit Card Trial) Bill 2015*. She participated in a local protest devoted to this issue and has been quoted in national media on the subject.

Sue regularly travels then, for a range of reasons, including to visit family members, as well as her environmental activism. Yet in my mind's eye she stands in her yard with the wind tearing through it.

In Ceduna, swirling winds frequently lift topsoil off the wheat farms and cloak the whole sky in an orange haze. Some time in 2008, I borrowed the Joan Didion omnibus from the Ceduna library, retreating guiltily into familiar readings by this American essayist as an escape from the strain of making and sustaining so many new relationships and constantly confronting my ignorance of the scene I had become temporarily a part of. I was drawn to Didion's descriptions of the malevolent Santa Ana, a hot wind that came 'whining' on down to Los Angeles from the north-east, 'blowing up sandstorms' and 'drying the hills and the nerves'.[2]

The West Coast's hot wind also had a strong effect. For some Aboriginal people, if it began out at sea it was likely the returning spirit of a drowned kinsman. For Sue, it served to remind her that while humans might seek to now extract a profit from ventures on country, mastery of this wild realm would prove illusory. 'Who's going to control the north winds?' Sue asked provocatively, when local disquiet spread about the process of potentially transporting mineral sands along conveyor belts also used for wheat and salt, while Iluka assured residents the thorium and uranium content in the heavy mineral concentrates were negligible.[3]

British anthropologist Tim Ingold writes that 'to feel the wind is not to make external, tactile contact with our surroundings but to mingle with them'.[4] Sue absorbs the wildness of this wind into herself, it 'infuses her entire being'.[5]

The term 'wild' is richly multivalent in Aboriginal usage. In anthropologist David Trigger's work in Queensland's gulf country, 'wild times' refers to the time of extensive violence on the colonial frontier, until people were 'quietened down'.[6] Deborah Bird Rose's Indigenous teachers told her that 'the wild' was ecologically diminished country, whereas 'quiet country' was that lived on and cared for by generations of Indigenous people. 'Wild people (colonisers) made wild country (degrading, failing),' summarises Rose.[7] Recall Aunty Sue explaining 'we don't live out there anymore'. Yet Sue's family tends to and is in renewed contact with water sources that are no longer depended upon in a material sense. Out the back is being cared for, again. In Aboriginal English 'wild' also means angry. Native title certainly made Aunty Sue frustrated and 'that wild'.

Out the back, humans might come to cower in the face of elemental forces—roiling heat and whipping winds sometimes combined to send our smaller, more informal camping parties hurrying back to town early. On still nights out the back on rockhole trips, however, we were thrilled by the howls of dingoes carrying across unknown distances. And in the deep quiet of a winter's evening in 2015 we thought at first that a fire smouldered on the horizon line before it too slowly changed shape as the hours passed, becoming a luminous moon suspended low over the salt lake.

Aunty Sue's hope is that *all* who travel with her out the back will make contact with something of this wildness.

Notes

Indroduction

1 This figure is for the Local Government Area; census data is available from the Australian Bureau of Statistics Website. <www.abs.gov.au>.

2 Morris (2013: 107).

3 Cowlishaw and Morris (1997).

4 See N. Brown and C. Brown (2005).

5 Wright (1991).

6 Mob is frequently used as a suffix in Aboriginal Australia. Often 'mob' designates a relationship to place: for example, Kooris in East Gippsland, Victoria 'identify themselves and others in terms of place, contrasting … the Lake Tyers "mob" with the Bairnsdale and Orbost mobs' (Keen 1999: 104). This convention was introduced to a wider audience with the publication of anthropologist Robert Tonkinson's 1974 book *The Jigalong Mob*. At Jigalong mission, Mardu people of the Western Desert forged a broad-based social identity, attesting to the possibilities for new ways of figuring relationships between place, experience and identity after colonialism has disrupted people–country relations. Mob can also be used in a more descriptive vein. At Yuendumu in the Northern Territory those whitefellas associated with implementing the federal government's 2007 Northern Territory Emergency Response are called 'Intervention mob' (Musharbash 2010:219), while in the northern Kimberley, members of the pastoral elite have been designated the 'million thousand mob' (Redmond 2007: 81).

7 Sider (2006: 276).

8 Tsing (1993).

9 This information is available from the website of South Australia Native Title Services (SANTS). See <http://www.nativetitlesa.org/our-news/sants-welcomes-far-west-coast-native-title-determination>. Last accessed 15 February 2016.

10 Three members of the High Court bench, Justice Dean, Justice Gaudron and Justice Toohey rejected the doctrine of *terra nullius* in these terms. Anonymous (1993: 15).
11 Borch (2001: 238).
12 Bartlett (1993: x).
13 However, the Crown had the right to extinguish native title without compensation, and had in fact done so over much of the continent. (Bartlett 1993: xx-xxii).
14 Attwood (2003); Peterson (1981); Yunupingu (1997).
15 Monaghan (2012: 48).
16 See, for example, Trouillot (2001).
17 Correy (2006: 337).
18 Weir and Ross (2007).
19 de Certeau (1984).
20 Austin-Broos (2009: 12).
21 Clifford (2013: 7).
22 The term 'hybrid scholar-activist' comes from anthropologist Stuart Kirsch (2006: xi), who worked with Yonggom people in Papua New Guinea affected by the environmentally disastrous Ok Tedi mine.
23 Hale (2006: 104).
24 Maher (1997: 222).
25 Bourgois (1995: 207).
26 Beckett (2008: 89).
27 Stanner (2009b: 48–49).
28 Stanner (2009b: 49).
29 Beckett (2008: 92).
30 Shostak (2000: 39)
31 Crapanzano (1980: 11).
32 Behar (2003).
33 Scheper-Hughes (1993: 28).
34 Cowlishaw (2009: 29).
35 The caption appears in Rose (1992). For an analysis of Hobble's stories see especially Rose (1991, 2001).
36 Beckett (2015); Beckett (2000).
37 Stewart (2007: 1).
38 Stewart (2007: 5).
39 Stewart (1996: 3).
40 Clifford (1988: 41).
41 Behar (1996).
42 Malinowski (1922: 3).
43 Hage (2010).
44 See, for example, Tuhiwai Smith (1999); Brady (2014).
45 See Berlant (2000); W. Brown (2001).

Chapter 1

1 Klein (1993: 182).
2 Klein (1993: 176).
3 Jackson (2013: 186).
4 I have been granted access to a selection of wonderful recordings done by Anderson and Walshe as part of a funded National Estates Grants Program, 'Oral History of the Koonibba Mission Project'. The interviews were conducted in 1996 and 1997, and have been lodged in the J.D. Somerville Oral History Collection, Mortlock Library of South Australia. The recordings are stored at OH 365.
5 Wark (2011: 41).
6 See Povinelli (2002); Lattas (1990). Charles Hale (2002) shows that limited forms of Indigenous recognition, and condemnation of the bad racist past, are also characteristic of what he calls 'neoliberal multiculturalism'.
7 I am drawing here on Hage (1998). For the history of Afghan cameleers in Australia, including accounts of the racial violence, abuse and suspicion their presence was met with, see Christine Stevens (1989). Phil Sparrow (2005) provides an explanation of the situation of Hazara people in Afghanistan and the reasons behind the waves of Hazara asylum seeking in Australia since 2001. The Baxter Immigration Detention Centre was in fact closed in 2007.
8 Strakosch (2015: 6).
9 Povinelli (2011).
10 Martin (2015: 115–16).
11 Simpson (2014: 11).
12 Simpson (2014: 16).
13 Monaghan (2012: 49).
14 This focus on lived experience distinguishes the literature I refer to, first, from an extensive specialised literature aimed at strengthening native title practitioners' professional practice. See, among many examples: Burke (2010); Fingelton and Finlayson (1995); Memmott (2011); Sutton (2003); Trigger (2010). Second, a voluminous literature describes juridical developments and provides an overview of the workings of the native title system. Key titles include: Strelein (2009); Ritter (2009b); and Brennan et al (2015a).
15 Smith and Morphy (2007b: 2).
16 Smith and Morphy (2007b: 6).
17 Weir (2012: 1).
18 See the profile of the relevant Prescribed Body Corporate, The Far West Coast Aboriginal Corporation. <nativetitle.org.au/profiles/profile_sa_farwestcoast.html>. Last accessed 16 March 2016.

19 The South Australian government's PACE (Plan for Accelerating Exploration) website provides further details. See <http://paceinvestors.pir.sa.gov.au/geology/eucla_basin and http://paceinvestors.pir.sa.gov.au/geology/gawler_craton>. Last accessed 27 January 2013.
20 Neale, Timothy, and Eve Vincent. 2017. Mining, Idigeneity, Alterity. Or, Mining Indigenous Alterity? *Cultural Studies*, 31. Advance online publication. DOI: 10.1080/09502386.2017.130.3435.
21 Ritter (2009a).
22 Greg Ogle et al. (2002: 5).
23 Dorbzinski (2004: 21).
24 Cohen (1992: 208).
25 See Scambary (2013: 10).
26 Dombrowski (2010:130).
27 O'Faircheallaigh (2006).
28 Weiner (2006).
29 Scambary (2013: 149).
30 'Signing of sand mining agreement,' *Aboriginal Way* (publication of the Aboriginal Legal Rights Movement Native Title Unit, South Australia), January 2008, p. 3. For details of this agreement, see the entry in the Agreements, Treaties and Negotiated Settlements Project website: <http://www.atns.net.au/agreement.asp?EntityID=4485>. Last viewed 10 August 2015.
31 Holcombe (2015); Scambary (2013: 4).
32 Tsing (2005: 4).
33 See 'About Iluka Resources'. Available from <http://www.ceduna.sa.gov.au/webdata/resources/files/JA_Project_info_sheet_Aug_2011.pdf >. Last accessed 15 February 2016. The information about the Nunga rates of employment was reported in a media release. See <https://www.iluka.com/docs/default-source/media-releases/media-release---iluka-suspends-jacinth-ambrosia-mining-concentrating-activities>. Last accessed 5 January 2017.
34 <https://www.iluka.com/docs/default-source/media-releases/media-release---iluka-suspends-jacinth-ambrosia-mining-concentrating-activities>. Last accessed 5 January 2017.

Chapter 2

1 Berndt and Berndt (1944: 242–43); Clarke (1997: 136).
2 N. Brown and C. Brown (2005: 78).
3 Lea (2008: 226).
4 See Langton (2013).
5 Rowley (1970, 1971, 1972).
6 Rowley (1972: xiv–xv).

7 Rowley (1972:v).
8 See Cowlishaw (1987).
9 Gibson (2008: 295).
10 Paradies (2006: 359).
11 Stanner (2009a: 69–70).
12 Merlan (1998: 170).
13 Merlan (2006: 101).
14 Muir and Morgan (2002); Rose (2002).
15 Neale (2013); Sutton (2011).
16 Collmann (1988: 1–2) makes pertient comments on this once pervasive tendency; for examples see Inglis (1964: 115); Reay (1945: 309).
17 McCorquodale (1997: 24).
18 I. Watson (2014: 172).
19 Fanon (1967: 109).
20 Fanon (1967: 111).
21 Fanon (1967:116).
22 Anderson (2003); Beckett (1988a); Carlson (2016); Langton (1993); Morton (1998).
23 Dodson (2003: 28).
24 On the last point see Vincent (2016: 241).
25 Malkki (1992).
26 Simone de Beauvoir (2011) developed these concepts to explain the way woman as object was defined in relation to—both against and through—man as subject. Woman, for de Beauvoir, was 'Other' to man, as indigenous people were British colonialism's 'Other', defined as an absence of the qualities the 'civilised' coloniser was assumed to possess.
27 Hall (1990: 223); Norman (2015: 20).
28 For a fulsome discussion of this important era see Carlson (2016: 69–84).
29 Hall (1990: 225).
30 Hall (1990: 225).
31 My use of the term governmentality references Foucault's (1991) famous thesis: from the mid eighteenth century, the object of governing subject peoples shifted away from the enjoyment of sovereignty over them to the governing of things. 'The population', specifically its bodily state of health, economic productivity and reproductive capacity, became the end of government.

Chapter 3

1 See, for example, Bauman (2006).
2 Peters-Little (1999: 4).
3 Brock (1993: 156).

4 Eckermann (2010: 6).
5 Brock (1995: 208).
6 Mattingley and Hampton (2008: 3). This experiment in 'systematic colonisation' was short-lived. Historian Stuart Macintyre explains (1999: 80), 'While the principal settlement, Adelaide, and its surrounds were carefully laid out by William Light, the surveyor general, the arrangement soon succumbed to land speculation and South Australia reverted to the status of an ordinary Crown colony in 1842.'
7 The document is reproduced in full on the ANTaR SA website at <http://antarsa.auspics.org.au/category/news/2010/09/read-the-letters-patent-of-19-february-1836>. Last accessed 12 July 2012.
8 Reynolds (2003: 127–52).
9 Reynolds (2003: 127–29).
10 Reynolds (2003: 136).
11 Reynolds (2003: 137).
12 Reynolds (2003: 140).
13 Reynolds (2003: 141).
14 Foster et al (2001: 2).
15 Brock (1995: 208–09).
16 Brock (1995: 215).
17 Foster et al (2001: 4)
18 Brock (1995: 215).
19 Foster (1989: 65). See also Foster (2000).
20 Foster (1989: 69–70) tells us that monthly ration distribution at Port Lincoln was first introduced in 1847 but after a series of murders in 1850 and a long drought, resulting in widespread Aboriginal starvation, ration distribution was 'stepped up' with additional distribution points at Venus Harbour and Salt Creek.
21 Faull (1988: 37).
22 Brock (1993: 64).
23 Faull (1988: 44).
24 Eckermann (2010: 12).
25 Eckermann (2010: 13–14).
26 Faull (1988: 314).
27 Faull (1988: 315). See Rose (1991) for Aboriginal accounts of the arbitrary cruelty meted out to Aboriginal workers within the northern pastoral industry.
28 Foster et al (2001: 46–47).
29 Foster et al (2001: 47).
30 Foster et al (2001: 49).
31 Burgoyne (2000: 114).
32 Burgoyne (2000: 115).
33 Burgoyne (2000: 115).

34 Burgoyne (2000: 115).
35 Burgoyne (2000: 115).
36 Burgoyne (2000: 115).
37 Burgoyne (2000: 118).
38 Stanner (2009c: 182–93).
39 Morris (1989: 84).
40 Foster el al (2001: 69).
41 Foster el al (2001: 69–70).
42 Lutz (n.d.: 33).
43 Dayman (1989).
44 Eckermnann (2010: 11). Kangaroo skins were sent to Adelaide to be auctioned, and eventually shipped to America where they were used to line railway carriages, for bookbinding and in gloves (Faull 1988: 52).
45 Brock (1993: 65); see also Faull (1988: 52).
46 Brock (1993: 65).
47 Brock (1993: 65).
48 Faull (1988: 55).
49 Brock (1993: 65).
50 Faull (1988: 317–18).
51 Eckermann (2010: 30).
52 Burgoyne (2000: 21).
53 Eckermann (2010: 30–31). This passage is indented in Eckermann's work but no reference for the original is given.
54 Eckermann (2010: 33).
55 Burgoyne (2000:14).
56 Brock (1993: 97–98).
57 Eckermann (2010: 233).
58 Brock (1993: 66).
59 Brock (1993: 80).
60 Brock (1993: 79–80)
61 Burgoyne (2000: 24).
62 See Eckermann (2010: 28, 145). The vital role of Aboriginal labour in various rural economies across Australia is highlighted by authors such as Beckett (2005).
63 Eckermann (2010: 123).
64 Brock (1993: 71).
65 Brock (1993: 63).
66 Brock (1993: 66).

Chapter 4

1 Brock (1993: 68).
2 Eckermann (2010: 51).

3 Foucault (1991: 136–37).
4 Brock (1993: 68–69).
5 Eckermann (2010: 125) says that Koonibba Nungas were 'induced' to sign a petition, in Wiebusch's temporary absence, by local 'patriots' who were hostile to the Lutherans in their midst. The historian Cameron Raynes (2009: 58) takes this same petition to be indicative of early signs of 'unrest' at Koonibba. Christobel Mattingley and Ken Hampton (2008: 204) note that 'anti-German feeling was strong enough' to warrant a petition, but they stress instead the petitioners' demand for a stake in their land: 'we want the benifit (sic) of this ground, as there is no satisfaction to the natives'.
6 Fabian (2002: 17).
7 Eckermann (2010: 20).
8 Eckermann (2010: 44).
9 See Berndt and Berndt (1945: 260–66).
10 Eckermann (2010: 211–12); on Bates, see White (1993: 56).
11 Eckermann (2010: 42).
12 Povinelli (2002: 54).
13 Eckermann (2010: 103).
14 Brock (1993: 71).
15 Brock (1993: 71).
16 Brock (1993: 67) shows that Nungas quickly grasped that letters 'were a powerful means of communication'. Letters were frequently dictated to, and read out by, European intermediaries. These letters enabled contact over long distances and provided a means for Aboriginal groups to inform other groups of their whereabouts and intended movements. European technologies were captured for Aboriginal ends, points out Brock. Examples of this kind abound in the literature dealing with the post-frontier period.
17 Brock (1993: 89).
18 Eckermann (2010: 44).
19 Burgoyne (2000: 41).
20 Burgoyne (2000: 25).
21 Eckermann (2010: 168–69).
22 Brock (1993: 14). For an analysis of racial thinking in this period see McGregor (1997).
23 Brock (1993: 6).
24 Mattingley and Hampton (2008: 55).
25 Gale (1964: 111).
26 Mattingley and Hampton (2008: 45).
27 Eckermann (2010: 107-109).
28 Brock (1993: 83).
29 Children's dormitories were a common feature of missions around

Australia, as childhood socialisation was key to missionary success. The dormitories served slightly different functions in different places and often accommodated children whose parents lived permanently on the same mission. There also seems to have been variation in terms of the regularity of, and restrictions surrounding, children's contact with their kin (see Blake 2001: 67–84; Choo 2001: 142–69; Tonkinson 1974: 122–24).

30 Human Rights and Equal Opportunity Commission (1997: 638).

31 Brock (1993: 16).

32 Brock (1993: 82–83). Historian Anna Haebich (2000: 199) shows that in South Australia the Protector continued, for some time after the passage of the 1911 Act, to remove Aboriginal children using the provisions of the *State Children's Act 1895*. This Act included a definition of a 'neglected child' as a child found 'sleeping in the open air, without home or settled abode' (Human Rights and Equal Opportunity Commission 1997: 636–37).

33 Eckermann (2010: 105–06).

34 Mattingley and Hampton (2008: 206–08). Kinnear tells her story more fully elsewhere (in Pring 1990: 47–66). Again she speaks fondly of the children's home but also details extremely fraught and upsetting relations with her biological family and mother, with whom she was reunited later in life.

35 Raynes (2009: 63–64).

36 Eckermann (2010: 157–58).

37 See, among others, Haebich (2000); Read (1999).

38 Human Rights and Equal Opportunity Commission (1997: 37).

39 Eckermann (2010: 110).

40 Raynes (2009: 70).

41 For example, Robert Tonkinson (1974: 69) argued that the 'Jigalong mob' remained 'tradition-oriented' although he described a situation quite different from the one at Koonibba. At the Jigalong mission, during the 1960s, Christianity had made few inroads. Ceremonial and religious life flourished despite the missionaries' presence. Tonkinson (1974: 135) argued that 'the mission, unwittingly and indirectly, has facilitated the retention of the Law and its focal manifestation, the religious life. By allowing large numbers of tradition-oriented Aborigines to congregate on a permanent basis at Jigalong, where they were fed, the mission has enabled them to pool their religious knowledge and has given them ample spare time to devote to religious discussion and activity'. Male initiation ceremonies involving sub-incision and circumcision continued in secret at Jigalong throughout the 1960s, and the missionaries dared not venture into the camp in which Aboriginal adults lived. At Koonibba, daily life had been transformed by the 1920s, by which time Christianity had certainly taken hold. It's Aboriginal people's memories of the mission that are oriented to the persistence and presence of the old ways on the mission.

Chapter 5

1 Brock (1993: 67).
2 Eckermann (2010: 107).
3 Burgoyne (2000: 38–40).
4 Burgoyne (2000: 39).
5 Musharbash (2008: 151–52).
6 Beckett (1994: 131).
7 Brock (1993: 79).
8 Brock (1993: 89).
9 Brock (1993: 90).
10 Brock (1993: 91–92).
11 Brock (1993: 92).
12 Brock (1993: 104–05).
13 Brock (1993: 108).
14 Brock (1993: 110–11).
15 Burgoyne (2000: 56).
16 For example Reay (1945).
17 Burgoyne (2000: 56–58).
18 Burgoyne (2000: 58).
19 For example Cowlishaw (2004: 126).
20 Brock (1993: 105).
21 Burgoyne (2000: 56).
22 Eckermann (2010: 177–80).
23 Gale (1964: 101).
24 Berndt and Berndt (1942: 204).
25 Gale (1964: 108).
26 Eckermann (2010: 189–90).
27 Eckermann (2010: 188–89).
28 See Gale (1964).
29 Eckermann (2010: 190).
30 Eckermann (2010: 201–02).
31 Jacobs (1983: 360–61).
32 Brock (1993: 7).

Chapter 6

1 Foley (2007: 172).
2 Weir (2013: 163–64).
3 Lydon and Burns (2010: 52).
4 Scambary (2013: 149).
5 Merlan (1989, 2006); Scambary (2007); Smith (2008); Weiner (2011).

6 Daley (pers com, 2015).
7 Edwards (2008: 79).
8 Peterson (1981: 115).
9 Bradshaw and Collett (1991: 22).
10 As recorded in the Agreements, Treaties and Negotiated Settlements database (ATNS). See <http://www.atns.net.au/agreement.asp?EntityID=1627>. Last accessed August 12, 2012.
11 Rowse (2012: 68).
12 Rowse (2012: 79).
13 Rowse (2012: 69).
14 *The Anangu Pitjantjatjara Yankunytjatjara Land Rights Act 1981* handed back over 100,000 square kilometres and the *Maralinga Tjarutja Lands Right Act* over 75,000 square kilometres (Mattingley and Hampton 2008: 82, 87). Philip Toyne and Daniel Vachon (1984) provide a wonderfully lively account of the campaign leading up to first act.
15 See Palmer (1990, 1999).
16 Merlan (2006: 97).
17 Merlan (2006: 97).
18 Jacobs (1983; 1988).
19 Jacobs (1988: 35–36).
20 Jacobs (1988: 38–39).
21 Jacobs (1988: 31).
22 Wolfe (1999: 183).
23 Jacobs (1983: 5).
24 See also Monaghan (2012: 49).
25 Babidge (2010: 189).
26 The Aboriginal and Torres Strait Islander Commission (ATSIC) was established in 1989 and combined the administrative roles of the former Department of Aboriginal Affairs, and the representative and advocacy roles of previous bodies. John Howard's Coalition government abolished ATSIC in 2005 (Bradfield 2006: 87–88).
27 Brock (1993: 105–07).
28 Wilson (2003: 48).
29 Pearson (1995: 95).
30 Pearson (1995: 95). See also: Cowlishaw (1995); Lavelle (2001); V. Watson (2001).
31 Povinelli (2002: 32).
32 Dauth (2011: 23).
33 Dauth (2011: 22).
34 Dauth (2011: 26).
35 Agius et al (2004: 207).
36 Weiner et al (2002: 4).
37 Brennan et al (2015b: 4).

38 Walker (2015: 20).
39 Brennan et al. (2015b: 6).
40 Monaghan (2012: 54).
41 Macdonald (2002).
42 See especially Mantziaris and Martin (2000).
43 W. Brown (1995); Fraser and Honneth (2003); Honneth (1995).
44 Honneth (2003: 111).
45 In Taylor and Gutmann (1992: 32).
46 In Taylor and Gutmann (1992: 25).
47 Coulthard (2014: 25). See also Simpson (2014).
48 Coulthard (2014: 25).
49 Correy et al (2011: 42).
50 Merlan (2006: 97).
51 Monaghan (2012: 50–55).
52 Monaghan (2012: 54).
53 Monaghan (2012: 48).
54 Letch (2010: 11-15).
55 Harrison (2003: 345).
56 Correy et al (2011: 42–43).
57 Correy et al (2011: 44).
58 Correy et al (2011: 50).
59 Sutton (2003: 5–6).
60 Sutton (2003: 5–6).
61 Monaghan (2007: 115).
62 Monaghan (2012: 49–50).
63 Monaghan (2007: 116).
64 Monaghan (2010: 240).
65 See Ramp (2006)
66 Bates (1966: 177).
67 Pilbrow (2013: 228).
68 Babidge (2010: 185).
69 Pilbrow (2013: 229).
70 Sansom (2007: 79).
71 Dousset and Glaskin (2007: 142); Palmer (2010).

Chapter 7

1 Richards and Haseldine (2012).
2 Gara (1995: 135).
3 Wilson (2003: 13).
4 See the library's archived website for this event: <http://www.slq.qld.gov.au/whats-on/calevents/general/exhibitions/transforming-tindale>. Last

accessed 23 June 2016. Thanks to Emma Kowal, who drew my attention to this exhibition and with whom I viewed it.

5 Wilson (2003:13–14). Ian Keen (1999) describes a similar scenario in East Gippsland, Victoria.

6 Wilson (2003: 17).

7 Dauth (2011: 31); Monaghan (2012: 52). In Ceduna, tribal names, territory and language are understood to be isomorphic. This assumption warrants scrutinising, but this theoretical task is tangential to my focus in this book on everyday experiences. I hope to elaborate on all of this in an article in preparation.

8 Paine (1996: 61)

9 G. Miller (2005b).

10 G. Miller (2005a); G. Miller et al. (2010).

11 Faull (1988: 336).

12 An interesting parallel is found in a Tanzanian case described by Jim Igoe (2006: 405). Here, as elsewhere in Africa, claims to indigeneity became salient in the 1990s. However, 'the ability to claim indigenous status is far from evenly distributed, much less the connections and ability to necessary to translate these claims into economic and political capital' via the NGO and aid sector. When a coalition's interests were communicated through a newspaper called *Voice of the Maasai*, other groups were dissatisfied, revealing complex machinations to do with inter-ethnic contests over recognition of cultural distinctiveness and indigeneity (Igoe 2006: 416).

13 Jacobs (1983: 360).

14 Monaghan (2012: 49).

15 Brock (1993: 63–64).

16 Eckermann (2010: 147).

17 Berndt (1941: 5).

18 Platt (1970: 63).

19 Capell (1971: 103).

20 Brock (1995: 217).

21 Brock (1993: 64).

22 Brock (1993: 64).

23 Ronald Berndt subsequently published three articles based on this short trip: an account of sleeping customs and dreams at Ooldea; an article about the Dreaming stories collected at the soak, then termed by him 'myths', as well as the population movements underway in this region (also summarised by Brock); detailed descriptions of the rites surrounding death and burial as relayed by various Ooldea residents and observed by a missionary working at Ooldea.

24 Berndt and Berndt (1942b: 311).

25 Berndt and Berndt (1942b: 311).

26 Berndt and Berndt (1942b: 312).
27 Berndt (1940: 286).
28 Berndt (1940: 289).
29 Berndt (1941: 5).
30 Berndt (1941: 5).
31 Berndt and Berndt (1942b: 312). The Berndts published their 'Preliminary Report of Field Work in the Ooldea Region' in a series of articles from 1942–1945.
32 Brock (1995: 217).
33 Tindale (1974: 135).
34 Tindale (1974: 136–37).
35 Wolfe (1999: 206-07).
36 Appadurai (1988: 37).
37 Hinkson (2014).
38 Ramp (2006).
39 Sutton (2003: 5).
40 Monaghan (2012: 49)
41 Macdonald (1997); Weir (2012: 2).
42 See Fabian (2002).

Chapter 8

1 Rosaldo (1993).
2 Bourdieu (2009: 105–06).
3 Bourdieu (2009: 109).
4 Bourdieu (2009: 105).
5 Stewart (1996: 9.
6 Glaskin (2007: 68).
7 In a fascinating footnote, in which non-Aboriginal employees within native title representative bodies become the object of Aboriginal people's anger, Correy et al (2011: 59 ff) speculate, 'It is just at the time when they are most at home with their own conscience that they become constituted as oppressors. Their generosity and goodwill is repaid with revolt and hate and not the tribute of recognition that the well-meaning liberal advocate is fully occupied in thinking they deserve. In going some way to humanising the colonising regime they have highlighted the unacceptability of the situation …Native title is still part of the limitations of a colonial regime and, in upholding the regime by democratising it, the regime is rendered even more unpalatable.' It is perhaps telling that this confronting observation appears in the 'underbrush of footnoting', with its ambiguous relation to the corpus of the main text: 'intimate, yet distanced, both within and without, providing therewith the raw energy, as well as the

mechanisms for making implicit and powerful connections [and claims], while at the same time denying them' (Taussig 1999: 66–68).

8 Morton (1997: 86–87).

9 Morton (1997: 87).

10 Morton (1997: 90).

Chapter 9

1 Berndt and Berndt (1942a: 168).

2 Berndt and Berndt (1942b: 317).

3 Berndt and Berndt (1942a: 143).

4 Berndt (1941: 4).

5 Berndt (1941: 8).

6 For example, Berndt (1941: 10).

7 Berndt and Berndt (1942a: 143).

8 Berndt and Berndt (1943: 371–72). Other comments in the Berndts' report pertain to the association of rockhole sites with fertility, about which it is inappropriate to say anything more as this knowledge is gender-restricted.

9 Downloaded from the website of the Department of Environment and Heritage, Government of South Australia at <www.environment.sa.gov.au/parks/>. Last accessed 13 January 2012.

Chapter 10

1 Sullivan (1995: 101).

2 Smith and Morphy (2007: 6).

3 Morphy (2007: 32).

4 Morphy (2007: 44–45).

5 Ritter (2009: 26).

6 For an excellent analysis of the politics of waste and dumpster diving, see Clark (2004).

7 Stoller (1989: 9).

8 Stoller (1989: 5).

9 Tsing (2005: 14–16).

10 Myers (1986: 60).

11 Feldman (1991: 165).

12 Vincent (2016).

13 N. Brown and C. Brown (2005: 75).

14 Golub (2014).

15 Fisher (2012: 175).

16 'Shame job' (letter to the editor), *West Coast Sentinel*, November 13, 2008, p. 4.

Chapter 11

1 Philip Holden travelled the 5,309-kilometre length of this dingo-proof fence in 1989. In his travelogue he explains that the fence is referred to as the 'Barrier Fence' in Queensland, the 'Border Fence' in NSW and the 'Dog Fence' in South Australia (Holden 1991: 7).
2 Holden (1991: 24, 33).
3 Holden (1991: 159).
4 I.e. Foucault (1980).
5 B. Smith (2008: 209–10).
6 Spivak (1987: 205).
7 Spivak (1987: 205).
8 Wolfe (1999: 2010).
9 Wolfe (1999: 2010).
10 Lattas (1993: 247)
11 Beckett (1988b: 2).
12 Lattas (1993: 245).
13 Wolfe (1999: 2010)
14 Lattas (1993: 260).
15 Dodson (2003: 40–41).
16 See Lea (2006).
17 Moreton-Robinson (2015: xi).
18 Moreton-Robinson (2015: 18).
19 The term 'visitors', often used throughout this local debate, is important to note: it provides an example of the way non-raced categories are used to describe and attempt to obscure a problem of race relations.
20 *West Coast Sentinel,* January 10, 2008, p. 1.
21 *West Coast Sentinel,* July 10, 2008, p. 4.
22 *West Coast Sentinel,* January 17, 2008, p. 1, p. 5.
23 *West Coast Sentinel*, April 3, 2008, p. 1.
24 Agamben (1998).
25 *West Coast Sentinel*, April 3, 2008, p. 1.
26 *West Coast Sentinel*, April 3, 2008, p. 4.
27 Lea et al (2012).
28 Povinelli (2011).
29 *West Coast Sentinel,* July 10, 2008, p. 4.
30 *West Coast Sentinel*, May 15, 2008, p. 4.
31 Lea et al (2012: 157).
32 *West Coast Sentinel,* January 10, 2008, p. 2.
33 *West Coast Sentinel*, May 15, 2008, p. 4.
34 *West Coast Sentinel*, May 15, 2008, p. 4. Aboriginal peoples' cognisance of whitefellas' aversion to rubbish has been noted by others. Zohl D* Ishtar, for example, shows that the senior women of Wirrimanu (formerly

Balgo) use rubbish to demarcate areas as their own, and discourage white interference (2005: 66). See also Lea et al (2012: 155).

35 See Langton (1993).

36 See Graeber (2007).

37 Berndt and Johnston (1942: 196).

38 Berndt and Berndt (1943: 368).

39 Berndt and Berndt (1944: 226).

40 Munn (1971).

41 Atkinson (2002: 204–25).

42 Richards and Haseldine (2012: 32–33).

43 Fanon (1967: 116).

Chapter 12

1 Biddle (2014: 438).

2 Probyn-Rapsey (2015).

3 See the discussion in Rose (2011: 64–66).

4 Indeed in 1980 a dingo did take nine-week-old baby Azaria Chamberlain from a tent in Central Australia. The Chamberlain family were camped at Uluru, then referred to as Ayres Rock, when a dingo snatched Azaria from the tent where she was sleeping. Her body was never found. Just two weeks before Azaria's death, the rock's chief ranger reported to his superiors that he was worried about the increasing confidence of the local dingo pack, warning that 'a dingo is well able to take advantage of any laxity on the part of a prey species and, of course, children and babies can be considered possible prey' (Bryson 2012:6). The fact that Lindy Chamberlain was prosecuted for and found guilty of the murder of her baby daughter defies imagination. The investigation into Azaria's disappearance, the Chamberlains' trial and the media's reporting of it constituted, says Australian writer John Bryson, 'a vast, stupendous fraud' (2012:13). Lindy Chamberlain's conviction was quashed in 1988. While this all served as a chilling reference point for me, it barely interested Aunty Sue who was far more concerned to pass on what she had been taught about dingoes and infants from the 'old people'.

5 Rose develops an analysis of the contemporary will-to-destruction, exemplified by the killing and defiling of wild dogs by graziers. Rose (2011: 1, 86–87) contrasts a scene of cruelty and dominance (ten dogs strung from a tree near Canberra) with an Indigenous ontology of 'connectivity'. More specifically, Rose (1992) points to the place of the dingo in Yarralin cosmology, as a generator of human life. For Yarralin people, humans are the progeny of dogs.

6 Rose (2006: 77).

7 Cultural theorist Chris Healy (2008: 185, 189, 194–95) has produced a nuanced analysis of whitefella walking practices along the Lurujarri Heritage Trail in the Kimberley. Healy categorises these as: 'aesthetic leisure', which stressed the experience of 'communion with the land to manage the stress of modernity'; 'mimetic primitivism', in which young men ripped off their shirts and 'rushed to answer the call of the wild'; and 'allo-fascination', a mode which placed Aboriginality at the centre of the experience of the trail so that the land travelled only became significant through the stories the Aboriginal guides told about it. Elements of the first and third modes are evident among Rockhole Recovery participants.
8 Berlant (2007).
9 Lea (2008: 167).
10 Reciprocal kin terms are used here, as they are across Aboriginal Australia.
11 Greer (2008: 93).
12 See also Gibson (2008: 293).
13 Poore (2001: 205).
14 Poore (2001: 230).
15 Poore (2001:196).
16 Poore (2001:197).

Epilogue

1 Ritter (2009b: 7).
2 Didion (2008: 217).
3 'Concerns over radiation from zircon sand', *West Coast Sentinel*, October 23, 2008, p. 3.
4 Ingold (2007: 19).
5 Ingold (2007: 29).
6 Trigger (1992).
7 Rose (2004: 4).

Bibliography

Newspapers and periodicals

Aboriginal Way (Publication of the Aboriginal Legal Rights Movement Native Title Unit, South Australia).

West Coast Sentinel.

Books, articles, etc.

Agamben, Giorgio (1998), *Homo Sacer: Sovereign Power and Bare Life* (Stanford, CA.: Stanford University Press).

Agius, Parry, et al. (2004), 'Comprehensive Native Title Negotiations in South Australia', in Marcia Langton, et al. (eds.), *Honour Among Nations: Treaties and Agreements with Indigenous People* (Carlton, Vic.: Melbourne University Press), 203–19.

Anderson, Ian (2003), 'Black bit, white bit', in Michele Grossman (ed.), *Blacklines: Contemporary Critical Writing by Indigenous Australians* (Carlton, Vic.: Melbourne University Press), 43–51.

Anonymous (1993), Mabo. The High Court Decision on Native Title (Discusson Paper), (Canberra: Commonwealth Government Printer).

Appadurai, Arjun (1988), 'Putting Hierarchy in Its Place', *Cultural Anthropology,* 3 (1), 36–49.

Atkinson, Judy (2002), *Trauma Trails, Recreating Song Lines: The Transgenerational Effects of Trauma in Indigenous Australia* (North Melbourne, Vic.: Spinifex Press).

Attwood, Bain (2003), *Rights for Aborigines.* (Crows Nest, NSW: Allen & Unwin).

Austin-Broos, Diane (2009), *Arrernte Present, Arrernte Past: Invasion, Violence, and Imagination in Indigenous Central Australia* (Chicago: University of Chicago Press).

Babidge, Sally (2010), *Aboriginal Family and the State: The Conditions of History* (Burlington, VT.: Ashgate).

Bartlett, Richard (1993) *The Mabo Decision, and the Full Text of the Decision in Mabo and Others v. State of Queensland With Commentary,* (Sydney: Butterworths).

Bates, Daisy (1966), *The Passing of the Aborigines* (London: Granada).

Bauman, Toni (2006), 'Nations and Tribes "Within": Emerging Aboriginal "Nationalisms" in Katherine', *The Australian Journal of Anthropology,* 17 (3), 322–35.

Beckett, Jeremy (ed.), (1988a), *Past and Present: The Construction of Aboriginality* (Canberra: Aboriginal Studies Press for the Australian Institute of Aboriginal Studies).

— (1988b), 'Introduction', in Jeremy Beckett (ed.), *Past and Present: The Construction of Aboriginality* (Canberra: Aboriginal Studies Press for the Australian Institute of Aboriginal Studies), 1–10.

— (1994), 'Kinship, mobility and community in rural New South Wales', in — Ian Keen (ed.), *Being Black: Aboriginal Cultures in 'Settled' Australia.* (Canberra: Aboriginal Studies Press for Australian Institute of Aboriginal Studies), 117–36.

— (2005), *A Study of Aborigines in the Pastoral West of New South Wales (1958 MA Thesis with new Introduction and Preface)* (Sydney: Oceania Monographs).

— (2008), 'Frontier encounter: Stanner's Durmugam', in Melinda Hinkson and Jeremy Beckett (eds.), *An Appreciation of Difference: W. E. H. Stanner and Aboriginal Australia* (Canberra: Aboriginal Studies Press), 89–101.

— (2015), 'George Dutton's Country: Portrait of an Aboriginal Drover', *Encounters with Indigeneity: Writing about Aboriginal and Torres Strait Islander Peoples* (Canberra: Aboriginal Studies Press), 1–27.

Behar, Ruth (1996), *The Vulnerable Observer* (Boston: Beacon Press).

— (2003), *Translated Woman. Crossing the Border with Esperanza's Story* (Boston: Beacon Press).

Berlant, Lauren (2000), 'The subject of true feeling: pain, privacy and politics', in Sara Ahmed (ed.), *Transformations: Thinking through Feminism* (London: Routledge), 33–47.

— (2007) 'Slow Death (Sovereignty, Obesity, Lateral Agency)', *Critical Inquiry* 33: 754–80.

Berndt, Ronald (1940), 'Aboriginal Sleeping Customs and Dreams, Ooldea, South Australia', *Oceania,* 10 (3), 286–94.

— (1941), 'Tribal Migrations and Myths Centring on Ooldea, South Australia', *Oceania,* 12 (1), 1–20.

Berndt, Ronald and Berndt, Catherine (1942a), 'A Preliminary Report of Field Work in the Ooldea Region, Western South Australia', *Oceania,* 13 (2), 143–69.

— (1942b), 'A Preliminary Report of Field Work in the Ooldea Region, Western South Australia', *Oceania,* 12 (4), 305–30.

— (1943), 'A Preliminary Report of Field Work in the Ooldea Region, Western South Australia', *Oceania,* 13 (4), 362–75.

— (1944), 'A Preliminary Report of Field Work in the Ooldea Region, Western South Australia', *Oceania,* 14 (3), 220–49.

— (1945), 'A Preliminary Report of Field Work in the Ooldea Region, Western South Australia', *Oceania,* 15 (3), 239–75.

Berndt, Ronald and Johnston, T, (1942) 'Death, Burial, and Associated Ritual at Ooldea, South Australia', *Oceania* 12: 189–208.

Biddle, Jennifer (2014), 'Breasts, Bodies, Art: Central Desert Women's Paintings and the Politics of the Aesthetic Encounter', in Timothy Neale, Crystal McKinnon, and Eve Vincent (eds.), *History, Power, Text: Cultural Studies and Indigenous Studies* (Broadway, NSW: UTS e-Press), 425–48.

Blake, Thom (2001) *A Dumping Ground: A History of the Cherbourg Settlement* (St Lucia, Qld: University of Queensland Press).

Bourdieu, Pierre (2009), *Outline of a Theory of Practice* (Cambridge; NY: Cambridge University Press).

Bourgois, Philippe (1995), *In Search of Respect: Selling Crack in El Barrio* (Cambridge; NY: Cambridge University Press).

Bradfield, Stuart (2006) 'Separatism or Status-Quo?: Indigenous Affairs from the Birth of Land Rights to the Death of ATSIC', *Australian Journal of Politics & History*, 52 (1), 80–97.

Bradshaw, Richard and Collett, Andrew (1991), 'Aboriginal Land Rights in South Australia', *Aboriginal Law Bulletin,* 2 (52), 20–21.

Brady, Wendy (2014) 'Indigenous Insurgency Against the Speaking for Others', in Timothy Neale, Crystal McKinnon and Eve Vincent (eds.) *History, Power, Text: Cultural Studies and Indigenous Studies* (Broadway, NSW: UTS e-Press), 112–21.

Brennan, Sean, et al. (eds.) (2015a) *Native Title from Mabo to Akiba: A Vehicle for Change and Empowerment?* (Sydney: Federation Press).

Brennan, Sean, et al. (2015b), 'The Idea of Native Title as a Vehicle for Change and Indigenous Empowerment', in Sean Brennan, et al. (eds.), *Native Title from Mabo to Akiba: A Vehicle for Change and Empowerment?* (Sydney: Federation Press), 2–13.

Brock, Peggy (ed.) (1989), *Women, Rites & Sites: Aboriginal Women's Cultural Knowledge* (Sydney: Allen & Unwin).

— (1993), *Outback Ghettos: Aborigines, Institutionalisation and Survival* (Cambridge; Melbourne: Cambridge University Press).

— (1995), 'South Australia', in Ann McGrath (ed.), *Contested Ground: Australian Aborigines Under the British Crown* (St Leonards, NSW: Allen & Unwin), 208–39.

Brown, Nina and Brown, Clare (eds.) (2005), *Talking Straight Out: Stories from the Irati Wanti Campaign* (Coober Pedy, S.A.: Alapalatja Press).

Brown, Wendy (1995), *States of Injury: Power and Freedom in Late Modernity* (Princeton, N.J.: Princeton University Press).

— (2001), *Politics out of History* (Princeton, NJ: Princeton University Press).

Bryson, John (2012) 'The Murder of Azaria: This Vast, Stupendous Fraud', *Meanjin* 79 (1), 6–13.

Burbidge, Belinda (2015) '"We are the kangaroo, we have the owl": Linguistic and emotional clues of the meanings of the bush in changing Wiradjuri being and relatedness', *The Australian Journal of Anthropology*, 26 (3), 414–27.

Burgoyne, Iris (2000), *Mirning: We Are The Whales* (Broome, W.A.: Magabala Books).

Burke, Paul (2010), 'Overlapping jural publics: A model for dealing with the "society" question in native title', in Toni Bauman (ed.), *Dilemmas In Applied Native Title Anthropology in Australia.* (Canberra: Australian Institute of Aboriginal and Torres Strait Islander Studies), 55–71.

Capell, Arthur (1971), 'The tragedy of the disapearing sounds', in Roderick Hulsbergen (ed.), *The Aborigine Today* (Dee Why, NSW: Paul Hamlyn), 93–110.

Carlson, Bronwyn (2016), *The Politics of Identity. Who Counts as Aboriginal Today?* (Canberra: Aboriginal Studies Press).

Choo, Christine (2001) *Mission Girls: Aboriginal Women on Catholic Missions in the Kimberley, Western Australia, 1900–1950.* (Crawley, W.A.: University of Western Australia Press).

Clark, Dylan (2004), 'The Raw and the Rotten: Punk Cuisine', *Ethnology,* 43 (1), 19–31.

Clarke, Philip (1997), 'The Aboriginal Cosmic Landscape of Southern South Australia', *Records of the South Australian Museum*, 29 (2), 125–45.

Clifford, James (1988), *The Predicament of Culture: Twentieth-Century Ethnography, Literature, and Art* (Cambridge, MA: Harvard University Press).

— (2013), *Returns. Becoming Indigenous in the Twenty-First Century* (Cambridge, MA; London: Harvard University Press).

Cohen, Bernice (1992), 'Multiple Use and Nature Conservation in South Australia's Arid Zone', *The Rangeland Journal*, 14 (2), 205–13.

Coleman, Dylan (2012), *Mazin Grace* (St Lucia, Qld: University of Queensland Press).

Collmann, Jeffrey (1988), *Fringe-Dwellers and Welfare: The Aboriginal Response to Bureaucracy* (St Lucia, Qld: University of Queensland Press).

Coulthard, Gren (2014), *Red Skin, White Masks. Rejecting the Colonial Politics of Recognition* (Minneapolis, London: University of Minnesota Press)

Correy, Simon (2006), 'The Reconstitution of Aboriginal Sociality through the Identification of Traditional Owners in New South Wales', *The Australian Journal of Anthropology*, 17 (3), 336–47.

Correy, Simon, McCarthy, Diana, and Redmond, Anthony (2011), 'The differences which resemble: The effects of the "narcissism of minor differences" in the constitution and maintenance of native title claimant groups in Australia', in Toni Bauman and Gaynor Macdonald (eds.), *Unsettling Anthropology* (Canberra: Australian Institute of Aboriginal and Torres Strait Islander Studies), 41–61.

Cowlishaw, Gillian (1987), 'Colour, Culture and the Aboriginalists', *Man, New Series*, 22 (2), 221–37.

— (1995), 'Did the earth move for you? The anti-Mabo Debate', *The Australian Journal of Anthropology*, 6 (1 & 2), 43–63.

— (2009), *The City's Outback* (Sydney: UNSW Press).

Cowlishaw, Gillian and Morris, Barry (eds.) (1997), *Race Matters: Indigenous Australians and 'Our' Society* (Canberra: Aboriginal Studies Press).

Crapanzano, Vincent (1980), *Tuhami: Portrait of a Moroccan* (Chicago: University of Chicago Press).

D* Ishtar, Zohl (2005), *Holding Yawulyu: White Culture and Black Women's Law* (North Melbourne, Vic.: Spinifex Press).

de Beauvoir, Simone (2011), *The Second Sex*, trans. Constance Borde and Sheila Malovany-Chevallier (New York: Vintage Books).

de Certeau, Michel (1984), *The Practice of Everyday Life* (Berkeley: University of California Press).

Dauth, Tim (2011), 'Group names and native title in south-east Australia', in Toni Bauman and Gaynor Macdonald (eds.), *Unsettling Anthropology* (Canberra: Australian Institute of Aboriginal and Torres Strait Islander Studies), 21–40.

Dayman, Lyn (ed.) (1989), *Pioneer Tales of the Far West Coast* (Ceduna Area School Library Local History Collection).

Didion, Joan (2008), 'Los Angeles Notebook', *Slouching Towards Bethlehem* (New York: Farrar, Straus and Giroux), 217–24.

Dodson, Michael (2003), 'The end in the beginning: re(de)finding Aboriginality', in Michele Grossman (ed.), *Blacklines: Contemporary Critical Writing by Indigenous Australians* (Carlton, Vic.: Melbourne University Press), 25–42.

Dombrowski, Kirk (2010) 'The White Hand of Capitalism and the End of Indigenism as We Know It', *The Australian Journal of Anthropology,* 21, 129–40.

Dorbzinski, Iris (2004), 'Wilderness protection within the Yellabinna Regional Reserve', *MESA Journal (Government of South Australia, Division of Minerals and Energy Resources),* (35), 21.

Dousset, Laurent and Glaskin, Katie (2007), 'Western Desert and Native Title: How Models Become Myths', *Anthropological Forum,* 17 (2), 127–48.

Eckermann, Clem (2010), *Koonibba: The Mission and the Nunga People* (Adelaide, S.A.: Openbook Howden Design & Print).

Edwards, Bill (2008), 'Aboriginal Land Rights', in Christobel Mattingley and Ken Hampton (eds.), *Survival in Our Own land: 'Aboriginal' Experiences in 'South Australia' since 1836.* (North Melbourne, Vic.: Australian Scholarly Publishing), 79–85.

Fabian, Johannes (2002), *Time and the Other: How Anthropology Makes its Object* (New York: Columbia University Press).

Fanon, Frantz (1967), *Black Skin, White Masks* (New York: Grove Press).

Faull, Jim (1988), *Life on the Edge* (Adelaide: District Council of Murat Bay, Ceduna, S.A.).

Feldman, Allen (1991), *Formations of Violence: The Narrative of the Body and Political Terror in Northern Ireland* (Chicago: University of Chicago Press).

Fingleton, Jim, and Julie Finlayson (eds.) (1995), *Anthropology in the Native*

Title Era (Canberra: Australian Institute of Aboriginal and Torres Strait Islander Studies).

Fisher, Daniel (2012), 'Running amok or just sleeping rough? Long-grass camping and the politics of care in northern Australia', *American Ethnologist,* 39 (1), 171–86.

Foley, Dennis (2007), 'What has native title done to the urban Koori in New South Wales who is also a traditional owner?', in Benjamin Smith and Frances Morphy (eds.), *The Social Effects of Native Title* (Canberra: ANU E Press), 167–84.

Foster, Robert (1989), 'Feasts of the Full Moon. The Distribution of Rations to Aborigines in South Australia: 1836–1861', *Aboriginal History,* 13 (1), 63–77.

— (2000), 'Rations, Coexistence, and the Colonisation of Aboriginal Labour in the South Australian Pastoral Industry, 1860–1911', *Aboriginal History,* 24, 1–26.

Foster, Robert, Nettelbeck, Amanda, and Hosking, Rick (2001), *Fatal Collisions: The South Australian Frontier and the Violence of Memory* (Kent Town, S.A.: Wakefield Press).

Foucault, Michel (1980), *Power/Knowledge: Selected Interviews and other Writings, 1972–1977* (New York: Pantheon Books).

— (1991), *Discipline and Punish,* trans. Alan Sheridan (London: Penguin Books).

— (1991) 'Governmentality' in Graham Burchell, Colin Gordon and Peter Miller (eds.), *The Foucault Effect* (Chicago: University of Chicago Press), 73–86.

Fraser, Nancy and Honneth, Axel (2003), *Redistribution or Recognition?: A Political-Philosophical Exchange,* trans. Joel Golb, James Ingram, and Christiane Wilke (London; New York: Verso).

Gale, Fay (1964), 'Administration as Guided Assimilation (South Australia)', in Marie Reay (ed.), *Aborigines Now* (Sydney: Angus and Robertson), 101–14.

Gara, Tom (1995), 'The N.B. Tindale collection at the South Australian Museum', in Jim Fingleton and Julie Finlayson (eds.), *Anthropology in the Native Title Era* (Canberra: Australian Institute of Aboriginal and Torres Strait Islander Studies).

Gibson, Lorraine (2008), 'Art, Culture and Ambiguity in Wilcannia New South Wales', *The Australian Journal of Anthropology,* 19 (3), 293–311.

Glaskin, Katie (2007), 'Claim, culture and effect: property relations and the native title process', in Benjamin Smith and Frances Morphy (eds.), *The Social Effects of Native Title* (Canberra: ANU E Press).

Golub, Alex (2014), *Leviathans at the Gold Mine: Creating Indigenous and Corporate Actors in Papua New Guinea* (Durham; London: Duke University Press).

Graeber, David (2007), 'Manners, Deference, and Private Property: Or, Elements for a General Theory of Hierarchy', *Possibilities: Essays on Hierarchy, Rebellion, and Desire* (Oakland, CA; Edinburgh: AK Press), 13–55.

Greer, Germaine (2008), *On Rage* (Carlton, Vic.: Melbourne University Publishing).

Haebich, Anna (2000) *Broken Circles: Fragmenting Indigenous Families 1800–2000* (Fremantle, W.A.: Fremantle Arts Centre Press).

Hage, Ghassan (2010), 'Hating Israel in the Field: On Ethnography and Political Emotions', in James Davies and Dimitrina Spencer (eds.), *Emotions in the Field: The Psychology and Anthropology of Fieldwork Experience* (Stanford, CA: Stanford University Press), 129–54.

Hage, Ghassan (1998), *White Nation: Fantasies of White Supremacy in a Multicultural Society* (Sydney: Pluto Press).

Hale, Charles (2006), 'Activist Research v. Cultural Critique: Indigenous Land Rights and the Contradictions of Politically Engaged Anthropology', *Cultural Anthropology,* 21 (1), 96–120.

— (2002) 'Does Multiculturalism Menace? Governance, Cultural Rights and the Politics of Identity in Guatemala', Journal of Latin American Studies, 34, 485–524.

Hall, Stuart (1990), 'Cultural Identity and Diaspora', in Jonathan Rutherford (ed.), *Identity: Community, Culture, Difference* (London: Lawrence & Wishart), 222–37.

Harrison, Simon (2003), 'Cultural Difference as Denied Resemblance: Reconsidering Nationalism and Ethnicity', *Comparative Studies in Society and History,* 45 (2), 343–61.

Healy, Chris (2008) *Forgetting Aborigines*, (Sydney: UNSW Press).

Hinkson Melinda (2014) *Remembering the Future: Warlpiri Life through the Prism of Drawing*, (Canberra: Aboriginal Studies Press).

Holcombe, Sarah (2015), 'Autonomy through Mining Wealth or Government Dependency: Operations of the Neoliberal State', *Hot Spots, Cultural Anthropology website.*

Holden, Philip (1991), *Along the Dingo Fence* (Sydney: Hodder & Stoughton).

Honneth, Axel (1995), *The Struggle for Recognition: The Moral Grammar of Social*

Conflicts, trans. Joel Anderson (Cambridge, MA: Polity Press).

— (2003), 'Redistribution as Recognition: A Response to Nancy Fraser', in Nancy Fraser and Axel Honneth (eds.), *Redistribution or Recognition?: A Political-Philosophical Exchange,* trans. Joel Golb, James Ingram, and Christiane Wilke (London; New York: Verso), 110–97.

Horton, David (2000), 'Aboriginal Australia (map)', (Canberra: AIATSIS; distributed by Geoscience Australia and Aboriginal Studies Press).

Human Rights and Equal Opportunity Commission (1997) *Bringing Them Home: A Report of the National Inquiry into the Separation of Aboriginal and Torres Strait Islander Children from their Families.* (Sydney: Human Rights and Equal Opportunity Commission).

Igoe, Jim (2006), 'Becoming Indigenous Peoples: Difference, Inequality, and the Globalization of East African Identity Politics', *African Affairs,* 105 (420), 399–420.

Inglis, Judy (1964), 'Dispersal of Aboriginal Families in South Australia (1860–1960)', in Marie Reay (ed.), *Aborigines Now* (Sydney: Angus and Robertson), 115–32.

Ingold, Tim. (2007) 'Earth, sky, wind, and weather', *Journal of the Royal Anthropological Institute* 13,19–38.

Jackson, Michael (2013), *The Politics of Storytelling* (Copenhagen: Museum Tusculanum Press).

Jacobs, Jane M. (1983), *Aboriginal Land Rights in Port Augusta (Unpublished MA Thesis)* (University of Adelaide).

— (1988), 'The construction of identity', in Jeremy Beckett (ed.), *Past and Present: The Construction of Aboriginality* (Canberra: Aboriginal Studies Press for the Australian Institute of Aboriginal Studies), 31–43.

Keen, Ian (ed.), (1994), *Being Black: Aboriginal Cultures in 'Settled' Australia* (Canberra: Aboriginal Studies Press for Australian Institute of Aboriginal Studies).

Keen, Ian (1999), 'Norman Tindale and me: anthropology, genealogy, authenticity', in Julie Finlayson, Bruce Rigsby, and Hilary Bek (eds.), *Connections in Native Title: Genealogies, Kinship and Groups* (Canberra: Centre for Aboriginal Economic Policy Research, The Australian National University), 99–106.

Kirsch, Stuart (2006), *Reverse Anthropology: Indigenous Analysis of Social and Environmental Relations in New Guinea* (Stanford, CA: Stanford University Press).

Klein, Richard (1993), *Cigarettes are Sublime* (Durham: Duke University Press).

Lalor, Myles (2000), *Wherever I go. Myles Lalor's 'Oral History',* ed. Jeremy Beckett (Carlton, Vic.: Melbourne University Press).

Langton, Marcia (1993), *"Well, I heard it on the radio and I saw it on the television": An essay for the Australian Film Commission on the politics and aesthetics of filmmaking by and about Aboriginal people and things* (North Sydney, NSW: Australian Film Commission)

— (1993) Rum, seduction and death: 'Aboriginality' and alcohol. *Oceania* 63, 195–206.

— (2013), *The Quiet Revolution: Indigenous People and the Resources Boom.* (Sydney: ABC Books/Harper Collins).

Lattas, Andrew (1990), 'Aborigines and Contemporary Australian Nationalism, primordiality and the cultural politics of otherness', *Social Analysis,* 25, 50–69.

— (1993), 'Essentialism, Memory and Resistance: Aboriginality and the Politics of Authenticity', *Oceania,* 63 (3), 240–67.

Lavelle, Ashley (2001), 'The Mining Industry's Campaign Against Native Title: Some Explanations', *Australian Journal of Political Science,* 36, 101–22.

Lea, Tess (2006), 'Cars, Corporations, Ceremonies and Cash: Hidden Co-dependencies in Australia's North', in Tess Lea, Emma Kowal, and Gillian Cowlishaw (eds.), *Moving Anthropology: Critical Indigenous Studies* (Darwin, N.T.: Charles Darwin University Press), 37–53.

— (2008), *Bureaucrats and Bleeding Hearts: Indigenous Health in Northern Australia* (Sydney: UNSW Press).

Lea, Tess, et al. (2012), 'Being Moved (On). The Biopolitics of Walking in Australia's Frontier Towns', *Radical History Review,* (114), 139–63.

Letch, David (2010), *Chain of Bays: Preserving the West Coast of South Australia* (Friends of Sceale Bay).

Lutz, E. E. (n.d.) *Memoirs of 68 Years Spent on the West Coast of South Australia, 1893–1961* (Ceduna Area School Local History Collection).

Lydon, Jane and Burns, Alan (2010), 'Memories of the Past, Visions of the Future: Changing Views of Ebenezer Mission, Victoria, Australia', *International Journal of Historical Archeology,* 14, 39–55.

Lydon, Jane (2009) *Fantastic Dreaming: The Archeology of an Australian Mission,* (Plymouth, U.K.: AltaMira Press).

Macdonald, Gaynor (1997), '"Recognition and justice": the traditional/historical contradiction in New South Wales', in Julie Finlayson and Diane Smith (eds.), *Fighting Over Country: Anthropological Perspectives*

(Canberra: Centre for Aboriginal Economic Policy Research, Australian National University), 65–82.

— (2002), 'The struggle for recognition: a native title story from Peak Hill, New South Wales', *Australian Aboriginal Studies,* (1), 87–90.

Macintyre, Stuart (1999), *A Concise History of Australia* (Cambridge; Melbourne: Cambridge University Press).

McGregor, Russell (1997), *Imagined Destinies: Aboriginal Australians and the Doomed Race Theory, 1880–1939.* (Carlton, Vic.: Melbourne University Press).

Maher, Lisa (1997), *Sexed Work: Gender, Race, and Resistance in a Brooklyn Drug Market* (Oxford; New York: Clarendon Press).

Malinowski, Bronislaw (1922), *Argonauts of the Western Pacific: An Account of Native Enterprise and Adventure in the Archipalegoes of Melanesian New Guinea.* (London: Routledge).

Malkki, Liisa (1992), 'National Geographic: The Rooting of Peoples and the Territorialization of National Identity among Scholars and Refugees', *Cultural Anthropology,* 7 (1), 24–44.

Mantziaris, Christos and Martin, David (2000), *Native Title Corporations: A Legal and Anthropological Analysis* (Annandale, NSW; Perth W.A.: Federation Press in co-operation with National Native Title Tribunal).

Martin, David F. (2015), 'Does native title merely provide an entitlement to be native? Indigenes, identities, and applied anthropological practice', *The Australian Journal of Anthropology,* 112–27.

Mattingley, Christobel and Hampton, Ken (2008), *Survival In Our Own Land: 'Aboriginal' Experiences in 'South Australia' since 1836* (North Melbourne, Vic.: Australian Scholarly Publishing).

McCorquodale, John (1997), 'Aboriginal identity: Legislative, judicial and administrative definitions', *Australian Aboriginal Studies,* 2, 24–35.

Merlan, Francesca (1998), *Caging the Rainbow: Places, Politics, and Aborigines in a North Australian Town* (Honolulu: University of Hawaii Press).

— (1989), 'The Objectification of "Culture": an aspect of current political process in Aboriginal affairs', *Anthropological Forum,* 6 (1), 105–16.

— (2006), 'Beyond Tradition', *The Asia Pacific Journal of Anthropology,* 7 (1), 85–104.

Memmott, Paul (2011) 'Modelling the continuity of Aboriginal Law in urban native title claims: A practice example' in Toni Bauman and Gaynor Macdonald, (eds.) *Unsettling Anthropology.* (Canberra: Australian Institute of Aboriginal and Torres Strait Islander Studies), 122–41.

Miller, Gladys (2005a), *Wirangu Picture Dictionary* (Adelaide: University of Adelaide).

— (2005b), *Wardugu Wirn: Hunting for Wombat* (Adelaide: University of Adelaide).

Miller, Gladys, et al. (2010), *A Dictionary of the Wirangu Language of the Far West Coast of South Australia* (Adelaide: Tjutjunaka Worka Tjuta Inc. and the University of Adelaide).

Miller, Patti (2012), *The Mind of a Thief* (St Lucia, Qld: University of Queensland Press).

Monaghan, Paul (2007), 'Authenticity, ideology and early ethnography—untangling Far West Coast Gugada', in Rob Amery and Joshua Nash (eds.), *Warra Wiltaniappendi: Strengthening Languages* (Adelaide: University of Adelaide), 113–18.

— (2010), '(Book Review) Daisy Bates, Grand Dame of the Desert by Bob Reece', *Aboriginal History,* 34 (1), 239–41.

Monaghan, Paul (2012), 'Going for Wombat—Transformations in Wirangu and the Scotdesco Community on the Far West Coast of South Australia', *Oceania*, 82 (1), 45–61.

Moreton-Robinson, Aileen (2015), *The White Possessive: Property, Power, and Indigenous Sovereignty* (Minneapolis: University of Minnesota Press).

Morphy, Frances (2007), 'Performing law: The Yolgnu of Blue Mud Bay meet the native title process', in Benjamin R. Smith and Frances Morphy (eds.), *The Social Effects of Native Title* (Canberra, ACT: ANU E Press), 31–57.

Morris, Barry (1989), *Domesticating Resistance: The Dhan-gadi Aborigines and the Australian State* (Oxford; New York: Berg).

— (2013), *Protest, Land Rights and Riots: Postcolonial Struggles in Australia in the 1980s* (Canberra: Aboriginal Studies Press).

Morton, John (1997), 'Why can't they be nice to one another? Anthropology and the generation and resolution of land claim disputes', in Julie Finlayson and Diane Smith (eds.), *Fighting Over Country: Anthropological Perspectives* (Canberra: Centre for Aboriginal Economic Policy Research, Australian National University), 83–92.

— (1998), 'Essentially Black, Essentially Australian, Essentially Opposed: Australian Anthropology and Its Uses of Aboriginal Identity', in Jürg Wassmann (ed.), *Pacific Answers to Western Hegemony: Cultural Practices of Identity Construction* (Oxford; New York: Berg), 355–85.

Muir, Jan and Morgan, Monica (2002), 'Yorta Yorta: The Community's Perspective on the Treatment of Oral History', in Mandy Paul and

Geoffrey Gray (eds.), *Through a Smoky Mirror: History and Native Title* (Canberra: Aboriginal Studies Press Native Title Research Unit), 1–9.

Munn, Nancy (1971), 'The Transformation of Subjects into Objects in Walbiri and Pitjantjatjara Myth', in Ronald Berndt (ed.), *Australian Aboriginal Anthropology: Modern Studies in the Social Anthropology of the Australian Aborigines* (Perth: University of Western Australian Press).

Musharbash, Yasmine (2008) *Yuendumu Everyday: Contemporary Life in Remote Aboriginal Australia* (Canberra: Aboriginal Studies Press).

— (2010), '"Only whitefella take that road": Culture seen through the intervention at Yuendumu', in Jon Altman and Melinda Hinkson (eds.), *Culture Crisis: Anthropology and Politics in Aboriginal Australia* (Sydney: UNSW), 212–25

Myers, Fred (1986), *Pintupi Country, Pintupi Self. Sentiment, Place, and Politics among Western Desert Aborigines* (Washington and London: Smithsonian Institute).

Neale, Timothy (2013), 'Staircases, Pyramids and Poisons: the immunitary paradigm in the works of Noel Pearson and Peter Sutton', *Continuum,* 27 (2), 177–92.

Neale, Timothy and Eve Vincent (2017). 'Mining, Indigeneity, Alterity. Or, Mining Indigenous Alterity?', *Cultural Studies*, 31. Advance online publication. DOI 10.1080/09502386.2017.1303435.

Norman, Heidi (2015), *What Do We Want? A Political History of Land Rights in New South Wales* (Canberra: Aboriginal Studies Press).

O'Faircheallaigh, Ciaran (2006), 'Aborigines, mining companies and the state in contemporary Australia: a new political economy or "business as usual"?', *Australian Journal of Political Science,* 41 (1), 1–22.

Ogle, Greg, Andrews, Declan, and Grady, Michelle (2002), 'Access Denied?: Prospects for Mining and Conservation in National Parks', (http://www.wilderness.org.au/campaigns/outback-australia/yumbarra_2003), 1-12.

Paine, Robert (1996), 'In Chief Justice McEachern's Shoes: Anthropology's Ineffectiveness in Court', *PoLAR: Political and Legal Anthropology Review,* 19 (2), 59–70.

Palmer, Kingsley (1990), 'Dealing with the legacy of the past: Aborigines and atomic testing in South Australia', *Aboriginal History,* 14 (2), 197–207.

— (1999), 'Favourite foods and the fight for country: witchetty grubs and the Southern Pitjantjatjara', *Aboriginal History,* 23, 51–60.

— (2010), 'Understanding another ethnography: The use of early texts in native title inquiries', in Toni Bauman (ed.), *Dilemmas in Applied Native Title Anthropology in Australia* (Canberra: Australian Institute of Aboriginal and Torres Strait Islander Studies), 72–92.

Paradies, Yin (2006), 'Beyond Black and White: essentialism, hybridity and Indigeneity', *Journal of Sociology,* 42 (4), 355–67.

Pearson, Noel (1995), 'From remnant title to social justice', *The Australian Journal of Anthropology,* 6 (1 & 2), 95–100.

Peters-Little, Frances (1999), 'The Community Game: Aboriginal self-definition at the local level', *AIATSIS Research Discussion Papers,* (10), 1–20.

Peterson, Nicolas (1981), *Aboriginal Land Rights: A Handbook* (Canberra: Australian Institute of Aboriginal Studies).

Pilbrow, Tim (2013), 'The Magic of Narrative in the Emplotment of State-Subject Relations: Who's Telling Whose Story in the Native Title Process in Australia', *Oceania,* 83 (3), 221–37.

Platt, John (1970), 'Some notes on Gugada and Wirangu', in Donald Laycock (ed.), *Linguistic Trends in Australia* (Canberra: Australian Institute of Aboriginal Studies), 59–63.

Poore, Megan (2001) *Being Ceduna: Survival on the Far West Coast of South Australia* (unpublished PhD thesis): Australian National University, Department of Archeology and Anthropology.

Povinelli, Elizabeth (2002), *The Cunning of Recognition: Indigenous Alterities and the Making of Australian Multiculturalism* (Durham: Duke University Press).

— (2011), *Economies of Abandonment: Social Belonging and Endurance in Late Liberalism* (Durham: Duke University Press).

Pring, Adele (1990) *Women of the Centre* (Apollo Bay, Australia: Pascoe Pub.)

Probyn-Rapsey, Fiona (2015), 'Dingoes and dog-whistling: a cultural politics of race and species in Australia', *Animal Studies Journal,* 2 (2), 55–77.

Ramp, Jason (dir.) (2006), *Wirrangul Women: Always Have, Always Will.* CAAMA Productions.

Raynes, Cameron (2009), *The Last Protector: The Illegal Removal of Aboriginal Children from their Parents in South Australia* (Kent Town, S.A.: Wakefield Press).

Read, Peter (1999) *A Rape of the Soul So Profound: The Return of the Stolen Generations,* (St Leonards, NSW: Allen & Unwin).

Reay, Marie (1945), 'A half-caste Aboriginal community in North-Western New South Wales', *Oceania,* 15 (4), 296–323.

Redmond, Anthony (2007), 'Some initial effects of pursuing and achieving native title recognition in the northern Kimberley' in Benjamin Smith and Frances Morphy (eds.), *The Social Effects of Native Title* (Canberra: ANU E Press), 79–90.

Reynolds, Henry (2003), *The Law of the Land* (Camberwell, Vic.: Penguin).

Richards, Marcina Coleman and Haseldine, Sue Coleman (2012), *Nyuly Gu Yadoo Mai (Our Good Food)* (Western Australia: Sue Coleman Haseldine).

Ritter, David (2009a), *The Native Title Market* (Crawley, W.A.: UWA Press).

— (2009b) *Contesting Native Title* (Crows Nest, NSW: Allen & Unwin)

Rosaldo, Renato (1993), 'Grief and a Headhunter's Rage', *Culture & Truth: The Remaking of Social Analysis* (Boston: Beacon Press), 1–21.

Rose, Deborah (1991), *Hidden Histories: Black Stories from Victoria River Downs, Humbert River and Wave Hill Stations* (Canberra: Aboriginal Studies Press).

— (1992), *Dingo Makes Us Human: Life and Land in an Aboriginal Australian Culture* (Cambridge; Melbourne: Cambridge University Press).

— (2001), 'The saga of Captain Cook: remembrance and morality', in Bain Attwood and Fiona Magowan (eds.), *Telling Stories: Indigenous History and Memory in Australia and New Zealand* (Crows Nest, NSW: Allen & Unwin), 61–79.

— (2002), 'Reflections on the use of Historical Evidence in the Yorta Yorta Case' in Mandy Paul and Geoffrey Gray (eds.), *Through a Smoky Mirror: History and Native Title* (Canberra: Aboriginal Studies Press Native Title Research Unit), 35–47.

— (2004), *Reports from a Wild Country: Ethics for Decolonisation* (Sydney: UNSW Press).

— (2006), 'What If the Angel of History Were a Dog?', *Cultural Studies Review,* 12 (1), 67–78.

— (2011) *Wild Dog Dreaming: Love and Extinction* (Charlottesville and London: University of Virginia Press).

Rowley, Charles (1970), *The Destruction of Aboriginal Society* (Canberra: Australian National University Press).

— (1971), *The Remote Aborigines* (Canberra: Australian National University Press).

— (1972), *Outcasts in White Australia* (Ringwood, Vic.: Penguin Books).

Rowse, Tim (2012), *Rethinking Social Justice: From 'Peoples' to 'Populations'* (Canberra: Aboriginal Studies Press).

Russell, Ali (dir.) (2010) *Keeper.* Ronin Films.

Said, Edward (1995) *Orientalism,* (London: Penguin).

Salter, Elizabeth (1971), *Daisy Bates* (London; Sydney; Melbourne: Angus & Robertson).

Sansom, Basil (2007), 'Yulara and Future Expert Reports in Native Title Cases', *Anthropological Forum,* 17 (1), 71–92.

Scambary, Benedict (2007), '"No vacancies at the Starlight Motel": Larrakia identity and the native title claims process', in Benjamin Smith and Frances Morphy (eds.), *The Social Effects of Native Title* (Canberra: ANU E Press), 151–66.

— (2013), *My Country, Mine Country: Indigenous People, Mining and Development Contestation in Remote Australia* (Canberra, ACT: Centre for Aboriginal Economic Policy Research, ANU).

Scheper-Hughes, Nancy (1993), *Death Without Weeping: The Violence of Everyday Life in Brazil* (Berkeley: University of California Press).

Sider, Gerald (2006), 'The Walls Came Tumbling Up: The Production of Culture, Class and Native American Societies', *The Australian Journal of Anthropology,* 17 (3), 276–90.

Simpson, Audra (2014), *Mohawk Interruptus: Political Life across the Borders of Settler States* (Durham; London: Duke University Press).

Smith, Benjamin and Morphy, Frances (eds.) (2007a), *The Social Effects of Native Title* (Canberra: ANU E Press).

Smith, Benjamin and Morphy, Frances (2007b), 'The Social Effects of Native Title: Recognition, Translation, Coexistence', in Benjamin R. Smith and Frances Morphy (eds.), *The Social Effects of Native Title* (Canberra: ANU E Press), 1–30.

Smith, Benjamin (2008), 'Still Under the Act? Subjectivity and the State in Aboriginal North Queensland', *Oceania,* 78, 199–216.

Sparrow, Phil (2005) *From Under a Leaky Roof: Afghan Refugees in Australia,* (Fremantle: Fremantle Arts Centre Press).

Spivak, Gayatri Chakravorty (1987), 'Subaltern Studies: Deconstructing Historiography', *In Other Worlds* (New York and London: Methuen), 197–221.

Stanner, W.E.H. (2009a), 'The Dreaming', in Robert Manne (ed.) *The Dreaming and Other Essays* (Melbourne, Vic.: Black Inc.), 57–72.

— (2009b), 'Durmugam: A Nangiomeri', in Robert Manne (ed.) *The Dreaming and Other Essays* (Melbourne, Vic.: Black Inc.), 19–56.

Stanner, W. E. H. (2009c), 'The Boyer Lectures: After the Dreaming', in Robert Manne (ed.), *The Dreaming and Other Essays* (Melbourne, Vic.: Black Inc.), 172–224.

Stevens, Christine (1989) *Tin Mosques & Ghantowns: A History of Afghan Cameldrivers in Australia* (Melbourne: Oxford University Press).

Stewart, Kathleen (1996), *A Space on the Side of the Road: Cultural Poetics in an 'Other' America* (Princeton, NJ: Princeton University Press).

— (2007), *Ordinary Affects* (Durham: Duke University Press).

Stoller, Paul (1989), *The Taste of Ethnographic Things* (Philadelphia: University of Pennsylvania Press).

Strakosch, Elizabeth (2015), *Neoliberal Indigenous Policy: Settler Colonialism and the 'Post-Welfare' State* (London: Palgrave Macmillan).

Strelein, Lisa (2009) *Compromised Jurisprudence: Native title cases since Mabo.* (Canberra: Aboriginal Studies Press).

Sullivan, Patrick (1995), 'Problems of mediation in the National Native Title Tribunal', in Jim Fingleton and Julie Finlayson (eds.), *Anthropology in the Native Title Era* (Canberra: Australian Institute of Aboriginal and Torres Strait Islander Studies), 97–103.

Sutton, Peter (2003) *Native Title in Australia: An Ethnographic Perspective* (Cambridge; Port Melbourne, Vic.: Cambridge University Press).

Sutton, Peter (2011), *The Politics of Suffering: Indigenous Australia and the End of Liberal Consensus* (Carlton, Vic.: Melbourne University Publishing).

Taussig M. (1999) *Defacement: Public Secrecy and the Labor of the Negative,* (Stanford, CA: Stanford University Press).

Taylor, Charles and Gutmann, Amy (1992), *Multiculturalism and 'The Politics of Recognition': An Essay* (Princeton, NJ: Princeton University Press).

Tindale, Norman (1974), *Aboriginal Tribes of Australia: Their Terrain, Environmental Controls, Distribution, Limits and Proper Names* (Canberra: Australian National University Press).

— (1976) 'Some ecological bases for Australian tribal boundaries' in Nicolas Peterson (ed.) *Tribes and Boundaries in Australia* (Canberra: Australian Institute of Aboriginal Studies), 12–29.

Tonkinson, Robert (1974), *The Jigalong Mob: Aboriginal Victors of the Desert Crusade* (Menlo Park, CA: Cummings Pub. Co.).

Toyne, Phillip, and Daniel Vachon (1984), *Growing Up The Country: The Pitjantjatjara Struggle for their Land* (Fitzroy, Vic.: McPhee Gribble).

Trigger, David (1992), *Whitefella Comin': Aboriginal Responses to Colonialism in Northern Australia* (Cambridge: Cambridge University Press).

— (2010) 'Anthropology and native title: Issues of method, claim group membership and research capacity' in Toni Bauman (ed.) *Dilemmas In Applied Native Title Anthropology in Australia* (Canberra: Australian Institute of Aboriginal and Torres Strait Islander Studies), 147–59.

Trouillot, Michael-Rolph (2001) 'The Anthropology of the State in the Age of Globalization', *Current Anthropology* 42 (1),125–38.

Tsing, Anna (1993), *In the Realm of the Diamond Queen: Marginality in an Out-of-the-way Place* (Princeton, NJ: Princeton University Press).

— (2005), *Friction: An Ethnography of Global Connection* (Princeton, NJ: Princeton University Press).

Tuhiwai Smith, Linda (1999), *Decolonizing Methodologies: Research and Indigenous Peoples* (London: Zed).

Vincent, Eve (2016), 'Kangaroo tails for dinner? Environmental culturalists encounter Aboriginal greenies' in Eve Vincent & Timothy Neale (eds.), *Unstable Relations: Indigenous People and Environmentalism in Contemporary Australia* (Perth: University of Western Australia Publishing), 212–51.

Walker, Brett (2015), 'The Legal Shortcomings of Native Title', in Sean Brennan et al. (eds.), *Native Title from Mabo to Akiba: A Vehicle for Change and Empowerment?* (Sydney: Federation Press), 14–22.

Wark, McKenzie (2011) *The Beach Beneath the Street: The Everyday Life and Glorious Times of the Situationist International,* (London; New York: Verso).

Watson, Irene (2014), 'In the Northern Territory Intervention, What is Saved or Rescued and at What Cost?' in Timothy Neale, Crystal McKinnon, and Eve Vincent (eds.), *History, Power, Text: Cultural Studies and Indigenous Studies* (Sydney: UTS ePress), 167–85.

Watson, Virginia (2001), 'Power and Politics: Debate over Native Title' in Stewart Lockie and Lisa Bourke (eds.), *Rurality Bites: The Social and Environmental Transformation of Rural Australia* (Annandale, NSW: Pluto Press), 72–85.

Weiner, James, Godwin, Luke, and L'oste-Brown, Scott (2002), 'Australian Aboriginal Heritage and Native Title: an example of contemporary Indigenous connection to country in Central Queensland', *Occasional Papers Series No. 1/2002* (WA: National Native Title Tribunal).

Weiner, James (2006), 'Eliciting Customary Law', *The Asia Pacific Journal of Anthropology,* 7 (1), 15–25.

— (2011), 'Conflict in the Statutory Elicitation of Aboriginal Culture in Australia', *Anthropological Forum,* 21 (3), 257–67.

Weir, Jessica (2012), 'Country, Native Title and Ecology' in Jessica Weir (ed.), *Country, Native Title and Ecology* (Canberra, ACT: ANU E Press), 1–16.

— (2013) 'Karajarri: Native Title and Governance in the West Kimberley' in Toni Bauman, Lisa Strelein and Jessica Weir (eds.), *Living with Native Title: The Experiences of Registered Native Title Corporations.* (Canberra: AIATSIS Research Publications), 147–74.

Weir, Jessica and Ross, Steven (2007), 'Beyond Native Title: the Murray Lower Darling Rivers Indigenous nations' in Benjamin R. Smith and Frances Morphy (eds.), *The Social Effects of Native Title* (Canberra: ANU E Press), 185–202.

White, Isobel (1993), 'Daisy Bates', in Julie Marcus (ed.), *First in their Field: Women and Australian Anthropology* (Carlton, Vic.: Melbourne University Press).

Wilson, Neva (2003), *Our Identity is our History and our Future* (Seaton, S.A.: South Australian Museum).

Wolfe, Patrick (1999), *Settler Colonialism and the Transformation of Anthropology: The Politics and Poetics of an Ethnographic Event* (London; New York: Cassell).

Wright, Judith (1991), *Born of the Conquerors: Selected Essays* (Canberra: Aboriginal Studies Press).

Yunupingu, Galarrwuy (ed.) (1997), *Our Land is Our Life: Land Rights—Past, Present and Future* (St Lucia, Qld: University of Queensland Press).

Index

www.ingramcontent.com/pod-product-compliance
Lightning Source LLC
LaVergne TN
LVHW050952080826
845145LV00005B/1483

* 9 7 8 1 9 2 5 3 0 2 0 8 0 *